David James Burrell, American Tract Society

The Gospel of Gladness

David James Burrell, American Tract Society

The Gospel of Gladness

ISBN/EAN: 9783337284701

Printed in Europe, USA, Canada, Australia, Japan

Cover: Foto ©Lupo / pixelio.de

More available books at **www.hansebooks.com**

THE
GOSPEL OF GLADNESS.

BY

DAVID JAMES BURRELL, D. D.

AMERICAN TRACT SOCIETY,
150 NASSAU STREET, NEW YORK.

CONTENTS.

CONTENTS.

THE
GOSPEL OF GLADNESS.

PREACHED BY DAVID JAMES BURRELL, D. D., AT THE MARBLE
COLLEGIATE CHURCH, OCTOBER 11, 1891.

" Rejoice in the Lord always: and again I say, Rejoice." Phil. 4:4.

A YOUNG man was looking forward to his wedding
day. It was the old story: his life was sweetened and
brightened by the constant vision of one fair face. The
arrangements for the festal occasion were all made and
the time was drawing nigh. The caterer had been engaged and the master of ceremonies, the festivities of the
occasion were all planned, when suddenly a strange thing
happened—the young man was converted. He met with
Jesus the Nazarene and surrendered all. But now what
was to be done about those festivities? Religion is a serious piece of business. Life had assumed a new and far
more important interest since Jesus had entered into it.
Was it a time for singing and merry-making? What
would the new Master say? The difficulty was solved in
the right way. Jesus himself was invited to the wedding.
The young man determined that he would have nothing
going on at his home which should be out of line with the
obligations of his new life or which his new Master could
not bless with his presence and his smile.

The time came, and Jesus was at the wedding; nor
did he deport himself there as a wall-flower or kill-joy, or
chill the pleasure of the feast by lowering looks : He moved
about among the happy guests with a bright light in His
eyes and a cheery word on His lips. Their myrtle branches
and chaplets of flowers, their laughter and dancing and
carrying of torches, did not offend Him. When the harp

and psaltery struck up he made no protest; when the nuptial hymn was sung he did not frown upon it. This Jesus was not a sanctimonious dreamer among the shadows, but a man among men. And when, to meet an unexpected need of the occasion, he turned the water into wine, it was very like what he has been doing ever since, by his bright presence transforming the perfunctory duties of a mechanical piety into the merry-making of a genuinely holy life.

His attendance at that wedding in Cana struck the key-note of his religion and of the Christian life.

A Christian who lives with his head hung down like a bulrush and casting looks of deprecation towards all innocent delights, gives a false impression of the religion which he professes and of the Saviour whom he loves.

Where shall we find a lawful joy and peace if not in the Christian life? If we are reconciled with God, if hell is behind us and heaven before us, if our consciences are clear, our hearts should be tuned, not to " Il Penseroso," but rather to " L'Allegro "—

> " Hence loathed Melancholy,
>   Of Cerberus and blackest midnight born,
>   In Stygian cave forlorn,
>   'Mongst horrid shapes and shrieks and sights unholy.
>   And haste thee, nymph, and bring with thee
>   Jest and youthful Jollity,
>   Sport that wrinkled Care derides,
>   And Laughter holding both his sides."

Why not? There are pleasures for evermore at the right hand of God.

One reason why we should rejoice is because we have a good God and we know it. We are not afraid of him ; we have made our peace with him.

The Puritans were a noble body of heroic men, but we have somewhat against them, in this, that they maligned God. Their conception of him as a consuming fire distorted all the tasks and pleasures of their common life.

In their eyes it was a sin to wear a starched ruff, to play a game of cricket, or to smile on the holy Sabbath, and to read the "Fairy Queen" was as the unpardonable sin. Up and down the sedgy roads wandered Oliver, the noblest of them all, muttering to himself and envying the owls that hooted among the leafless boughs, and the toads that croaked among the leaves and grass, because they had no "certain fearful looking for of judgment."

We have not so learned our gracious God. We were indeed under condemnation and had need to be forgiven, but the cross has put our melancholy to an open and eternal shame.

Could we with ink the ocean fill, were the whole world of
      parchment made,
Were every single stick a quill and every man a scribe by trade,
To write the love of God alone would drain the ocean dry,
Nor could the scroll contain the whole though stretched from
      sky to sky.

God has shown himself in providence and grace to be the best of fathers. We draw nigh to him not in the spirit of bondage again to fear, but in the spirit of adoption whereby we cry, Abba, Father.

A second reason why we should rejoice is because our God has given us a pleasant world to live in.

He might have made the sky of a dun color, as dismal as the roof of some subterranean vault, dripping with slime, bats clinging to the walls, and the chill of the dreary place creeping into the very marrows of one's bones. But he did not. He made the sky so brilliantly beautiful as to put rubies and diamonds and sapphires to shame. He placed the shining sun in mid-heaven, and lit the stars at night and set them swinging like lanterns at the top-masts of an innumerable Armada sailing through the ocean of infinite space.

He might have made the earth like yonder moon, the

memorial of some catastrophe of ages long ago, scarred and blistered and barren. But he did not. He carpeted the earth with green pastures, and planted it with gardens whose perfume is like to that of Hesperus, with birds singing among the trees and flowers blooming everywhere, from the buttercup by the brookside to the edelweiss on the snow-capped summits of the Alps.

He might have made the ocean a steaming pond of foulness, shored with asphalt like the Dead Sea, and with jackals and hyenas prowling near. But he did not. He made it a vast reservoir of pellucid sweetness, baring its bosom to the commerce of the nations and opening its arms to receive the murmuring brooks and rolling rivers.

And best of all, this world so beautiful is everywhere and always vocal with the praises of God. The stars in their courses are

> "For ever singing as they shine,
> 'The hand that made us is divine.'"

On every grass-blade, on the white vesture of the lily, is written the Name which is above every other. The ocean rolls the praises of Him who holds its waters in the hollow of his hands. An undevout man cannot appreciate the beauty of this world. No poet can adequately sing its splendors unless, like Coleridge in the Valley of Chamouni, he can distinctly hear "earth with its thousand voices praising God."

A third reason why a Christian should make merry and be glad is because a golden opportunity is his.

"Is life worth living?" That depends. If a man has no purpose, no lofty aspiration for his own or others' good, it is an open question. Among the hymns of Isaac Watts there is nothing more suggestive than the comparatively unknown bit of wisdom which he calls "insignificant existence."

> There are a number of us creep
> Into this world to eat and sleep,
> And know no reason why we're born
> But only to consume the corn,
> Devour the cattle, fowl, and fish,
> And leave behind an empty dish.
> The crows and ravens do the same,
> Unlucky birds of hateful name;
> Ravens or crows might fill their place,
> And swallow corn and carcasses;
> Then if their tombstone, when they die,
> Be n't taught to flatter and to lie,
> There's nothing better will be said
> Than that "they've eat up all their bread,
> Drunk up their drink, and gone to bed."

To live thus is surely not worth the while.

But God never intended this for any man: at the feet of every even the humblest soul on earth he places a ladder, and along its rounds of possibility reaching up unto useful life and character he bids us climb. "Add to your faith, virtue; and to virtue, knowledge; and to knowledge, temperance; and to temperance, patience; and to patience, godliness; and to godliness, brotherly kindness; and to brotherly kindness, charity." This is God's purpose for every man; that he make the most of himself, not merely growing in character, but enlarging his influence to the betterment of all around him. No man is ruled out; if any is a ne'er-do-weel or a good-for-naught, it is his own fault. God's voice is always calling; his hands are always beckoning; his grace is always drawing us higher and higher towards the stature of a perfect man.

And fourthly, as Christians we have reason to rejoice because we belong to an honorable family. Blood tells. He is a poor sort of fellow who does not aspire to leave a name that his children will be proud of. Tuft-hunters are despicable; but fortunate are all sons and daughters who can honor their forebears.

After all, however, there is no lineage so honorable as

that which belongs in common to all, to wit, "He was the son of Seth, who was the son of Adam, who was the son of God."

Our human nature is ruined, but it is a splendid ruin. Will, heart, and conscience lie shattered and crumbling, like the stones and the capitals of some old temple of the gods. But in silence there walks the spirit of a disrobed Levite who looks forward to the promised restitution of all things. Man at his best was but a little lower than the angels; man at his worst is still a child of God.

But a Christian is something more: not only has he God's breath in his nostrils; not only is God's image impressed upon his never-dying soul; but, as the Buddhists would say, he is a "twice-born man." In him the restitution is begun and will continue until the last stone of character is laid with shoutings of "Grace, grace unto it!" He is born from above, out of darkness into light, out of the sepulchre of sin and shame into newness of life.

One more reason why those who have made their peace with God in Jesus Christ should rejoice is because they have a splendid outlook.

It is a dreadful thing to have one's hopes and purposes all circumscribed within the narrow horizon of this present life. It is an inexpressibly dreadful thing to have no present interest in the great verities that reach out into the eternal ages. A man who is without God, and therefore without hope, should never smile; his soul should be enveloped by the shadows of a ceaseless melancholy.

Why is it that those who visit Paris always make their way behind the massive splendors of Notre Dame to the little building where the bodies of the unknown dead are exposed to view? What is it that draws our gaze towards the sad features of the suicide? We can scarcely understand the utter wretchedness that moves one to leap from "the ills we have to those we know not of."

> " Where the lamps quiver
> So far in the river,
> With many a light
> From window and casement,
> From garret to basement,
> She stood with amazement,
> Houseless by night.

> " The bleak wind of March
> Made her tremble and shiver,
> But not the dark arch
> Or the black flowing river ;
> Mad from life's history,
> Glad to death's mystery
> Swift to be hurled,
> Anywhere, anywhere
> Out of the world."

But for us the present hand-breadth of life is of little import. Its afflictions are but for a moment. Its tasks will be over in a day or two, and beyond—all things are beyond. The milk and honey are beyond the wilderness. The vistas of eternity open up beyond the death-bed.

If the heat and burden of the day seem sometimes unendurable, we may assure ourselves, as did Godfrey's Crusaders, who, footsore and discouraged, lifted their eyes and saw afar off the gleam of the domes of Jerusalem, and plucking up courage hastened on to enter its sacred gates. The domes of heaven are just yonder. " O mother dear Jerusalem, when shall I come to thee?"

These are some of the reasons why one who believes in Jesus Christ should rejoice evermore ; why no stings should ever overcome him ; why no dark spirit of melancholy should ever dim the lustre of his eye.

If there are those who say, " We have our pleasures, though we are not followers of Christ," let them consider well whether they have any right to pleasure until their peace is made with God. How dare they rest upon their beds this night if it be certain that death before daybreak would bring them unprepared before the judgment bar of God? Are not their pleasures dearly bought if to enjoy them they must silence the voice of conscience and reason and blot out the vast solemnities of the eternal life? Is not their laughter but as the crackling of thorns? Are they not like those miners of Cornwall who, at work beneath the sea, are driven from their labors in tempestuous times by the roar of the storms above them?

All the delights of an unholy life are shallow and fleeting, for

<blockquote>
" Pleasures are like poppies spread ;
You seize the flower, its bloom is shed ;
Or like the snowfalls in the river,
A moment white, then gone for ever."
</blockquote>

But the follower of Christ can well afford to laugh and make merry as he journeys heavenward. He has done the right thing ; his conscience is clear ; the smile of God is over him.

I point you to the cross, to the saving power of the blood. Let those dying lips of the Saviour speak to thy soul to-night, saying, "Thy sins be forgiven thee," and the change will be like the break of day.

Then you and I, forgiven and happy, blessing God and making merry in our hearts, may journey on heavenward, with all the ransomed of the Lord who shall come to Zion at length with songs and everlasting joy upon their heads.

THE

TRYSTING - PLACE.

PREACHED BY DAVID JAMES BURRELL, D. D., AT THE MARBLE COLLEGIATE CHURCH, OCTOBER 18, 1891.

"Enter into thy closet." Matt. 6:6.

JERUSALEM is said to have been builded "as a city compact together." Its streets were narrow and its homes were crowded. The city lay upon the crest of a mountain range; and, surrounded by natural defences, it was a refuge for the people of all the neighboring country in times of danger. On the occasion of the great annual festivals the Jews came crowding there from every part of the known world. It was not an extraordinary thing for ten millions of people to be gathered in and around Jerusalem during these annual services, as it is written, "Thither the tribes go up."

And here we notice a strange circumstance: though every available foot of space in Jerusalem was of the utmost value, and though the dwellings were small and crowded, yet there was probably not one home in Jerusalem that did not have a little chamber up towards the house-top reserved for meditation and communion with God. It was to such an upper room that the prophet went when he laid himself upon the body of the widow's son and cried, "O Lord, let the child's soul return unto him again." It was to such a retreat that David went, tottering along the winding stairway, heart-broken and sobbing, "O Absalom, my son, my son, would God that I had died for thee!"

Might it not be well for us to stand in the ways and search out the old paths and walk therein? We have apartments in our homes for every other use, but none for secret prayer. Yet let us not overmuch restrict the definition. The old poet Lovelace says,

> " Stone walls do not a prison make
>   Nor iron bars a cage ;
> Minds innocent and quiet take
>   That for their hermitage."

It is equally true that four walls do not a closet make. The important matter is that we shall be apart from the world. "The world is too much with us." In the quiet street we may shut to the doors by letting down our eyelids, and be alone with God. Out on the stormy sea the sailor, swinging in his hammock, calls back the memories of boyhood and repeats the words he learned at his mother's knee :

> " Now I lay me down to sleep,
>   I pray the Lord my soul to keep."

And his hammock is his closet. The Arab on the broad desert, as the sun sweeps across mid-heaven, falls upon his knees crying, "Allah, il Allah!" and the boundless waste is his closet. Our Lord, who was homeless, kept his tryst in solitary places by the lake-shore or under the shadows of the olive-trees.

> "Cold mountains and the midnight air
> Witnessed the fervor of his prayer."

Three things are pre-requisite to the building up of a noble life and character, to wit: The knowledge of self, the knowledge of God, and the bringing of self into an at-one-ment with God. And these three are all to be had, better than elsewhere, in the trysting-place.

I. *To know one's self* lies at the outset. But this is no easy matter. I make the acquaintance of everybody else more readily than of myself. I know my wife and children, my friends and neighbors, my acquaintance of an hour ago, better than I know this man. Nor will I ever know him better unless I go apart to be alone with him.

(1.) In the closet I discover, to begin with, that *I am;* nor is this an unimportant matter. Bancroft says that one of the most notable discoveries ever made, in its bearing on human progress, was when Descartes, wandering alone by the banks of the Danube, cried out on a sudden, "Ich bin Ich!" In that moment, as he faced himself, his own individuality stood out against all custom, history, and tradition, and he saw himself a man. At the basis of life and character lies self-consciousness. I have gone a great ways when I have learned that I travel along through personal tasks and sorrows and responsibilities, alone, to the Judgment Bar of God.

(2.) *I always will be.* We are accustomed to think it necessary that the certainty of death should ever be kept before us. "King Philip, thou art mortal!" was the cry with which the Macedonian monarch was awaked to the royal duties of each day. The thing that we have to have dinned into our ears is not that we are mortal, but that we are immortal. The rolling of the hearse through our streets, the waving of the black plume, ever remind us that we must die; but the thing that we forget is that death does not end all. We live for ever. God's breath is in our nostrils and we are as immortal as the eternal God. We all have intimations of immortality, but amid the hurly-burly of life we give little heed. We must needs go apart to hear the still voice of the angel that speaks within us, " Thou shalt live and not die !"

(3.) *I am not what I ought to be.* A man in a crowd may scoff at total depravity, but when he goes alone, by himself, he knows there is something in it. The fops of the time of Louis XIV. were said to be young until they died of old age; but such an one in the solitude of his chamber, stripping off his disguises, washing off the powder from his wrinkles and baring his lean infirmities, could not but perceive himself to be a decrepit old man. We are all the while posing before the world, seeming to be better than we are; we need to go into solitude, not to "see oursels as ithers see us," but to see ourselves as we are; and then we cry, " God be merciful unto us !"

(4.) *I have aspirations to be better than I am.* The best as well as the worst that is in me is discovered in the trysting-place. Out in the mountains, alone and forsaken, the Psalmist lamented, " All thy waves and thy billows have gone over me ! Why art thou cast down,

O my soul, and why art thou disquieted within me?"
Then catching sight of a wounded deer, fleeing, with hot
eyes and panting sides, an arrow quivering in its flanks,
towards the babbling water, he cried, "As the hart
panteth after the water brooks, so panteth my soul after
thee, O God!" In like conditions we find that while we
are not what we should be, our hearts are an hungered
and athirst to be more like God.

II. *To know God.* If to know ourselves, as Thales
said, is wisdom, then to know God is far better, for Jesus
said, "This is life eternal, to know God and Jesus Christ
whom he hath sent." But where shall we make his
acquaintance? Where do we take hold upon the confidence of any friend? On 'Change? In the market-
place? In the crowded street? No; but apart, in the
solitude, where we pour out the story of our sorrows and
know him as our friend. In like manner, if we are to
know God, it must be by going apart to commune with
him.

(1.) We shall discover at the outset that "*God is.*"
Nor is this of little moment. No man indeed is an atheist in these days. Is it written, "The fool hath said, There
is no God"? Nay, but "The fool hath said in his heart,
There is no God." That is, his wish is father to the
thought. He seeks to eliminate God from his daily life.
His walk and conversation are such as deny God. No
man is intellectually an atheist, but we all make too little
of God; we idealize him, dogmatize about him, and forget him. If we thoroughly believed in him, felt his being,
apprehended him, what manner of persons would we be!

(2.) *God is near by.* We do not deny God; we simply put him afar off. St. Paul, preaching to the scientific men of Athens and with special reference to a certain Unknown God, said, " He is not far from every one of us." We have gotten too far away from our Bibles and become too familiar with the purely scientific conception of God's law. Force, the universal soul, a something or nothing that maketh for righteousness, an eyeless, armless, heartless ghost of a God, what is that to me, or what is that to any man? We go apart and talk with Him; He comes and puts his hand upon us, looks down into our faces, answers our need. He is nearer now than touching, nearer than seeing, nearer than the nearest friend that ever stood beside us.

(3.) *We have certain definite relations with him.* And these relations are filial. We are received by the spirit of adoption, whereby we cry, " Abba, Father." It is much to be doubted if the sense of this blessed Fatherhood can come to us amid the fret and worry of our common life. The interchange of love among kinspeople is never in public places; it is in the solitude that God speaks to us, saying, " My son, my daughter."

(4.) *He has great expectations concerning us.* " As I live, saith the Lord, I have no pleasure in thy death." He has so loved us as to give his only-begotten Son to suffer and die for us. Here in the secret place, as we stand beneath his cross, the love that passeth understanding is revealed to us.

III. We are now upon our knees and the nexus is complete. The soul is brought into oneness with God.

(1.) Here is the beginning of spiritual life; souls are new-born in the solitude. If Saul is converted at high noon on a dusty thoroughfare, he must needs be blinded for a season that so his spiritual birth shall be in the secret place. The beginnings of all life are out of sight. The foliage of the vine is woven in hidden looms, and the juices of the grape are distilled in subterranean laboratories. So, for the most part, souls coming into the kingdom have the joyful beginnings of their higher life in the trysting-place.

(2.) Here we renew our strength. To-night I shall pass out into the unknown country where no man has ever journeyed before me. How dare I venture into the land of darkness and of danger without a divine hand to protect me? And at daybreak I shall venture into another *terra incognita*, an unexplored land of duty and responsibility and danger. There will be pestilence walking and arrows flying all about me. How dare I venture forth into that new day without first grasping the hand of the Almighty and Omniscient One? "I cannot go up hence unless the Lord go with me."

(3.) Here I am invigorated by the Spirit and the help that I need for spiritual growth is given me. Nor is it possible for me to receive it so well otherwise or elsewhere. There must needs be insulation if the body is to be surcharged with electricity. In like manner the Spirit touches us when we are in the secret place. His voice is a still small voice, and, like the prophet, we must put our faces between our knees if we would hear it.

(4.) And finally, here we take hold upon Omnipotence, and entering into participation of divine strength, we become co-laborers with God. The Lord Jesus, in his secret communings with the Father, pressed upon the long arm of the lever that uplifts the world ; and so do we in the secret place.

To your knees, therefore, O men and women cumbered with much serving at home or in the market-place ; give yourselves time and opportunity to hear God saying, "Seek ye first of all the kingdom, and the rest shall be added unto you." To your knees in the secret place, O young men and women beginning life's voyage; look towards the other shore and see how far the horizons stretch away. Life is a hand-breadth : eternity is for ever. To your knees, O fathers and mothers in Israel whose hairs are white like the almond-trees in blossom. Hear God calling ; mark him beckoning to the joys which eye hath not seen and ear hath never heard.

> " More things are wrought by prayer
>   Than this world dreams of. Wherefore let thy voice
>   Rise like a fountain night and day ;
>   For what are men better than sheep or goats,
>   That nourish a blind life within the brain,
>   If, knowing God, they lift not hands of prayer
>   Both for themselves and those who call them friends ?
>   For so the whole round earth is every way
>   Bound by gold chains about the feet of God."

WILD OATS.

A SERMON PREACHED BY DAVID JAMES BURRELL, D. D., AT THE
MARBLE COLLEGIATE CHURCH, OCTOBER 25, 1891.

"He that soweth iniquity shall reap calamity."
(New Version) Prov. 22:8.

ABOUT 1600 A. D. there lived in England an eccentric literary genius, by name John Lyly, who conceived the thought of expressing things disagreeable in periphrases and elegant circumlocutions. Death was called a departure from the fellowship of the living, or the paying of the debt of nature. Stealing was misappropriation, or a confusion of *meum* and *tuum*. Lying was prevarication; another favorite name for it was "malingering." This fashion of never calling a spade a spade was known as "euphuism." We have not wholly departed from it at this late day. A trace is found in the expression "sowing one's wild oats." The phrase is intended to comprehend pretty much all the vices of young manhood; and, like charity, it covers a multitude of sins, such as inebriety, personal impurity, profanity, baccarat, and if there be any other of the youthful vices too shocking for ears polite, this phrase embraces it. We are all sowing something or other. The field is the world. Some go forth in their young manhood and womanhood bearing precious seed—wheat for the world's hunger, the fine wheat of kindly lives and generous deeds—and they will doubtless come again with rejoicing, in the great garnering-time, bringing their sheaves with them. And there are others who go heedlessly sowing the wind, to reap the whirlwind. You meet them reeling through the streets; they are to be found carousing in upper chambers; squandering their time and earnings in the pleasures of the green baize field, or pursuing their way in the black and dark night to the house of the strange woman. Their lips are blistered with drink; red-eyed, thick-tongued, addle-brained, they are sowing wild oats. Nay, let us drop the metaphor: they are sowing iniquity, and they shall reap calamity. They are sowing phosphorus and tinder, and, except they repent, they shall of a surety reap the fires of hell.

It would be well, all around, if there were less of sentimentalism and more of sound common sense with respect to the follies of our fast young men. We want more of Anglo-Saxon and less of Lyly's euphuism. In my judgment the fathers and mothers are, in many cases, largely responsible for the vices of their sons. At many an upper window to-night mothers will be watching and hearkening for the unsteady steps of the wayward ones. God be praised for mother's love! But there is one thing that ought to be said: If your son is a scapegrace, a drinking, carousing, licentious, good-for-naught, it behooves you at the outset to face the awful fact. It is a terrible thing to be the parent of a ne'er-do-weel. I know how it is: he comes home at midnight or towards the wee sma' hours reeling between two boon companions, and you help him to bed and tuck the clothes tenderly about him; and next morning when he comes down, eyes red and brain ready to split with aching, you stroke the damp hair from his forehead and pamper and coddle him with sympathy and hot coffee, until he imagines himself a poor misused fellow, and indeed something of a hero. Oh let him know the dreadful truth! Let him know that, while your mother soul is full of compassion, as the soul of a pure woman it loathes and abhors his bestiality. Let him know that you mourn for him as for one who has "Ichabod" written on his brow, "The glory hath departed."

Young women, moreover, ought to have a clear understanding respecting this matter. There are some who think it a rather nice and clever thing to be familiar with scapegraces. Oh if they only knew, if they did but apprehend the thousandth part of what it signifies, they would rather press their lips to the surface of a white hot cylinder, they would rather clasp hands with a leper, they would rather bathe in the reeking vileness of a cesspool, than give their friendship to a fast young man.

Not long ago a mother called upon me with reference to her wayward son who had brought shame upon himself and her. She was in great trouble; but as to any frank statement of the case, she quite resented it. In the course of our conversation she observed, "Boys will be boys," and presently, "He'll live it down, I am sure he'll live it down." Never were two greater mistakes than these.

I. "Boys will be boys." If by that you mean that a young man is fairly entitled to get all the legitimate enjoyment that flows from good blood and healthful spirits, I say, Yea and Amen to it. We live in a pleasant world, and God means that we shall enjoy it. But if you mean that boys must or may take their turn at playing fast and loose with the moralities and proprieties and decencies, then I say a thousand times no! There is not a particle of truth in it. Moreover it is a libel on vigorous and healthful young manhood. In the name of thousands and tens of thousands of manly young fellows whose hands were never soiled with money filched at the gambling-table, whose intellects were never befogged with drink, whose lips were never blistered by unlawful love, I protest against it. Paul had a young friend in Ephesus to whom he wrote, "Be strong; quit thyself like a man: flee, also, youthful lusts. Let no man despise thee; let no man take thy crown." In that great city, with its stadium and amphitheatre and marble baths, the youth was surrounded by innumerable temptations; he could easily have excused himself for indiscretion on the ground of custom. "They all did it." The "young bloods" of Ephesus reeled past him sowing their wild oats; and where are they now? What impression did they leave on the after ages? Timothy kept himself unspotted from the world, a vigorous, healthy, manly young man. There are multitudes of clerks and artisans, some sons of aristocrats, many young handcraftsmen, who loathe the thought of dissipation. Their hands are steady, their eyes are clear, their laughter as pure as the laughter of a child. Cheery fellows they are, with clear consciences, who can look their mothers in the face and kiss their sisters' lips without leaving a sooty stain; brave young fellows who are making a successful fight for manhood, panoplied with the whole armor of God.

In Paul's eighth chapter to the Romans our attention is called to the two levels of life.

(1.) The low level of the flesh. Here abide the self-pleasers, the mammonites, the epicures, all who are merely getting and enjoying, pampering the senses and having a good time. Their life is not a whit better than that of the beasts that perish. Their aphorism is, "Let us eat and drink, for to-morrow we die." Bring out the skeleton and place it at the feast! "*Dum vivimus, vivamus.*"

(2.) The higher level of spirit, where men and women

live who realize that they were created in God's likeness, who believe in eternity and the endless life, who live not for themselves only, but for the good of others and the glory of God. Among the dwellers on this level are multitudes of young men who are fighting the Hydra, building character, and making their lives tell for truth and righteousness.

For all such there are three safeguards. One is conscience: a sentinel stationed on the outer walls to give warning of danger. Alas for the young man who hurts his conscience or defies it! " Look out for the engine when the bell rings!"

Another is the sense of honor:

> " Whene'er you feel your honor grip,
> Let that aye be your border."

When James Harper was leaving home to make his fortune in the city, his mother's last word was, " My boy, you have good blood in you." So I say to you, young men, Be mindful of the fact that God's breath is in your nostrils and that you live for ever.

And still another safeguard, and most important, is faith. " Above all, taking the shield of faith, wherewith ye shall be able to quench all the fiery darts of the adversary." The young man who trusts to himself is bound to fail. There is no better motto than the old Saxon legend —a wine-glass with one foot broken, and upon it the inscription, " Hold thou me up."

II. We now turn to that other false sentiment, " He 'll live it down." And I say here, as I said to that mother, He never will. Can a man take fire into his bosom and not be burned? Sin always works an irreparable damage; vice leaves a terrible residuum.

(1.) It rots one's self-respect. It " eateth like a canker," like a gangrene, spreading to all the adjacent parts.

(2.) It pollutes the memory. A man may be forgiven; and when God forgives he forgets and casts the sin behind his back, blots it out, sinks it in the depths of the unfathomable sea; but the man himself must remember it. John B. Gough was wont to say that he would give his good right arm if he could for ever banish from his mind and memory the scenes of his early youth.

(3.) It indisposes the soul for better things; it crowds out all nobler purposes. You cannot sow Canada thistles in your field and expect a crop of wheat. Oh the dreadful waste! Youth is the seed-time. At fifteen John de Medici was made cardinal. At seventeen the learned Grotius began to practise law. At nineteen Lafayette distinguished himself as the friend of our republic. At twenty-two Newton worked out the law of attraction. At twenty-seven John Calvin wrote his "Institutes," which have formulated the doctrinal statements of all later years. At twenty-seven Napoleon took the bridge at Lodi and made himself the first captain of his age. And the best Man who ever lived, the noblest and manliest, died at thirty, saying of his life with all its noble purposes and vast ambitions, "It is finished." The world has a large place of usefulness for young men.

(4.) It enslaves in the fetters of habit. The saddest walk I know is along the road from Tam O'Shanter's inn to Alloway. On either side are the glories of Ayrshire and in the distance the banks and braes o' bonnie Doon. But one can only remember that along this road Robbie Burns staggered many a time, the fire of genius in his brain quenched by the fumes of drink. He has left his epitaph, written by his own hand, for us to ponder. Here it is :

> " Reader, attend, whether thy soul
> Soar fancy's flights beyond the pole,
> Or darkly grub this earthly hole
> In low pursuit,
> Know prudent, cautious self-control
> Is wisdom's root."

(5.) It ruins the body. Vice hangs its banners on the outer walls. It reddens the eyes, blears the features, soddens the flesh, and unnerves the whole man. The good Book tells us that the bones of the wicked are full of the sins of their youth, and if you wish to verify that, go to the museum of any hospital and ask to see the bones of the wicked, and mark how they are twisted and scarred by sin.

(6.) It destroys the soul. To be carnally minded is death. There is no room in heaven for the fast young man; if by some inadvertence he were to find his way there, he would be miserable amid the ascriptions of divine praise, and would be moved to cry out, " Where is Gehenna? that I may go and mingle with mine own."

A king, dying, imagined that he would be met on the other shore by a royal escort to lead him to a throne. He saw, however, in the distance a wretched hag, repellant beyond all imagining, who leered and ogled and beckoned and called, " Know ye not me? I am your sin, and am come to abide with you for ever!" This is the worst of all—the soul is the author of its own endless pain. The wicked make their bed and must lie in it.

It is comforting to know, however, that no matter what the mistakes of our past life have been, if we repent the Lord is ready to forgive. He is a great forgiver. And whether we have fallen into the temptations which are peculiar to young manhood or not, we have all sinned and come short of the glory of God. " Though your sins be as scarlet, they shall be white as snow; though they be red like crimson, they shall be as wool."

Nor is there any other way. In vain did Lady Macbeth cry, "Out, damned spot!" or seek cleansing by contrition.

> "Will all great Neptune's ocean wash this blood
> Clean from this hand? No, this my hand will rather
> The multitudinous seas incarnadine."

There is no deliverance from the shame and endless sorrow except at the fountain filled with blood drawn from Immanuel's veins.

Then, being forgiven of the mislived past, let us put on the whole armor of God, and henceforth apply ourselves to the service of truth and righteousness. Do you remember the words of Sir Walter Scott when death had laid its hand upon him? "Lockhart, be a good man. This is the sum and substance of all. Be a good man!" The poet-laureate has said the same thing in other words:

> "Howe'er it be, it seems to me
> 'T is only noble to be good."

JOB'S DAUGHTERS.

DELIVERED BY DAVID JAMES BURRELL, D. D., AT THE MARBLE
COLLEGIATE CHURCH, ON SABBATH EVENING NOV. 1, 1891.

" And in all the land were no women found so fair as the daughters
of Job: and their father gave them inheritance among their
brethren."—Job 42:15.

IT is a long lane that has no turning. Job had suffered
all the ills that human flesh is heir to ; but his captivity
was turned at last. He had stood the siege like a man.
No chastening, for the present, seemeth to be joyous but
grievous, but in the end it worketh the peaceable fruits of
righteousness to them that are exercised thereby. His
bodily pains are now over: his blood flows warm and
swift, and his flesh has come again like the flesh of a little
child. His fortune, also, is amply restored to him: he
has fourteen thousand sheep, six thousand camels, and a
thousand yoke of oxen. It is a true saying that godliness is profitable even for the life that now is. And his
friends have returned to him. You remember the epi-
gram :

> " Friends are like melons. Shall I tell you why?
> To find one good, you must an hundred try."

Matthew Henry says that Job's friends were mere swallows; they flitted in the fall and were back again in the spring. And his family is again built up. He had buried all his children, but God had repaired the breach. He has seven new sons and three daughters. As to his querulous wife, perhaps she had died and another taken her place; or rather let us hope she had learned her lesson and lived on. The patriarch's life was prolonged one hundred and forty years, and at length he was gathered to his fathers like a shock of corn in due season. All 's well that ends well.

We have to do particularly with these three daughters. There must have been something notable about them or they would not have been mentioned. You have probably observed how little is said of the women in ancient chronicles. Nor is this silence without reason. Those were days of stern conflict and pioneering. It was the formative period, and the women were rocking the cradle and ministering to the needs of generations yet to come. They were not mentioned therefore unless there was some special occasion for it.

I. These daughters of Job were remarkable for their beauty. " In all the land were no women found so fair as the daughters of Job."

Whether beauty is a good gift or not depends. It depends upon the use made of it. If you have ever been at Holyrood you sought at once the romantic spot beneath the great arched window where Mary of Scots made love to her devotees. But up the great stairway there is a place of deeper interest still—a blood-spot on the floor of the hall where her secretary Rizzio died for love of her. Yonder is the little door through which the assassins crept; yonder the bed-chamber through which they dragged him; yonder the entrance at which the beautiful queen stood screaming out her fear and fury. Near by is the window at which she stood, conscience-smitten, while the mob beneath called out the name of Darnley and thrust upon her sight a banner bearing this legend, "Oh, Lord, avenge him!" Her husband at that moment was Bothwell who had murdered Darnley. Her beauty was like a gallows-noose to all who were entangled in it. What a casting away of power was here!

Yet beauty is a divine talent, and may be gloriously used for God. The orphan girl who was seized to be the consort of Ahasuerus had beauty and piety along with it. When her people were in danger and the voice was heard under her window, "Who knowest but thou art come into the kingdom for such a time as this?" she communed with God and answered, "I will go in unto the king!" Never did woman care for her toilet more studiously than she that day; never was beauty more dazzling than hers. Her life in her hand, she set out for the wassail hall. The guards stood aside for the vision of beauty. She paused at the threshold. God help her now! God help her to use her marvellous beauty for him. The portal is crossed; she stands in sight of the revellers. Her coming there is like a burst of daybreak upon a boisterous night. Her beauty smites upon their eyes. There is a moment of bewildered surprise, then slowly the king lifts his sceptre: "Queen Esther, what wilt thou?" Her life is saved; her people are rescued from death; her beauty has done its appointed work.

The secret of beauty, after all, is the shining through of a consecrated spirit. I have passed a chancel window which seemed but a heterogeneous collection of fragments, as homely as the unsymmetrical features of the homeliest face. But I passed it again when the light was shining within, and lo! there stood the Madonna and her Child. So it is that a Christlike spirit transforms the plainest face and gives it a nameless charm.

II. These daughters of Job were remarkable also for their character. This appears in their several names, for in those times a name meant something.

(1.) *Jemima*, an old-fashioned name, meaning " Light of the Morning." Let it stand (to answer our purpose) for the influence of young womanhood at home. She had two sisters, loving and helpful. She had seven brothers, and boys were boys in Job's time as well as now. You can't put an old head on young shoulders. Nor can any one living estimate the influence of a gentle sister among a group of boisterous lads. There was the old father, too, who had seen trouble, sore trouble. And that cross-grained, embittered mother. What an opportunity for this Light of the Morning to do a gracious work!

(2.) *Kezia*, meaning Cassia, or "Breath of the Garden." Let her stand for the influence of young womanhood in social life.

Society, whether we like the constitution of it or not, is a fact, a tremendous fact. And it furnishes a coigne of vantage for many earnest people who are minded to do good. Society is not everywhere as bad as we are given to understand. Those who have the *entrée* of its charmed circle are not all *décollete* in modes and morals. In the time of the Roses virtue was a laughing-stock, marriage was a farce; all bonds were loosened in social life. The cavalier was usually a rake, and his fair ladye no better than she ought to be. Rivers of blood were shed for a woman's glove. Bull-baiting and cock-fighting were aristocratic pleasures. Bishops and dignitaries sat down together at the gambling-table. A man was not reckoned a gentleman unless he was carried to his bed from beneath the table of the banquet hall. We have made a great advance upon those times. Thank God, society is not what it used to be. Occasionally the old spirit creeps out, and namby-pamby pages come in chewing their canes, and queen's maids giggling and simpering; but our best society is clean and sweet and oftentimes godly. Snobs and dandies and frivolous young women are not the truest expression of our social life. There is scarcely a larger province of influence than is here afforded to a young woman of broad culture and sound principle. Miss Havergal was devoted to society; and with her sweet face and sweeter voice she sanctified it. In all her pleasures she lived in the spirit of her hymn,

> "Take my life and let it be
> Consecrated, Lord, to thee!
> Take my voice and let it sing
> Only, always for my King."

A visitor in the English House of Commons is struck with the lattice-work above the Speaker's chair, behind which are seen faces and figures flitting to and fro. These are English women, for no woman enters the House of Commons. But what matters that so long as a woman holds the sceptre of the British Empire? In our public and civil life there are walls of separation by which our women are excluded from many duties and responsibilities. This, however, is of little concern if they wield the sceptre as queens in our social life.

(3.) *Karen-happuch*, meaning " All - plenteousness."

Let Karen-happuch stand for the influence of young womanhood in the church of God. We are sometimes reminded—as if it were occasion for reproach—that women
constitute the majority of the church. This, however, is
nothing strange. The wonder is, considering what Jesus
Christ has done for womankind, that any woman should
hesitate for a moment to fall down and worship him. A
missionary passing through Cairo in company with an
accomplished Arab was amazed to see him, when approached by a wretched old creature, a withered hag, spit
at her and spurn her with his foot. He reproached him,
only to meet with this reply: "Pooh! she is only my
mother!" As a rule, a pagan woman has no thought of
equality in this life nor hope of it in the life hereafter, except on the chance of being born again and born a man.
All that the women of Christendom have to-day of right
and equality with their brother man is due to the gracious
offices of that Christ who "was of a woman born," and
whose disciples were instructed to teach that in his kingdom there is neither male nor female, but all are upon a
level of perfect equality in Him.

III. These daughters of Job were remarkable also for
their inheritance. "Their father gave them an inheritance
among their brethren." This was a rare thing in those
days; usually the eldest son received a double portion,
and the younger sons made haste to carry off everything

that was left.   In our times the daughters share the best
of everything with the sons, and above all they have equal
hope and part in the priceless bequest of the gospel of
Christ.

This inheritance means, to begin with, life at the cross.
All sons and daughters are equal here, and all alike being
conscious of sin may here array themselves in fine linen,
clean and white, which is the righteousness of saints.

What else?   The joy of service.   In our time women
are pressing to the front in Christian usefulness.   None
can complain that her spiritual power is " cabin'd, cribbed,
confined."

What else?   Participation in the heavenly glory.
" Now are we sons—and daughters—of God, and it doth
not yet appear what we shall be; but when He shall appear we shall be like him, for we shall see him as he is.
Eye hath not seen, ear hath not heard, it never hath entered into the heart of man to conceive, the things which
God hath prepared for them that love him."

"A COWARD,
AND WHAT BECAME OF HIM."

" And Pilate gave sentence that what they asked for should be done."
Luke 23:24 (N. V.).

A SERMON DELIVERED BY DR. BURRELL, ON SABBATH EVENING,
NOVEMBER 8, 1891.

WE all have an intense abhorrence of a coward; and this is to the credit of our human nature. For in the whole range of nature and humanity what is more repellant? Sir Walter Scott had a brother whom it is safe to say you never heard of. His name was Daniel. When a lad he went to the West Indies, and in a revolt among the negroes he showed the white feather and fled. His name was never mentioned after that; if reference was made to him, he was called " our relative." When he died he was buried secretly and no weeds were worn for him. He was a coward. That tells the story.

There was an old king of the Macedonians, by name Perseus, who for a similar reason was left out of the chronicles. Once when the battle raged fiercely he fled; he was overtaken by some of his captains and was found to have wrapped up his purple robe and placed it on the saddle before him, and was carrying his diadem under his arm. At sight of his pale face they turned back, one on the pretence of tying his shoe, another of watering his horse; and thus he vanishes from view.

It is bad enough to be a physical coward, but worse to be a moral coward, to show the white feather when principle is at stake; to have convictions but no courage behind them; to recognize the evil but lack courage to say no.

Fix your eyes on Pilate. An o'er close contact with an evil world had ploughed furrows across his face; sensuality had left its impress there. He had come up from Cæsarea a little while ago to keep peace during the great annual festival, for the Jews were a turbulent race. He made his headquarters at the castle of Antonia and doubtless kept well in-doors; for he was the best hated man in all Jerusalem and deserved it. Not long before he had built an aqueduct and taken money out of Corban, the sacred treasury of Israel, to pay for it. And when the people remonstrated he sent a band of Roman soldiers in Jewish disguise and slaughtered many of them. A little later he set up in Jerusalem a Roman standard on which was the name of an emperor to whom divine honors were paid. The Jews rose and besieged the Governor's gates until he recalled the idolatrous symbol and allowed them to have their way. And just recently, while a band of Galilean peasants were engaged at the altar, Pilate, having an accusation against them, sent a detachment of

Roman troops and "mingled their blood with their sacrifices." No wonder the Jews hated him and gnashed their teeth at him.

On the morning of this April day he was awakened bright and early by a beating at his gates. He doubtless arose from his couch with reluctance and muttering maledictions on these troublesome Jews. They had brought a prisoner for trial. Last night, at the conclave of the Sanhedrin, he was accused of blasphemy, of making himself equal with God. But no Roman magistrate would take cognizance of a theological indictment. So they must needs trump up charges against him. First, he had perverted the nation. Second, he had forbidden payment of tribute to the Emperor. Third, he had proclaimed himself a king. Pilate must determine upon this case: there was no escape. And you, friend, must also decide what you will do with Jesus who is called the Christ.

It is because of the connection of Pilate with this criminal case that he has come down through the centuries execrated in the words, " I believe in Jesus Christ who was crucified under Pontius Pilate." Now mark the circumstances which aggravated his cowardice.

(1.) He had heard about Jesus and knew him. His wonderful works and words and name were in the air. He had had, moreover, an interview with Jesus. He had asked him, " Art thou a king?" And Jesus answered, " Thou sayest it, but my kingdom is not of this world. I am come to reign in the province of truth." So he knew about Him. What will he do with Him?

(2.) Observe again, he had been warned concerning him. Not only had his conscience rung the alarm—as conscience warns us all—but a special admonition had been given him. His wife Procula had dreamed in the waking hours of the morning — the hour when Israel thought all dreams came true--and tradition tells us the dream. She saw a conflagration that consumed homes and temples and palaces, licked up forests and burned the heavens like a parched scroll, so that nothing could extinguish it. There were cries of the homeless and fear-stricken and dying. Then a lamb appeared, and as it lifted its eyes, all sounds were hushed. It mounted the flaming pyre; its side was pierced, blood gushed forth, and the fires were quenched. Then the lamb assumed human form and the appearance was, as the dreamer said,

> "Of a man divine and passing fair
> And like your august prisoner there."

Therefore she said, "Do no harm to that just man."

(3.) Observe again how Pilate's cowardice was aggravated by his attempts at evasion and compromise. He entreated the people, "Why, what evil hath he done?" He might as well have sung a lullaby to a cyclone. "Crucify him!" was the answer. "Crucify him!" And then he sent him to Herod—a happy thought. But Herod was too old a schemer to be caught napping. He would not be responsible for the decision of this perplexing case; so he sent the prisoner back. Pilate must judge him; so must you and I. Here is this Jesus, and what will he do with Him?   A great problem confronts him.   He said, "I will chastise him and let him go."   Oh shame upon him for a Roman magistrate!   The man is either guilty or innocent.   If guilty, he should die the death; if innocent, let him go.   Compromise never pays.   "Nothing is settled until it is settled right."   In 1787, at the making of our Constitution, the fathers were brought face to face with the slavery question.   They compromised; and we have been reaping the whirlwind ever since for their sowing of the wind.   Then in 1820 came Henry Clay with his Missouri Compromise: "No slavery north of 36o 30' except in Missouri."   That "except in Missouri" was to be the rankling thorn for years in our country's side.   Then in 1852 Stephen A. Douglas proposed his Kansas-Nebraska bill. It was a compromise, and it settled nothing.   The earth was rumbling even then.   In 1861 the heavens reverberated to the thunder of our artillery, and the whole land was sodden with tears and blood.   It is true in religion as in politics that no question is settled until it is settled right.   No man nor church nor theological seminary can afford to split the difference in spiritual things.

But what was the occasion of this man's cowardice?

(1.) To begin with, he was a trifler.   He lived in an age of cynicism; the foundations of religion were broken up.

> "On that hard Roman world disgust
>   And sated loathing fell;
> Deep weariness and sated lust
>   Made human life a hell."

And this man grew up in it. He had been a soldier. He had mingled with the soldiers at the camp-fire, cracking jokes about the gods and making sport of sacred things. And now, facing this divine Truth-giver, the irony of his retort—" What is truth?"—was but the outcome of his pernicious habit. Some of you, perhaps, have been wont to trifle in like manner. Our college boys are singing,

> " There was a man in our town,
>   And he was wondrous wise,"

to the tune of Antioch, on which our fathers bore aloft the praises of the Incarnation, "Joy to the world, the Lord is come!" But it should be understood that we cannot make light of any serious matter without ultimately paying for it.

(2.) Another reason for his cowardice : he was not his own man. He had no opinions of his own. He went to the people, to his wife, to the priests for advice. Oh, man, think for thyself! Do not farm out your opinions. Let no priest nor newspaper, no synod nor Sanhedrin, do your thinking for you. Let no man take thy crown. Quit thyself like a man.

It behooves us to have convictions of our own. Let us live by them, stand for them, and be willing in their defence, if need be, to die. If ever we are in doubt we have a sure Counsellor, as it is written, " If any of you lack wisdom, let him ask of God, who giveth to all men liberally and upbraideth not, and it shall be given him." Jas. 1 : 5.

(3.) Another reason for Pilate's cowardice was his

sycophancy. The people touched the raw spot when they said, " If thou let this man go thou art not Cæsar's friend." The Cæsar at this time was Tiberius, a jealous tyrant who owned Pilate body and soul. It would not do for Pilate to offend him lest he drop out of the line of promotion. At all hazards he must be Cæsar's friend.

What was the result? A little while after Tiberius was off the throne and Caligula was on. And Caligula said, " Go bring me Pilate ; he must answer to certain charges concerning an aqueduct, a Roman standard, and a murder at the altar." And a little later Pilate was an exile and a wanderer. He ended his own life at Lake Lucerne ; and there is a legend that once a year a spectre rises from the water, wringing its hands as Pilate did when he disclaimed responsibility for Jesus' death—wringing its hands and looking towards heaven.

> " By God abhorred, by man despised,
>   Shunned by the fiends below,
> Where shall the wretch, to hide himself
>   And hide his meanness, go ?"

But bide a wee. Let us not be too hard upon Pilate, for there may be some moral cowards among us. Let me give you a parting word, the motto of the Guthrie family, " *Sto pro veritate* "—Let us stand for the truth, the truth against the world. There is nothing better than that.

We are all in Pilate's place. The Lord Jesus stands in judgment before us. What are you going to do with Him? What think ye of him? Will you chastise him and let him go? Will you send him to Herod? You cannot shift the jurisdiction: he will evermore come back to you. Will you meet him with mock heroics, admiration of his manhood and rejection of his divine claim? Out upon all mere sentimentalism! The most cowardly thing that ever was said about Jesus was, "*Ecce Homo!*" Let us be logical and sensible. Christ was what he claimed to be or else an impostor who deserved to die. He either bore our sins in his own body on the tree or else the world for nineteen centuries has been deluded by him.

Here he stands before us. You and I must say whether he is to be our Christ or not. It is cowardice to believe the truth and not be willing to stand for it, and to suffer and die for it if need be. This is a most important moment, out of which may flow eternal issues for some of us.

> "Once to every man and nation
>   Comes the moment to decide,
>   In the strife of truth and falsehood,
>   For the good or evil side."

Make up your minds as to this Jesus, and having formed your judgment, stand by it. Do right! Do right! Do right though the heavens fall, and God bless you in doing it!

THE
STORY OF A BLIND BEGGAR.

DELIVERED BY DR. BURRELL, ON SABBATH EVENING,
NOVEMBER 15, 1891.

"And it came to pass that, as he was come nigh unto Jericho, a certain blind man sat by the wayside begging." Luke 18:35–43.

THE Passover was the great annual festival of all Jew-
ry. If we could have stood upon some high lookout we
should have seen the pilgrim bands winding their way
along all the thoroughfares towards the Holy City. One
of the caravans, at this time, was notable for the fact that
the Nazareth prophet was there. He was going to his
death. As he walked before his disciples "they feared."
A majestic sorrow was resting heavily upon him. Farrar
calls it the "transfiguration of self-sacrifice." He was
passing under the shadow of the cross. His disciples all
believed that he was going to Jerusalem to rule in regal
splendor. In vain did he speak to them of his approaching death; they could not apprehend it; they "were not
able to bear it." It was towards evening when the pilgrims reached the lower ford of the Jordan, crossed, and
drew nigh to Jericho the key city of the Holy Land. As
they approached the gate there were beggars along the
way who called aloud for help. One of them was desper-

ately in earnest, crying, " Jesus, thou Son of David, have mercy on me !" For some reason Jesus answered not. He is always the prayer-hearer ; but sometimes he tarries, and we must abide his time, He entered Jericho with his disciples and spent the night with Zacchæus the broker. The next morning he resumed the journey ; and as they issued from the western gate, the beggar who had been so importunate the night before was there with another wretched comrade, crying, " Jesus, thou Son of David, have mercy on me !"

Let us fix our eyes on this man.

I. Observe, he was a beggar. It is hard to be poor. Not many of us sympathize with Luther in his saying, " I thank God I am a poor man." The newspapers tell of a strange thing which happened yesterday at the Recorder's office. A German lad who had left his home and widowed mother a few months ago was brought to the bar for stealing. It transpired that on reaching Castle Garden he set out in a vain quest for work, finding a few odd jobs and sending a dollar or two to his old mother in Germany. Then the boy was adrift again. Hungry and desperate, he went down to the river's edge, but his old mother's face seemed to be looking back at him from the water and he turned again to the streets ; then in sudden impulse he committed the lawless deed. It was proven on examination that at the time he was on the very verge of starvation ; and as necessity knows no law, the Recorder acquitted him. One of the earliest memories of my boyhood is a pathetic song :

> " Pity, kind gentlemen, friends of humanity,
>   Cold blows the wind and the night 's coming on ;
> Give me some bread for my mother in charity ;
>   Give me some bread; and then I 'll be gone."

The world is full of such happenings and such appeals. Everywhere the struggle to keep the wolf from the door goes on.

II. To add to his misery this beggar was blind. What could be worse? Do you remember Milton's lament in "Samson Agonistes," written after the light had vanished from his own poor eyes?

> "Oh dark! dark! dark! amid the blaze of noon,
> Irrevocably dark, total eclipse without all hope of day."

If we must suffer loss of all our senses, let them go—taste, hearing, touch—but oh let us keep our eyes!

III. The climax of his misery, however, is reached in this—the beggar was blind in the valley of Jericho—the most beautiful spot on earth, the garden of balsam, the vale of fragrance, "the field of paradise." This expanse of beauty and fragrance and fruitfulness was the gift that Anthony selected for Cleopatra as the consummate token of his love. Bartimæus heard the people, as they passed by, commenting on the beauty of the morning, on the glory of the landscape round about, but he saw nothing. "How fair the skies," said one, "and the pastures how green!" "How beautiful the vineyards, just purpling for the vintage!" Vainly he rolled his eyes and saw it not.

We note the parallel in our relation with God. We are as penniless as Bartimæus in the coin that passes current in the realm of spiritual truth, for all our righteousnesses are as filthy rags. We are as blind by nature as Bartimæus, for we cannot see the wonders that lie beyond our finger-tips. Up to very recent days it was the custom of the Persian princes to put out the eyes of all who could by any possibility lay claim to the throne. So the apostle writes, "The god of this world hath blinded the eyes of the children of disobedience, lest the light of the glorious gospel should shine in unto them." The great verities are all around us—God, holiness, eternal glory—but these are to be spiritually discerned, and alas! we have only fleshly eyes.

Our carnal minds are enveloped in night "amid the blaze of noon." Nor is there any hope that we shall ever appreciate the sublime things of the spiritual world unless, perchance, the loving God with power to heal shall come this way.

And here he comes! Let us turn our eyes from the blind beggar to Jesus. For here is the incarnation of God.

I. Observe, he is passing by. No wonder the beggar cries aloud, "Have mercy on me!" and with renewed earnestness again and again, "Jesus, thou Son of David, have mercy on me;" for, mayhap, it is his last chance. Now or never! The suggestion to us is of "opportunity." The word itself is eloquent. It is from *ob portus*, that is, "at the entrance of the harbor." There is many a pleasure boat that sails gayly past the harbor, to and fro, and never enters it. There is many a galley laden with treasure that seeks one port and another but never enters this. Many a soul laden with glorious hope and possibilities anchors at the entrance until driven by the last tempest out upon the boundless sea for ever. Oh seize thine opportunity! I would to God we were not so afraid to act upon a noble impulse. A business man knows his opportunity when a bargain is at stake and does not hesitate to seize it. In the administration of Andrew Jackson a representative of France approached him with the offer of an immense tract of territory lying along our Mississippi valley. At that time France was involved in an imbroglio with England, and her exchequer needed an immediate replenishing. The offer of this vast area of territory was made for the consideration of fifteen millions of dollars—a mere bagatelle—but the bargain must be closed at once. It may be that the President strained his prerogative a trifle; but in securing the Louisiana purchase he gained for us a territory larger than the entire area of the original colonies and the richest in the land. It takes genius to apprehend a bargain. It takes genius to apprehend one's opportunity and grasp it. This is true in spiritual as in temporal things. I am here to-night with a flag of truce from the kingdom of heaven, to say in behalf of my Lord that if any man will this moment accept the benefits of the atonement of Christ he shall have eternal life. But the promise is only for this moment. "To-day is the day of salvation." Alas if, heaven being within our very grasp, we lose it!

> "There is a tide in the affairs of man
>   Which, taken at the flood, leads on to fortune ;
>   Omitted, all the voyage of our life
>   Is bound in shallows and in miseries."

II. Observe that Jesus is standing still. What is it that has arrested his steps? Prayer. A beggar's cry. "Prayer moves the hand that moves the world to bring salvation down." I know what some people are saying— that prayer has merely a reflex influence, that it affects the petitioner, but has no power over the great God. Strange that we should be so much more sensible in temporalities than we are in spiritual things. How would it seem if a banking institution should notify its depositors that henceforth no more checks or drafts would be honored? "You may keep on presenting them; it will be good exercise for you to keep walking to and fro, but as to paying, we have decided to do no more of it." Not so have we learned the promises of God. When he says,

"Ask, and ye shall receive; seek, and ye shall find; knock, and it shall be opened unto you," he means every word of it. So in this case it was prayer that arrested the Saviour's steps.

It was the right sort of prayer, however. We sometimes "ask and receive not, because we ask amiss." As to this prayer of Bartimæus, note that

(1.) It was an intelligent one. He knew whom he was addressing: "Jesus, thou Son of David." This "Son of David" was a Messianic title, and its use showed that the suppliant believed in Jesus as the very Son of God. He might have been unable to set forth the rationale of prayer, but he grasped it. If we would pray aright we must at the outset apprehend that God is and that he is the rewarder of them that diligently seek him.

(2.) This prayer was importunate. "Be still," they cried; "hold thy peace!" But he would not. The sword of Abd el Mourad is displayed in one of the mosques of Constantinople. If you express wonder that a weapon so effective should be a mere wooden thing carved from a plane-tree, the attendant priest will answer, "Ay, but you forget the arm of Abd el Mourad." So prayer is nothing at all except for the strength of a fervid soul behind it.

(3.) It was a specific prayer. It went straight to the mark. There was no exordium nor peroration nor circumlocution. One thing only did this beggar want, one thing only did he ask: "Oh that I might receive my sight!" He had ten thousand other wants, no doubt, but this was over all.

When the Czar of Russia wished to build his railway from St. Petersburg to Moscow he sent for Winans, the American engineer, to make the survey. The route as outlined turned aside for hills and chasms, and sought contact with all towns and villages along the way. The

Czar drew a straight line across the diagram from St. Petersburg to Moscow, saying, "Go straight there; turn aside for nothing." And this is the right method of prayer. Let us come to the point. If we desire anything let us ask it.

(4.) It was also the prayer of faith. How do we know that Bartimæus had faith? Because he threw away his cloak when Jesus called him. All his earthly wealth might have been, and probably was, in that poor garment. But he could well afford to part with it in view of the great benefit which he felt sure was coming to him. Throw away your tattered cloak, my friend, as you draw near to Christ—that vicious habit, that darling sin, your carnal ambition or self-righteous pride—whatever it is, away with it! If you expect and desire your prayer to be heard, you will cast everything before the feet of God.

III. Now observe Jesus with his hands outstretched and saying, "Receive thy sight; thy faith hath saved thee." I would that we might have had an instantaneous photograph of Jesus in this attitude. It would be a perfect picture of God. For what is God? The scientist says Law. But Law means justice; and justice to the sinner is eternal death. Others tell us "God is Light." But if that be all we may as well look elsewhere for help and comfort. Light never cooked a dinner for a hungry man. The coldest thing in the universe is the white solar ray. No, God is Love above all. That tells the story and satisfies us.

Jesus said, "Receive thy sight," and the eyes of Bartimæus were opened. There were the oliveyards, the vineyards, the beauty of the skies above and the earth beneath, but nothing anywhere was so beautiful to him as the face of the Physician bending over him.

And it is written he followed Jesus and gave glory to

God. The pilgrim band moved onward to the Holy City. As they turned the spur of Olivet and came in sight of Jerusalem those that went before him and those that followed after cried, " Hosanna! Hosanna to the Son of David! Blessed is he that cometh in the name of the Lord!" And in all that joyous company there was none with a heart more rapturous or eyes brighter with enthusiasm or voice more resonant with grateful praise than Bartimæus, who a little while ago was a beggar, blind, friendless, and hopeless, in the valley of Jericho.

The sequel is not recorded, but it is easy to conjecture. He lived a few years, more or less, and then some kind friend closed his eyes, while others gathered about him said, " Bartimæus is dead." He had, however, but crossed the " covered bridge that leads from light to light through a brief darkness." And there his eyes were opened on the heavenly landscapes. " Oh the transporting, rapturous scene that opens to his sight!" But in heaven as on earth the fairest object he saw was Jesus' face, marred, but divinely beautiful. In humble gratitude he lives to-day, still " following him and giving praise to God."

THE
TWICE-TAUGHT LESSON.

" For they considered not the miracle of the loaves."   Mark 6:52.

DELIVERED BY DR. BURRELL, NOVEMBER 22, 1891.

THE quietest and least imposing of Christ's miracles was the feeding of the five thousand.   There was no display, no manifestation of power, as at the raising of Lazarus or the healing of the ten lepers.   It is safe to say that only a few of the people were aware of what was being done until it was over.   A lad with a basket, five loaves of bread, and a dozen men passing to and fro distributing the food which they had received from Jesus' hands.   No one knew how it was done.   Here was the hiding of power.   He might have waved a wand above the lad's basket and pronounced a mystic formula, but there was no demonstration of any sort.   It was a beautiful apologue of providence.   The same Christ is feeding us always, and in much the same way.   A farmer goes out with his apron full of wheat and scatters it over the ploughed ground; a little later he drives the reaper through the yellow harvest, and his garners are full.   So wholly does God conceal himself in this matter that we scarcely think of him in connection with it.   Yet he must needs watch over every kernel of grain, see that the sun duly shines upon it, that the showers are distilled from heaven upon it, that the chemicals of the soil are properly adjusted to it.   He must protect it from insect and vermin, from drought and torrent, that the handful may become a binful and the multitudes be fed. It is always the same quiet miracle of the loaves. He might, indeed, despatch a procession of angels to scatter the wheat, sending before them an orchestra with harps and cymbals, and uttering his word of command to the scattered wheat, " Live and multiply;" so that in an instant the growing grain would appear above the soil and ripen in an hour into a yellow harvest bending its head to the sickle. Then we should exclaim, "Behold the hand of the Almighty!" Yet year by year all this is being done in the beautiful processes of natural law, so effectively that summer and winter, seed-time and harvest, never fail; so silently indeed that heedless folk forget to say grace at table. We see the ploughman and the reaper, but how rarely do we see Jehovah behind them. We learn not the lesson of providence; we consider not the miracle of the loaves.   •

But if the multiplication of the loaves was unimpressive, there were other events that day which greatly wrought upon the people's wonder: the eloquence of Jesus, his marvellous presentation of spiritual truth, his miracles of healing, tokens of his divinity every way. They were inclined to receive him as that Son of David who had been prophesied to come in the last times and restore the kingdom to Israel. " Let us rally around him," they said, "and escort him to the Holy City, where hundreds of thousands in attendance on the annual feast will join us in proclaiming him King of the Jews !" These were the whisperings that passed among them. The disciples, enthusiastic and ambitious to occupy places of honor in the new kingdom, readily fell in with the suggestion. All that was passing in their hearts was known to Jesus. He must thwart their intent. His high purpose

was the redemption of the race. The throne of Judæa
was no more to him than a child's rattle to an archangel.
He therefore called his disciples aside and bade them
enter the little boat that was tied to the shore and to betake themselves to the other side of the lake. It is written significantly, "He constrained them to get into the
boat." They may have remonstrated. The sky may
have been dark with portents of the approaching storm.
He was but a landsman; they were sea-faring men and
knew the dangers of the little lake. But he constrained
them to go. Then, remaining with the people for a little, he
quietly dispersed them and betook himself to the solitude
of the mountain. Into that Holy of Holies we may not
intrude. It was his wont in this manner to hold frequent
intercourse with his Father alone. The forest was his
closet, the solitude was its closed door, and the sky above
was its open window towards Jerusalem. Here we leave
him.

The story now resolves itself into a drama in three
scenes.

I. The storm. While Jesus was in the mountain alone
the disciples, in their little boat, were moving out towards
the middle of the lake. The night closed around them.
There was a dead hush. The air was heavy and oppres-
sive. Not a breath stirred the sails. They knew the
meaning of this ominous calm ; nor had they long to wait.
Down through the gorges came the rushing wind; the
shrouds whistled, the timbers creaked ; they sprang to
the sails and lowered them, then to the oars; and until
the fourth watch of the night they toiled for their lives.

"If our Lord were only here !" they cried. "Oh if
our Lord were only here !" Once before he had been
with them under similar circumstances. The wind had
burst upon them while he lay asleep in the stern of the

little boat; and, weary as He was, they were reluctant to disturb him, until the worst came to the worst; then they bent over him, crying, "Master, Master, we perish!" Half rising and taking in the situation at a glance, he said, "Why are ye so cowardly, O ye of little faith?" Then facing the tempest, his garments and flowing hair blown backwards by the wind, he stretched forth his hands, saying, "Peace, be still!" and so quieted his angry child. Little wonder that they longed for his presence now. But it was for this very reason that he had brought them into the storm, that they might learn the lesson of his providence. In our very childhood we are taught to long for the fleshly presence of our Lord.

> "I wish that His hands had been placed on my head,
>   That his arms had been thrown around me,
> And that I might have heard his kind voice when he said,
>   'Let the little ones come unto me.'"

It was for this that He said, "It is expedient that I go away." We must trust him in his absence. "I will not believe," said Thomas, "except I put my finger into the print of the nails." If we thus insist he may condescend to convince us, "Reach hither thy hand and thrust it into my side, and be not faithless but believing," but, for all this, the greater blessing is upon the higher faith that grasps the invisible. "Blessed are they which not having seen have yet believed." Oh for a simpler, deeper, sublimer faith in the invisible, intangible, yet present and ever helpful Christ! In whom, though now we see him not, yet, believing, we rejoice with joy unspeakable and full of glory.

II. The rescue. It is written that while they were toiling at the oars through the weary night "he saw them." He was at the least three miles away, the night was dark, the billows were high, and the foam was tossing over the little boat; but through all he saw them. Oh wonderful eyes of the Lord! They pierce through infinite space. All the roofs are lifted off before them; they see the pain, the plotting, the shame and heart-ache; they see it all. Wonderful, wonderful eyes of the Lord! How comforting to us, who seem at times so far away, to know that we are never out of his sight! Let us be assured that our present trouble and all the uncertainties of our future are plain to him.

> "So on I go, not knowing:
>   I would not if I might.
>   I 'd rather walk with God in the dark
>   Than go alone in the light.
>   I 'd rather walk by faith with him
>   Than go alone by sight."

He not only saw them, but in the fourth watch of the night, the darkest and most hopeless hour, He came to them walking on the sea. The hieroglyph of the ancient Egyptians to denote impossibility was two feet upon the water; but the thing which is impossible with men is not only possible but easy for God. The sea is his and he made it. Let Xerxes move back his throne, lashing the tides in vain fury. God made the boundaries of the mighty deep and said, " Thus far shalt thou come and no farther, and here let thy proud waves be stayed!"

And when the disciples saw him they were afraid, saying, " It is a spirit!" His figure was outlined against the dark sky. They were seafaring men and afraid of the supernatural, the sort of men who in our times nail a horseshoe to the mast. This fear of the supernatural betrays a wrong adjustment in our moral nature. We are all prone to it. These fishermen had faced many a storm, but at sight of that dim figure against the sky their limbs shook and their flesh crept. Ah many a time when we have been in dire distress of pain or sorrow God has come to us in such strange guise of providence that we also have been afraid of him.

And he said unto them, " Be of good cheer; it is I; be not afraid." Our providences are all strange to us now. We consider not the miracle of the loaves and are scarcely more mindful of the miracle of the storm. Oh for more faith in providence! One day we will understand.

> " God moves in a mysterious way
> His wonders to perform;
> He plants his footsteps in the sea
> And rides upon the storm."

III. The swift voyage. We marvel at the speed with which our " ocean greyhounds " are in these times traversing the seas. Six days and a trifle over to cross the Atlantic! But never was a passage like this before us, for in the twinkling of an eye, when they had taken Jesus aboard, the little ship was at the place whither they went.

We are still learning our lesson. God is a great helper in every sphere and department of human life.

(1.) In the hard struggle for success. He who, in a legitimate calling, is striving for a competency or a fortune, may attain his end much more certainly by receiving Jesus on board the ship. It is a true saying that " Godliness is profitable for all things," not less for a man's temporal weal than for his spiritual life.

(2.) In the stress of adversity. When God's children are in trouble he loves to deliver them. His ear is open to their cry, and nothing is too hard for him. A band of Covenanters in old Scotland, men, women, and little children, driven from their conventicle and fleeing for life, as they climbed the hills saw just across the ravine the bloody Claverhouse and his men. They were helpless to escape.

It was evident that an hour would seal their doom. The old minister knelt down in their midst and prayed: "O God, this is the hour of thine opportunity. We are helpless unless thou come. These weary bairns can flee no more. We cast ourselves upon thy mighty power. Twine our enemies around these hills. O Lord, confuse them and deliver us! Cast the lap of thy garment over puir auld Saunders and these frail bairns." Then the thing happened which men laugh at—the incredible thing, a special providence. The mist crept up the valley while the little band of Covenanters were praying, rose higher and higher, until it stood as an impenetrable wall between them and bloody Claverhouse. God had indeed confused their enemies and twined them among the hills. He had cast the lap of his garment over his little ones. Yet why should this seem wonderful? It is but the story of our daily bread if we would only believe it. Or must we be brought into the storm that we may consider the truth of providence? Is the tempest a needs be?

(3.) In agonizing for salvation. All night long, nine weary hours, they toiled at the oars; their hands were blistered, their strength exhausted, their hope was gone. Then he came. And thus it ever is. When we have done our utmost God must save. And what is salvation but his most special providence? We are delivered not by might nor by power, but by the Spirit of the Lord. Our part of the doing is simply to believe. "This is the work of God," said Jesus, "that ye believe on him whom God hath sent."

(4.) In the last hour. Blessed is the man who, when he enters Charon's boat, finds that the boatman is not Charon, but Christ. "I will not fear, for thou art with me; thy rod and thy staff they comfort me." In London Tower is an inscription cut upon the wall by some prisoner who may have spent his life in darkness and suffered death centuries ago on Tower Hill:

" A passage perilus maketh a port pleasant."

There will be no storms in the better land, and no need to learn there the lesson of providence. It will be clear to us that every moment while we were on earth he was caring for us. And heaven will largely consist in the apprehension of this truth. Our heaven would begin here and now if only we could believe thoroughly in God.

TWENTY REASONS

FOR BELIEVING THE BIBLE TO BE THE WORD OF GOD.

PREACHED BY DR. BURRELL, NOVEMBER 29, 1891.

" But continue thou in the things which thou hast learned and hast been assured of, knowing of whom thou hast learned them; and that from a child thou hast known the Holy Scriptures, which are able to make thee wise unto salvation through faith which is in Christ Jesus. All Scripture is given by inspiration of God, and is profitable for doctrine, for reproof, for correction, for instruction in righteousness: that the man of God may be perfect, thoroughly furnished unto all good works."

2 Tim. 3:14-17.

THE young man to whom these words were addressed by the aged Paul was pastor of the Christian church in Ephesus. He was surrounded by temptations there. Ephesus was the chief emporium for a considerable portion of the trade of Asia, a resort for fashionable people who wished to lose themselves in the whirl of vice and sensuality, and it was also a distinguished seat of pagan learning. The young pastor had, therefore, to meet all the temptations incident to a life of sordid enthusiasm, carnal pleasure, and worldly wisdom. But against these he was fortified by the training which he had received, not merely from Paul, his spiritual foster father, but from his mother Eunice, and that other excellent woman his grandmother Lois. From these he had gotten a faithful tuition in the Holy Scriptures, which are able to make men wise unto salvation and to serve them in times of moral conflict as a weapon—"the sword of the Spirit which is the Word of God." In this letter, full of faithful counsel and admonition, the aged apostle bids the young pastor be mindful of those rudiments of faith and morals which had been thus imparted to him in early life. "Continue thou in the things which thou hast learned and hast been assured of." How many a youth in the fret and hurry of our metropolitan life has need of similar counsel. There never was a time in the history of the world when temptations addressed the young and unwary in voices so numerous and alluring as in these days. The life of commerce makes its vociferous claims; the life of pleasure beckons from the doorways and calls from the windows along the way; and presumptuous folly arrayed in the garb of wisdom cries aloud at the corners of the streets that the old truths are superannuated, that the Bible is untrustworthy, that religion is but a refined form of superstition, and that the *zeitgeist* is more important than the Spirit of God. Now let the hallowed past stand forth to help and strengthen! Let memory recall the voice of the dear mother who "just knew, and knew no more, her Bible true," and the voice of the village preacher, so far away in the glamour of the vanished past, commending the Cross, the old-fashioned Book, and the precepts of a holy life. O young man, continue thou in the things which thou hast learned and hast been assured of, knowing of whom thou hast learned them! Be not carried away with every wind of doctrine and destructive criticism. Stand by your principles. Be loyal to your convictions; and let the truths which have commended themselves to the world for centuries be yours to serve as an anchor of the soul, sure and steadfast, until you are quite confident that our forebears have been grievously duped, history imposed upon, and the race ensnared by the Christian faith. Think well before leaving the old landmarks. Hold fast your Bible. To leave that is to be without an anchor in the storm. Remember and give heed to the lessons of long ago!

If, however, we are to affix our faith to the Scriptures and cling to them amid the storms of opposition and iconoclastic wisdom, we must be able to give a reason for doing so. An earnest man ought never to be at a loss when asked why he believes the Scriptures to be the word of God. It is my purpose here to enumerate some of our reasons for holding to the old Book. The method of this argument is cumulative. One point may not be conclusive, but twenty may have the force of progressive approach to demonstration. Our glance at these considerations must be merely cursory and suggestive. It is believed, however, that their total force will be convincing to earnest and unbiassed minds.

1. There is *an antecedent probability* of a revelation from God. It is implied from our relations with him. If he is our Father he would scarcely leave us in doubt as to the great problems which reach out into the eternal ages. It would seem that a good father must speak to his sons and daughters in their distress and bewilderment, telling them definitely of his love, his justice, his purposes concerning them. A good king puts up finger-boards to guide wayfarers through the forest and along the perplexing roads. If God is our King shall he not tell us

how to reach the kingdom?   Is it reasonable to suppose that if, as the pagan Aratus said, "We are also his offspring," he would leave us without an answer to our questions "Whence?" and "Whither?"   Plato lamented that he was adrift upon a raft with no rudder at his hand nor star above to guide him, yet he ventured the hope that some time the gods would give the bewildered race a good stanch boat.   This was but the expression of the universal instinct.   If there is a God it would appear that somewhere there must be a clear and distinct revelation of him.   There is a Bible somewhere.   Where?   We believe, for reasons that follow, that our Scriptures are this Word of God.

2. *The Scriptures make this claim.*   And let it be noted that among the world's sacred books there is no other that arrogates to itself a real and inerrant divineness. The Bible is full of a " Thus saith the Lord."   Its claim of inspiration, like its doctrines of God and Immortality, is to be read everywhere between the lines.   The claim is made, moreover, in explicit terms, as where it is said, " Holy men of God spake as they were moved by the Holy Ghost," 2 Pet. 1 : 21 ; and again in our text, "All Scripture is given by inspiration of God, and is profitable for doctrine, for reproof, for correction, for instruction in righteousness : that the man of God may be perfect, thoroughly furnished unto all good works."   The word inspiration is *theopnustos :* literally, God-breathed.   All Scripture thus God-breathed is true, inerrantly true and profitable for us.

If it be said that this claim is not sufficiently definite or conclusive, we answer that the proof thus furnished within its own pages of its plenary inspiration is as complete and satisfactory as that which it furnishes to substantiate the immortality of the soul or the divineness of Jesus

Christ. It is as complete indeed as its proof of any of the great doctrines which we regard as vital to the integrity of the Christian faith.

3. *The Truth of the Bible*, its absolute, faultless truth. The claim of such inerrancy is made not for the Scriptures as they are current among us, but for the original autographs as they came from the pens of the holy men who wrote as they were moved by the Spirit of God. If it be said that no one living has ever seen that original parchment, we answer, By the same token no living man has ever seen the original Christ. We have the same reasons precisely for believing in the errorlessness of the original copy of the written Word as for accepting the sinlessness of the Incarnate Word. Both alike have suffered in " transcription." All copyists of the Incarnate Word have alike misrepresented him in their walk and conversation ; yet even the mistakes of believers in their earnest yet inadequate efforts to copy his perfect life and character are evidences in favor of the guilelessness of Christ himself. In like manner the small errors, literal and numerical, which have crept into the Scriptural text in the process of transcription through these hundreds of years do but furnish strong presumptive proof of its original inerrancy as it was received from the divine mind for transmission to men. If there had been errors in the original, misstatements of fact, contradictions of science, fabulous history, it would be incredible that the wisdom of the world should not have discovered them long, long ago. It seems clear, however, that the errors in our received versions are such as were most likely to come, nay, such as could scarcely have come otherwise than in the process of transcription. We boldly affirm that as yet the destructive critics have not been able to produce a single error or discrepancy which is not most

reasonably and fairly accounted for in this way, not one which can be logically or conclusively or reasonably traced to the original autograph.

4. *Its Literary Worth.* Let *dilettanti* scholars speak with modesty in disparagement of the Scriptures in view of the fact that the wisdom of the centuries conspires to praise them. Sir Isaac Newton said, "We account the Scriptures of God to be the most sublime philosophy." John Milton said, "There are no songs comparable to the songs of Zion, no orations equal to those of the prophets, and no politics like those which the Scriptures teach." Daniel Webster said, "From the time that at my mother's feet or on my father's knee I first learned to lisp verses from the sacred writings they have been my daily study and vigilant contemplation. If there be anything in my style or thoughts to be commended, the credit is due to my kind parents in instilling into my mind an early love of the Scriptures." It is fair to say that by universal consent there is no book in universal literature which at any point of literary merit approaches the Scriptures.

> "A glory gilds the sacred page
>   Majestic like the sun;
> It gives a light to every age,
>   It gives but borrows none."

5. *Its Unity.* Here are sixty-six books upon a large variety of themes embraced under the general head of religion: the work of forty writers of various nationalities and of all grades of natural ability and culture, speaking divers tongues, writing at intervals along a period of 1,600 years, representing all degrees of racial development from barbarism to noblest enlightenment. And here is the strange thing: these sixty-six books thus composed when

bound together constitute one harmonious and consistent whole. Shall we say that this is a fortuitous circumstance? The folly of such a statement would immediately be recognized in any other sphere. If forty persons of different tongues, temperaments, and degrees of musical culture were to pass through the organ-loft of this church at long intervals and strike sixty-six notes, which when combined should yield the theme of the grandest oratorio earth ever heard, the man who would regard that as a fortuitous happening would by universal consent be deemed a fool. The conclusion would be irresistible that one controlling mind was behind it.

6. *Its Completeness.* The uninspired word *finis* at the end of the book is as true as if it were in the body of it. There was to be no *addendum*, no *erratum*. The book when finished with the testimony of the last evangelist was closed for ever. That word *finis* means, " I am complete ; let the future ages supplant or supplement me if they can !"

The text-books that were used when we were boys and girls at school are all obsolete. Such as are in current use by our children must be revised from year to year ; the latest editions must be had in every case. But strange to tell, the first edition of the Scriptures is the one in universal demand. Our desire is to get back to the oldest, to the original, for what must be in spiritual things the best authority for this and every age. In other words, marvellous to tell, the Bible written so long ago must have been adapted to all future progress—a book full and complete, measuring out to the entire race its supply for all kinds of moral needs from the beginning to the end of time.

7. *Its Freshness.* No other book bears reading over

and over and over again. We tire of the noblest and best on
a third reading. But these marvellous pages are like spices,
which the more they are rubbed give forth the more of
fragrant sweetness. Old Dr. Elliot sitting by the window
with a Bible on his knees, being asked what he was reading, answered, " The news, always the news." The poet
Goethe said, " The Bible becomes more and more beautiful the more I study it."

8. *Its Antiquity*. It was in large portion an old volume when Cecrops founded Egypt. We speak of Chaucer as the father of our literature, but the book of Job
was three thousand years old when Chaucer opened up
his " well of English undefiled." Dr. Johnson read the
book of Ruth aloud in a literary club at a time when infidelity was rife. " Where did you find it?" exclaimed his
hearers. Great was their amazement when he answered,
" This pastoral was written twenty-five hundred years before the discovery of America."

9. *Its Indestructibility*. The fires have not been able
to burn it. There have been eras of persecution when
the great cities of the world were lit with bonfires of Bibles;
and through all these centuries the hot fires of adverse
criticism have been kindled against it; yet out of them all
this blessed Book has come without the smell of fire upon
it. The Bible records no miracle more wonderful than its
own survival. Other books of moral truth have either
yielded to criticism or grown obsolete through the progress of the ages. Our libraries are cemeteries. Here
are three epitaphs which are at first sight scarcely recognized — *Novum Organum*, *Hydriotaphia*, *Eikonoklastes*.
Who cares for them now? Yet *Novum Organum*, by
Bacon, introduced the inductive system of philosophy.
Hydriotaphia, by Sir Thomas Browne, was a thesaurus of

general information such as the world has seldom seen.
And *Eikonoklastes*, by John Milton, was his manifesto
against the divine right of kings. Thus the great books
die, but one book lives!—lives in spite of persecution and
the rasure of time—lives gloriously and will survive all.

10. *Its Propagation.* It is printed in 300 languages
and scattered over the world like leaves of the tree of life.
The interest which it excites in the universal mind, and
by which it is separated infinitely from all books of human
origin, is attested by the fact that within forty-eight hours
after the new version was issued two million five hundred
thousand copies were disposed of. The telegraphic wires
were kept busy, to the exclusion of other—and, strangely
enough, less important—work, while transmitting the four
Gospels from New York to Chicago in a telegram of
more than one hundred thousand words.

11. *Its Influence on Character.* "It is the power of
God unto salvation to every one that receiveth it." We
may not explain the subtle metaphysical force in this volume—a force that grips hold of the sinner and somehow
transforms him, changes his heart, conscience, brain, and
will, and makes him a new man every way. The Chan-
cellor of Queen Candace was converted by reading the
53d chapter of Isaiah ; and Lord Rochester, a vicious infidel, was converted some centuries later by reading the
same portion of this book. And this sort of thing is going on the world over all the time. Has any other book
such power? Do the Shastras, the Zendavesta, the Koran,
the Analects of Confucius turn men about in this way,
reform them, transform them, and set their faces towards
truth and righteousness and heaven and God? An old
Highlander said to Claudius Buchanan, "I cannot argue,
I cannot present any theological facts or reasons, I can-

not explain the process or philosophy of revelation; but I know this, that when I was a man with an ungovernable temper and an evil character, this Book got hold of me and *quelled the tiger in me*."

We will abide the issue: stand on a Broadway corner and take a hundred men at random from among the passers-by who say that they believe in these Scriptures, and take another hundred at random from those who reject them; let the two companies stand facing each other and contrast their characters. We will abide the issue. The best men of the world to-day are, as a rule, conspicuously and undeniably those who believe in the Scriptures of God.

12. *Its Power over the Nations.* Take a map and draw lines separating the nations that receive the Bible from those who are without it, and you have divided between barbarism and civilization, between thrift and poverty, between charity and selfishness, between tyranny and freedom, between light and the shadow of death.

The three prominent nations of the earth to-day are America, England, and Germany. Our Government is indisputably founded on the principles of the Bible. The preamble of our Declaration of Independence was borrowed from Paul's sermon on Areopagus, and our whole political fabric is permeated with the moral teachings of Christ. England has a Christian queen who explicitly avows that the Bible is the secret of her country's greatness. And as for Germany, at the close of the Franco-Prussian war Père Hyacinthe declared to his people that the reason for their defeat lay in the fact that every German soldier marching against Paris had a Bible in his knapsack.

13. *Its Code of Morals.** It is superfluous to say that

the ethics of the Scriptures are furnishing all the moral standards of the world. The courtesies, proprieties, humanities of our civil, social, and domestic life are traced to the Sermon on the Mount. The jurisprudence of every civilized people on the globe is taken from the Decalogue. The Decalogue and the Sermon on the Mount are the two brief summaries of scriptural morality, and between them stands Jesus Christ, the exemplar of both these symbols and the only perfect Man the world ever saw.

14. *Its Doctrines.* The Bible is the only book in existence that boldly and conclusively touches the great spiritual problems. It is the only book that makes a distinct utterance with reference to the nature and character of God, and to the nature and character and destiny of man. It not only sets forth the great moral and spiritual truths, but it so simplifies them as to bring them within the grasp of not merely philosophers but the humble folk. As it is written, " Except ye become as little children ye shall in no wise see the kingdom of God." And a curious fact is this : the truths thus presented are capable of codification. No one ever heard of a doctrinal system belonging to Islam or Confucianism or any other religion except ours. There is a system of truths represented in the œcumenical creeds of christendom which is substantially—nay, absolutely—identical among all the multitudinous families of the church militant. These truths are strung together in logical and coherent order, as if intended to furnish thus a necklace of pearls for the adornment of the Bride of God.

15. *The Science of the Scriptures.* And here I am aware we are setting foot on delicate ground ; for it is a somewhat shop-worn claim of a certain class of scientific people in these times that the Scriptures are as far as pos-

sible from accuracy at this point. It stands, nevertheless, that no scientific statement in the Scriptures has ever been disproved; while on the other hand they furnish the basis for cosmology, anthropology, philology, geology, astronomy, and every other important science. If it be claimed that the Scriptures be not *en rapport* with certain scientific hypotheses of these times, we answer that if it were we should scarcely regard it as divine, for God does not guess at anything. It is worthy of note in this connection that in 1801 there were more than eighty theories before the French Institute with respect to natural science, every one of which was alleged to contradict the Bible. Where are they now? Every one of them has died the death; but the old Book lives.

It used to be said that the Bible was all wrong in the statement that "the host of heaven cannot be numbered." This was alleged to be one of its scientific blunders. Hipparchus counted the host of heaven and made them 1,022; Ptolemy, two centuries later, substantially agreed with him, making the total 1,026; but as the scope of vision was artificially enlarged some thousands or hundreds of thousands more came into view. At length Lord Rosse's telescope enabled the human eye to see something like four hundred millions. To-day the stars of heaven are as innumerable as the sands of the seashore. There are more solar systems within our line of vision now than there were fixed stars in the ancient times. The skies are filled with nebulæ, clouds of star-dust! The Bible was right: the host of heaven cannot be numbered. Thus it is found, as in every other particular where the Scriptures have been assailed by criticism, that they did but anticipate the approved results of science in these after days.

16. *Its History*. All other chronicles — as those of Cæsar, Herodotus, and Thucydides—are but the records of an episode or period of events; but the Bible is the one universal history. It carries us back through the nations, past the earliest communities, beyond the primitive chaos, to the remotest origin of things. "In the beginning, God."

The attempts to cast reproach on Scriptural history have been vain. In Genesis 9 : 27 we have the cardinal truth of ethnology set forth in the seemingly commonplace words, "God shall enlarge Japheth, and he shall dwell in the tents of Shem; and Canaan shall be his servant." This is a statement of literal historical truth. In the tenth chapter of Genesis we come upon a catalogue of names as dry as a city directory, which is in fact a procession of the nations, and yielding a more comprehensive survey of history than was ever written elsewhere. And in every particular where the records of this venerable Book have been aspersed the researches of the archæologist among the monuments of the past have seemed to vindicate them.

17. *The Prophecies*. Seventeen of the books of the Bible are prophetic. Of the tens of thousands of predictions which they contain, not one has miscarried yet. Many of them remain to be fulfilled; but the observation of the past gives us abundant reason to believe that every one shall be fulfilled. The owl and the bittern, dwelling amid the ruins of innumerable cities on which the curse of divine judgment was pronounced in olden times, declare the truth of the divine prophecies. Not one faileth.

18. *The Tone of Authority*. It might be supposed that a book dealing with truths that lie beyond the evi-

dence of the senses would speak with some reservation. But there is no *if* or *perhaps* in our Bible; it speaks with a voice of authority. And indeed our souls demand this. With respect to the great problems we wish no guesses, we will accept no peradventures; we must know. Nor can we know except by a definite divine *ipse dixit*. It is thus the Scriptures speak, "Yea and amen." "Thus saith the Lord," "Verily, verily I say unto you." To put an *if* into the Decalogue or the Sermon on the Mount or the Apocalypse, or to put a *perhaps* in the third chapter of John with its announcement of the great truth of Redemption, would be to destroy the force of all. The Bible, professing to announce the great truths of eternity, must utter forth no uncertain sound. It speaks as the oracles of God.

19. *Its Adaptation to Human Wants.* There is no experience in life where the Scriptures do not yield us help and comfort. In pain, sorrow, poverty, discouragement, the anguish of death, it helps and holds us up. This was beautifully stated by Coleridge in his words "It finds me." Wherever we are, whatever we do, however we suffer, this blessed Bible finds us.

20. *Its Plan of Salvation.* This is, after all, the crowning proof of its divineness. In every human heart, down below all other wants and aspirations, there is a profound longing to know the way of the spiritual life.

The whole world is all the while crying, "What shall I do to be saved?" Of all the books in the world the Bible is the only one that answers this universal cry. There are others that with more or less correctness set forth the precepts of right living; but there is none that suggests a way of blotting out the record of the misspent past or of escaping from the penalty of the broken law.

All through the Scriptures, from the Garden of Eden to the Apocalyptic vision of the City of God, walks the majestic figure of One who claims to be the deliverer of the soul from sin. In the midst of the sacred oracles stands the Cross throwing its shadow four ways towards all the horizons of human life. Out of this blessed Book comes the voice, heard always and everywhere, " He that believeth on the Lord Jesus Christ shall be saved "—saved here and hereafter, saved from the shame and bondage and penalty of sin.

It is of little use, however, to study the Scriptures from the outside, or, by viewing them objectively, to prove their divineness. A Bible on the shelf is a vain thing. There are multitudes of people who know the Scripture by heart yet in their hearts have none of it. The truth is to be had not by looking at it in the distance but by appropriating it, by assimilating it, as bread is eaten and becomes a part of our physical life. The best proof of inspiration is that which a man gets by making the blessed Scriptures his own and feeling their power in his own inward peace and the renewal of his daily life. There is no evidence so satisfactory as that whereof the aged evangelist wrote, " That which we have heard, which we have seen with our eyes, which we have looked upon and our hands have handled of the word of life, declare we unto you." A lifeboat is a beautiful piece of mechanism. The ingenuity of man has taxed itself to make it a marvel of strength and symmetry. But if a shipwrecked mariner, clinging to a spar in mid-ocean with the waves beating over him, were to look at the lifeboat drawing near as a wonderful mechanical contrivance or as a mere thing of beauty, he would be regarded as a desperately foolish man. We are all in a bad case spiritually—the danger is of eternal death. We have scarcely a spar to cling to. And this Bible is our lifeboat. If we feel the need of salvation, in God's name let us honor and receive it. Nay, let us cry aloud, " Save me ! Take me aboard of this stanch ship and carry me safe to land !" The Scriptures are indeed the " power of God unto salvation " to every one who thus receiveth them. To the unsaved they are as a storehouse of wonders ; but to such as believe they are as the mighty arms of God. Oh that they may hold us and save us all !

> " Within this sacred volume lies
> The mystery of mysteries.
> Happiest they of human race
> To whom the Lord hath given grace
> To read, to think, to fear, to pray,
> To lift the latch and ope the way."

A GENUINE INSTANCE OF FAITH-CURE.

PREACHED BY DR. BURRELL, DECEMBER 6, 1891.

"Thus saith the Lord, I have heard thy prayer, I have seen thy
tears: behold, I will heal thee." 2 Kings 20:5.

WE are here introduced to a sick-chamber. King
Hezekiah is in the very article of death. The physicians
have given him up. In the ordinary course of nature
there is no hope of recovery. He has every possible
comfort: a pillow of down for his aching head, purple
hangings about his couch, attendants with quick eyes for
every want. The physicians move about his room with
anxious faces. Ask them about their patient and they
will answer, "He is a very sick man, but we are hopeful
of pulling him through." They know the issue but are
reluctant to announce it. No one dares to tell Hezekiah
that death is at his door. Oh the mistaken kindness of
keeping the great secret from those who are on the borders of the unknown world!

The door opens softly and a man enters, clothed in
the hair-cloth robe of a prophet. Would that we might
have seen him: his serious face, his wonderful eyes—eyes
that had gazed through heaven's open windows and seen
the King in his beauty, that looked upon the Christ seven
hundred years before His advent coming from the hills of
Edom with garments dyed red in the wine-press of redemption. This man approaches the bedside of the dy-

ing king. He has a message, and it is not easy to deliver it, for this good king is his own familiar friend. But the shortest way is the best; he cannot break it gently: "Thus saith the Lord, set thy house in order, for thou shalt die." Dread message! And "the king turned his face to the wall." In that moment none must see the tokens of the struggle within him. We also must presently face the dread announcement. Will it appall us? What is our thought of death? Is it, as Abd-l-Kadah said, "a black camel kneeling at the gates of all"? Or is it, as Milton says, "The golden key that opes the palace of eternity"?

While the king lies with his face towards the wall it is evident by the moving of his frame that some mighty emotion has taken hold upon him. He has passed the possibility of human help and is reaching up after the strength of God. He is praying. At such a moment all are impelled to pray. The most ungodly cries, "O God!" when sudden death confronts him. It is an intuition that God alone can be a help to the needy in the supreme hour "when the blast of the terrible ones is as a storm against the wall."

Let us keep our eyes for a while upon this praying king. He is pleading for the restoration of his health. And this is the prayer which multitudes who scarcely pray for anything else are offering in these days. Hezekiah's petition will prevail, though the pallor of death is now upon his face, and we shall presently see him going about his customary tasks. So here is a genuine case of faith-cure. And, where there is so much of quackery and foolish superstition, it is a relief to find a valid, indisputable instance of the prayer that heals. We may profitably devote some attention to it.

I. Our first consideration is, in general terms, that *God hears prayer and answers it.* He announces himself distinctly as the hearer of prayer.   No soul in trouble ever called on him and had reason to complain, " There is none that regardeth."   He keeps no suppliant waiting at his gates.   His ear is ever open to the supplication of the least of his little ones.

And he answers.   His honor is expressly pledged to it.   Here is the promise : " Ask, and it shall be given you ; seek, and ye shall find ; knock, and it shall be opened unto you."   And then, as if he had surmised that some would question the full scope and boundless reach of the promise, he doubled it by iteration : " For whosoever asketh receiveth, and he that seeketh findeth, and to him that knocketh it shall be opened."   Had there been an *if* or a *perhaps* or a *peradventure*, there might be room for questioning ; but the word is " shall," and God's honor and veracity stand back of it.

The prayer of healing falls under the general rule. There is nothing unique or peculiar about it.   Its answer is subject to the usual conditions.   It is no harder for God to cure diseases than to do anything else.   Nothing indeed is too difficult for him.   During his ministry on earth it was his pleasure to heal what physicians would call desperate cases.   When he was in a certain place a ruler came to him saying that his little daughter twelve years old, the light of his eyes, was dying.   She was already past all human help.   Christ arose and went with him.   On reaching the home he bent over the dying child and said, " *Talitha cumi ;*" and immediately she arose and sat up.

As he descended from Olivet after the delivery of his wonderful Sermon on the Mount, the cry of a leper was heard.   His was a hopeless case.   Standing afar off with his finger upon his lip he called, " Unclean ! Unclean !" and then, " Lord, if thou wilt, thou canst cleanse me !" And immediately the Lord said, " I will ; be thou clean."

And the leper's flesh came to him as the flesh of a little child.

At the foot of the Mount of Transfiguration a boy lay writhing in a convulsion. An evil spirit possessed him. No power on earth could heal demonism. The disciples had tried their skill upon this lad in vain, and their enemies at the moment were deriding them. The Lord came into the midst saying, "O ye of little faith, how long shall I bear with you?" Then to the demon within the child he said, "Come out of him;" and in an instant the restoration was complete.

While he was passing along the street, on one occasion, a poor woman who was afflicted with a chronic malady, and who had spent all she had upon physicians and was no better for it, forced her way through the crowd and touched the hem of his garment. Such was the healing virtue in him that, hopeless as her case was, the warm blood of perfect health began at once to flow through her veins, healed by a touch! And the Master said, "Daughter, go in peace; thy faith hath saved thee."

By the wayside a blind beggar sat, so hopelessly blind that no oculist on earth would have undertaken his case. As Jesus passed by he cried, "Jesus, thou Son of David, have mercy on me." "What wilt thou?" "Oh that I might receive my sight!" "Receive thy sight!" And he opened his eyes and followed Jesus, glorifying God.

All these and multitudes of others who appealed to Jesus were beyond all human help. But no case was too difficult for this Good Physician. He gloried in exercising his power on the hopeless ones. And he is the same yesterday, to-day, and for ever. The prayer for healing, like all other prayers, when made in pursuance of such conditions as are divinely prescribed, is sure of a hearing at the throne of the heavenly grace.

II. If the prayer for healing is to receive an answer, it *must be the prayer of faith.*   What is faith?   More than a mere belief that we shall receive what we ask for.   It is the vital bond of union between the soul and God.   It is the blending of the human with the divine life.   A petitioner who has faith may ask what he will and it shall be done unto him.

It must be understood, however, that *sickness may be in pursuance of the divine will.*   It is a grievous error to suppose that our pains and maladies have never a good purpose in them.   " No chastening for the present seemeth to be joyous, but grievous ; nevertheless afterwards it yieldeth the peaceable fruit of righteousness to them which are exercised thereby."   If it be God's pleasure that we shall suffer for some good end, we may not presume to cross his beneficent and holy will.   Paul had some mysterious affliction which he called his " thorn in the flesh." It may have been a chronic malady ; perhaps, as some suppose, an acute disease of the eyes.   Whatever it was, he entreated most earnestly to be relieved of it.   As he says, " I besought the Lord thrice that it might depart from me."   And with what result ?   " He said unto me, My grace is sufficient for thee ; for my strength is made perfect in weakness."   How did Paul receive this strange answer to his prayer ?   " Most gladly therefore," he says, " will I rather glory in my infirmities, that the power of Christ may rest upon me."

Observe again that *death is a divine ordinance.*   None of God's angels has been so maligned as this bright-visaged messenger.   How dismal our fate would be were we compelled to live on and on for ever, bearing our burdens and bowing more and more under our decrepitude, yet never transported to a higher and better life.   No, blessed be God for the ordinance that dooms us to die!

> "To die, to end
> The heartache and the thousand natural shocks
> That flesh is heir to—'t is a consummation
> Devoutly to be wished."

The prayer of faith must be at every point and every way *acquiescent in the divine will.* Only a son or daughter of God can offer it; and the proof of our filial relation with God is in this spirit of acquiescence. For if we are his children we know that all things are working together for our good. Let us get the pattern of our prayer at Gethsemane. There the cup of purple death was pressed to the lips of the Saviour, and he cried in an agony of supplication, "Oh my Father, if it be possible let this cup pass from me!" And again, and then once more, "Oh my Father, if this cup may not pass from me, thy will be done!" All prayer, including the prayer for healing, must be offered in the spirit of this supplication. It is scarcely possible that the wisest of Christians should expect to improve upon it.

III. The prayer for healing *must be reasonable.* The principles of common sense are to be applied in the religious province as everywhere else. We are invited, when approaching the mercy-seat, to produce our cause and bring forth our strong reasons. King Hezekiah was able to give three reasons for greatly desiring the restoration of his health: He had no heir—for Manasseh was not born until three years after this event—and the line royal would be cut off. Still further, his kingdom was under assault. The hosts of Sennacherib had laid siege to Jerusalem. The king would fain deliver his country from the invader. "Lord, spare me until I shall have put the Assyrians to flight!" Moreover, he was in the midst of a great reform. He had opened the temple and greatly beautified it. He had restored the Passover feast, which had passed into utter disuse. The pilgrims were now wending their way from all directions towards Jerusalem to worship God. He had destroyed the serpent idol, crying, "Nehushtan! It is a brazen thing!" He had restored the Psalter to its place in public worship and had arranged a canon of the Scriptures. "Now, Lord, spare me," he prayed, "until I shall finish my work!" It is much to be feared that many supplications for healing are made with no good reason to sustain them. Why should a useless life be lengthened? Why should a sinner, dying in his sins, be spared by a gracious God who foresees that recovery must simply mean the deepening of his shame and the darkening of his doom? If any among us is afflicted with any malady let him, before he asks for recovery, be sure that he can give a valid reason why he should desire it or the Lord grant it.

Then, too, a prayer for healing must pay deference to *the use of means.* This is in the line of common sense. The king, having made known his desire to God, called upon his physicians to do their best for him. The remedy used was a poultice of figs, the usual application for a virulent ulcer in those days. In case of desperate illness let us also pray and send for the doctor. Faith without works is dead. Had a " Christian Scientist " been present in the sick-chamber of Hezekiah when the physician applied the fig-poultice, he would in all likelihood have pronounced him a fool; but if the Lord had been there and expressed his mind, he would probably have said that there was indeed a fool on the premises, but it was not Hezekiah. For there is no greater folly in the universe than to divorce religion from common sense. If a man pray for bread shall he expect the Lord to put a loaf in his hands? Nay, rather, the Lord will strengthen his sinew and give him a spade, and say, " Go dig and earn your bread." As a rule, the answer to prayer is through second causes. The most preposterous of dupes is the man who folds his hands, opens his mouth, and expects the Lord to provide for him.

Now the sequel. Isaiah had turned to leave the sick-chamber, had reached the outer court of the palace, when a message came from God. He straightway returned and delivered it. "Thus saith the Lord, I have heard thy prayer, I have seen thy tears; I will heal thee." The king's life was prolonged fifteen years. His first act was to visit the temple, where he offered up a joyous thanksgiving. And at once he proceeded to improve his new lease on life. He not only continued the reforms which he had undertaken, but, as it is written, " he made a pool and a conduit and brought water into the city "—fresh water for the people of Jerusalem. That was a great thing to do.

But at length the supplement of his life was over, and death came after all. Did the voice say again, " Get thy house in order, for thou must die "? Nay, there was no need. He was ready for the coming of the King. Are we ready? A housewife expecting a guest would prepare her house by sweeping out the last particle of dust, leaving no spot on the white curtains, and arraying herself in her best apparel. There is no telling; perhaps the King will come this night to us. Let us prepare ourselves by the cleansing of our souls from sin—and for this the fountain is opened at Calvary—and by having our work done. When the Lord had said, " It is finished!" he added, " Into thy hands I commend my spirit."

While Dr. Janeway's friends were praying about his dying bed, praying for his recovery, he said, " Keep me not from my crown. Voices are calling, hands are beckoning. Oh could you but see! Could you but see what I am seeing now! Keep me not from my crown, good friends! I long to go. Come, Lord Jesus, come quickly!"

"IF" AND "WHY?"

PREACHED BY DR. BURRELL, DECEMBER 13, 1891.

"So Ahab sent unto all the children of Israel, and gathered the prophets together unto Mount Carmel. And Elijah came unto all the people and said, How long halt ye between two opinions? If the Lord be God, follow him; but if Baal, then follow him. And the people answered him not a word." 1 Kings 18:20, 21.

HERE was an event of colossal importance. A contest of gods! Things had been going wrong in Israel. There was a confusion of worship. The king was essentially a weak man, and his consort was strong-minded and an idolatress. She had brought from her Assyrian home the rites of Baal and Astarte. The high hills were smoking everywhere with pagan sacrifices. The people were bewildered. Whom were they to worship as the true God?

The slopes of Mount Carmel were thronged by the multitude who had come to witness the Lord's controversy. Far below on one side rolled the sea; on the other was the rocky bed of Kishon, dry these many months and seeming like a chasm storm-riven in the earth. Far yonder was Esdraelon, the ancient battlefield of Israel. And on all sides famine! The leaves of the forest were withered and charred. The vineyards and olive-yards were brown. The meadows were scorched as if by the fiery breath of some offended deity. It was now three years and more since Elijah had suddenly appeared in the king's palace and abruptly said, "As the Lord liveth, it shall not rain except by my word." The days passed and the months, and the heavens were as brass. No rain, no rising mists from the Mediterranean, no gracious morning dews. It was a land of utter desolation that met the eyes of those who, gaunt with hunger, looked off from Carmel's slopes that day.

The priests of Baal were there, four hundred and fifty in number. They represented the State religion. There was still among the people a half-shamed clinging to the worship of that God who with a stretched-out arm had brought them forth from the land of Egypt the house of their bondage. It was hard to forget the pillar of cloud, the quails, the manna, the smitten rock, the brazen serpent, the tottering walls of Jericho. It was hard to forget how in Esdraelon yonder the stars in their courses had fought against Sisera. But it was no easy matter to resist the allurements of the State religion. Baal was worshipped with imposing rites and ceremonies and splendid processions. The new faith was under the patronage of the queen ; the courtiers had no alternative but to say, "Baal is the God." The people aped the court. The temple of Jehovah was practically deserted. The shrines of the Assyrian deities were thronged with worshippers.

To-day there was to be a settlement ; Baal and Jehovah cannot both be God. Let them defend their respective claims. The Lord's altar shall have a bullock, and Baal's altar shall have a bullock, and the devotees of each shall call upon their deity ; and the God that answereth by fire let him be God. The preparations are made ; the priests of Baal are there in force, and over against them a solitary prophet of the Lord. Just before the signal for the controversy, the prophet stands forth to admonish the people: "How long halt ye between two opinions?" The figure is that of a bird hopping from twig to twig—an expressive picture of fickleness and indecision. "How long halt ye between two opinions? If the Lord be God, follow him; if Baal, then follow him!" And all the people answered, "It is well spoken."

It was indeed well spoken. And how mightily the Lord vindicated himself that day! The priests of Baal in the morning began their cry, "O Baal, hear us!" and continued it until the sun had crossed mid-heaven. Hoarse and frenzied, they still called upon their idol; but there was no voice nor any that regarded. The hollow caves and beetling cliffs returned their cry, "O Baal, hear us!" As the day wore on, the prophet of the Lord stood forth and taunted them with rude and merciless irony, "Cry aloud, for he is a god! Either he is on a chase, or upon a journey, or engaged in conversation, or, peradventure, he sleepeth and must be awaked!" Still they persisted in their vain entreaties until the sun sank towards the western sea, as if to symbolize the discomfiture of the fire-god. Then Elijah stood forth in the presence of the multitude and made his simple prayer, "O God of my fathers, hear me this day and let all the people know that thou art God!" There was a moment of breathless silence. Then it came—a blazing fleece out of heaven! Nearer, nearer, until it fell upon the altar. It consumed the bullock; it consumed the stones of the altar; it lapped up the water in the trenches. Silence for a moment more, and then a loud cry, "The Lord is God!" Ten thousand voices caught it up and ten thousand more, until there was a rolling flood of acclamation, "The Lord is God!" Old Kishon heard it and sent it echoing back. The rocky slopes and beetling cliffs of Esdraelon, that had reverberated to many a battle shout, returned the cry. The sea yonder was calmed as if to listen—"The Lord he is the God! The Lord he is the God!"

But if the Lord be God, why do ye not follow him?

Mark the impressiveness of the logic. There was no evading it. So long as any there could remember the scene, the dripping altar, the frenzied priests, the quiet voice of the prophet, the descending fire, it seemed impossible to withhold homage from Jehovah as the only living and true God. He had sublimely vindicated his majesty. There was no need of ever again reopening the controversy. Those who returned from Carmel to their homes said one to another that evening, "This has settled it for ever and ever: the Lord alone is God." They went away convinced. In a month they had measurably forgotten. In a year the fires were kindled again upon the high places in honor of Baal, and the people in circling dance went round about the altars worshipping the fire-god.

Blame them not. Alas for the fickleness of our human nature! We are not men and women, but birds hopping from twig to twig. We have seen the Lord's controversy, have marked the vindication of his majesty over and over again; and our impressions have vanished "like the snowfall in the river." We too have our idols, wealth, honor, and pleasure, the world, the flesh, and the devil. Is there any god in our pantheon that can help or deliver us? They are all put to shame every day, yet we go on serving them. What have they ever done for us? Have they built up character? Have they relieved suffering? Have they dispelled ignorance? Have they helped or gladdened the troubled soul? Have they made the world better in any way? "O Baal, hear us!" but there is no voice nor any that regardeth! And still we go on kissing our hands and devoting our lives to our blind and helpless idols.

If the Lord be God, why do we not follow him? Here are two suggestive words, "if" and "why."

"IF *the Lord be God*." But there is no *if*.

(1.) There is no *if* in nature. Stand in the solitude and cry aloud, "O Jehovah, answer me if thou art God!" and mark how multitudinous the voices that reply, "The Lord he is the God." The murmuring of brooks, the lapping of sea-waves, the rolling of the thunder, the hum of the insects, the sweep of the tempest, the music of the spheres—all everywhere are saying, "The Lord is God." The heavens declare his glory, the firmament showeth his handiwork. Day unto day uttereth speech and night unto night showeth knowledge of him. There is no speech nor language; their voice is not heard; yet their line is gone out through all the earth and their words to the end of the world. Their "line" is gone forth like an electric wire from the central throne of Deity, over which perpetually passes this message, "The Lord is God."

A red republican in Paris during the Reign of Terror was telling in a street-corner group how they were going to pull down the churches, to pull down the crucifixes and shrines and everything that could perpetuate religion, when a peasant standing by said quietly, "You must not forget, citizen, to pull down the stars." So long as there is a star in heaven, a tree in the forest, a brook rippling towards the rivers, or a river rolling to the sea, so long as a bird sings or a flower blooms, so long as there is one grass-blade left in the meadows, there will be an oracle through which a voice will proclaim, "The Lord he is the God."

(2.) There is no *if* in providence. In history every-

where there is a power that makes for righteousness.
Time is a shuttle flying to and fro and casting the threads
in and out, red and purple and golden—blood of battlefield, glory of the blessed times of peace; and the theme
of the pattern is *the Triumph of Goodness*. Who sits at
the loom? Looms do not weave without a weaver. "The
fool hath said in his heart, There is no God."

> He works in all things ; all obey
>   His first propulsion from the night.
> Wake thou and watch. The world is gray
>   With morning light.

(3.) There is no *if* in grace. The story of redemption
is eloquent of God. If for Carmel we read Calvary, we
have the very consummation of the Lord's controversy.
There was the great theistic argument. The sacrifice was
laid upon the altar. It was not the voice of a solitary
prophet but of a ruined race that cried, "O God of our
fathers, hear us, and let us know that thou art God!"
Then the fire fell, the fire of divine justice, and consumed
the sacrifice. As it is written, "He was made a whole
burnt-offering for us." The angels of heaven who had
leaned upon their harps and waited for the stupendous
denoument must have shouted when it was finished,
"Who is like unto our God, glorious in holiness, fearful
in praises, doing wonders?" Never on earth was seen
such a demonstration of Jehovah's power. There is no *if*
in grace. It is settled for ever that Jehovah is the God.

What then? WHY *do ye not follow him?* This is the
answerless question. There are pretexts innumerable and
subterfuges and makeshifts, but no man can present a valid
excuse for withholding his love and service from the true
God. All excuse will be put to shame in the judgment.
"The hail shall sweep away the refuges of lies."

It would be vain and superserviceable to canvass the frivolous subterfuges; their name is legion. A few by way of illustration must answer.

There are those who plead *honest doubt*. But this is scarcely sincere. An honest doubter is not contented until he has moved heaven and earth to resolve his doubt. It is related of Zaid, the sage of Mecca who had broken with the national religion, that he stood with his back to the temple crying, " If I knew thee I would worship thee; but alas, I know thee not." Thus day after day he prostrated himself and moistened the ground with his tears. So if honest doubt is really in our way, so important are the issues involved in these spiritual problems we must be upon our knees continually until we have settled it. We must be agonizing to rid ourselves of it.

There are others who plead *a want of feeling*. This again is quite invalid; nor would it be advanced in any other than the province of religious things. The question is one not of feeling but of fact. If a grocer were to present his bill to-morrow and you should answer, " I recognize the justice of this claim, but I have no feeling about it; I somehow fail to apprehend it, and therefore I refuse to settle it," men would pronounce you akin to a fool. So I say the question of feeling does not affect the case. This lethargy, this listlessness, is greatly to be lamented; but the thing to be attended to immediately is duty. Duty is a debt, a debt to God. If the Lord be God it is your duty to follow him; and an honest man will pay his honest debts.

Or possibly you desire *time for deliberation*. This also is a delusion and a snare. You have had time enough. If ten years were given you what would you do with them? Would you settle the problem of the Trinity, of the Incarnation, of the divine decrees? Would you be any nearer to an acceptation of the fundamental truths of personal sin and a glorious Saviour? The plea for further time is practically no more nor less than sinful procrastination. What you need is not more reflection, but a moving of your stubborn will. And in the meantime every moment of delay is a distinct violation of the divine law; for indecision is at this moment decision against God.

Thus there is no *if* with reference to the Godhood of Jehovah, and there is no *why* as to our refusal to honor him. The most unreasonable thing in the world is the withholding of the soul's homage from the true God. The truth is, "The god of this world hath blinded the eyes of them which believe not, lest the light of the glorious gospel of Christ, who is the image of God, should shine unto them."

It is not for me to say that this is the moment on which depends your eternal destiny. But it may be. The wise thing to do is to cut the Gordian knot. If you have been waiting, hesitating, procrastinating, there is at this moment before you a distinct possibility of beginning the service of Jehovah and so entering upon spiritual and eternal life. If you are persuaded that the God who has manifested his grace on Calvary in giving his only-begotten and well-beloved Son to die for us is the only living and true God, it behooves you as reasonable and right-minded men to set out forthwith to follow him.

The most miserable man in all the multitude who shall turn away from the great assize to dwell in endless night will be that one against whom sentence is passed, "He knew his duty and did it not." Be wise therefore to-day.

"THE RIGHT OF A MAN BEFORE THE FACE OF GOD."

PREACHED BY DR. BURRELL, DECEMBER 20, 1891.

" He will not turn aside the right of a man before the face of the
Most High."   Lam. 3:35.

THE question of human rights has from the beginning
held a prominent place in courts and councils and on bat-
tlefields.   The most notable events of history are such as
mark the progress of this controversy.   Runnymede was
a milestone; the Reformation was another; Waterloo
another.   The nearest approach to a formal settlement of
the question thus far was when our fathers issued the civil
manifesto, " All men are created free and equal and with
certain inalienable rights."

These rights which the individual holds in relation to
his fellow-men are intangible things, but they are infinitely
worth striving for and defending.   We think the more of
St. Paul because he stood upon his rights at Philippi.
The magistrates had commanded him to be beaten and
cast into the inner prison.   While he sat there in the
night, his feet fast in the stocks, strange things happened,
so that in the morning the magistrates were constrained
to give orders for his release.   But to their consternation
the man refused to go.   Paul insisted on his rights.   He
fell back on the *Lex Porcia* which forbade the scourging

of a Roman.   "They have beaten us openly and uncondemned, and have cast us into prison, being Roman citizens, and now do they thrust us out privately?   Nay, but let them come and take us out."   And so the magistrates did, and we respect Paul for the position which he took that day.

It is not, however, to the rights of a man with respect to his fellow-men that we now direct our thought, but to his rights before the face of God.   There is a general impression that God does as he pleases without any reference to sanctions or immunities of ours.   This, however, is far wide of the truth.   God is never arbitrary.   Shall not the Lord of all the earth do right?   In the long run, when we review his dealings with us from the standpoint of eternity, we shall see that his ways were just and righteous altogether.

I. One of our rights with respect to God is life.   This is a natural right.   It is written that when God created man he breathed into his nostrils the breath of life so that he became a living soul.   In this particular man was created in the divine likeness.   His life was a spark thrown off from the infinite life of Deity.   It is impossible, therefore, to think of annihilation or of "conditional immortality" in connection with him.   He must live for ever because he partakes of the divine life.   He is as immortal as God is.   It is written that when man had fallen from his high estate of innocency "it repented God that he had created him."   At this point the question arises, If He was so disappointed in the outcome, so grieved and regretful, why did he not destroy man?   Because he could not.   In giving his own indestructible life to his creature, breathing His breath into his nostrils, he voluntarily put it out of his own power to annihilate him.

The doctrine of immortality is not seriously questioned

by thoughtful men.   It is a striking coincidence that the two most dramatic soliloquies in English literature are both concerned with this truth.   "To be or not to be" was not, after all, the real question that confronted the melancholy Dane.   It was, rather, how to meet the endless life.

> " To die, to sleep;
> *Perchance to dream !   Ay, there's the rub.*
> For in that sleep of death what dreams may come,
> When we have shuffled off this mortal coil,
> Must give us pause."

In like manner Cato, sitting in a meditative attitude with a disquisition on " Immortality " upon his knees and a drawn sword on the table before him, speaks thus :

> "The soul, secure in its existence, smiles
> At the drawn dagger and defies its point.
> The stars shall fade away, the sun himself
> Grow dim with age and nature sink in years ;
> But thou shalt flourish in eternal youth
> Unhurt amidst the war of elements,
> The wreck of matter, and the crush of worlds."

Our life is the only created thing in the universe that has not in it the seed and certainty of death.   An oak may resist the storms of a thousand years, but it falls at last.   Our bodies are never free from disease ; it is only a question of time when each shall return to the dust as it was.   But the soul has in it no seeds of decay.   Its eyes never grow dim, its blood does not stagnate, and whenever the query is propounded, " If a man die, shall he live again ?" its answer is instant, " I shall live and not die !"

II. The second of our rights before God is freedom. This again is a natural right.   It belongs to us by virtue of the fact that God created us in his own likeness.   How he could have done this without giving us each a sovereign will, is unthinkable. To be like God I must have a will and an unhindered right to exercise it.

In this again man is unique among all created things. The sun goes forth out of its chambers in the morning to run its race and has no alternative. God speaks and it obeys. The sea rolls to and fro as He directs. "Thus far shalt thou come and no farther; and here let thy proud waves be stayed." But to you and me he says, "Thou shalt," and if I please I may make answer, "I will not." There is no other being in the universe that can thus defy God. If he would win me he must reason with me. If he would capture me he must draw me with the cords of a man. The two great moral symbols of the Scriptures are the Decalogue and the Sermon on the Mount; and each of these is set before us not merely with an *ipse dixit*, but on rational grounds. "I am the Lord, thy God, which have brought thee out of the land of Egypt, out of the house of bondage. *Therefore* thou shalt have no other gods before me." In like manner the Sermon on the Mount closes with a distinct concession that a man may disregard the divine injunction, though to his eternal and irremediable ruin. As it is written, "Therefore whosoever heareth these sayings of mine and doeth them, I will liken him unto a wise man, which built his house upon a rock: and the rain descended and the floods came and the winds blew and beat upon that house, and it fell not; for it was founded upon a rock. And every one that heareth these sayings of mine and doeth them not, shall be likened unto a foolish man, which built his house upon the sand: and the rain descended and the floods came and the winds blew and beat upon that house, and it fell: and great was the fall of it."

It thus appears that God has placed it beyond his

power to interfere with the exercise of our freedom. We drive our oxen with a whip, but we ourselves as rational beings are divinely led as with leading strings. " Come now, saith the Lord, let us reason together: though your sins be as scarlet, they shall be as white as snow ; though they be red like crimson, they shall be as wool."

If, notwithstanding his goodness, we persist in sin, he can only suffer us to have our way. "Ye will not come unto me that ye might have life." "O Jerusalem, Jerusalem, how often would I have gathered thy children together, even as a hen gathereth her chickens under her wings, and ye would not !"

III. We are entitled to the full benefit of the moral law. This also is a natural right. We are normal beings. As God himself is the source and centre of law, so we, being made in his likeness, are made under law ; and we may claim all the benefits and privileges of it. No other creature has a similar prerogative. The stocks and stones are not so. The vegetable and animal kingdom have no relation to moral distinctions. The fig-tree that was cursed by the Son of God and withered away was not wronged and could make no complaint against him, for it was wholly outside the province of the moral law. We, however, as God's children, have a distinct claim upon him. If it were conceivable that he should impose on us, we should have the right to protest against it. He could not, however, impose upon us. There are those who be-lieve in a more or less arbitrary decree of election and of reprobation. God is sovereign, but there is absolutely nothing unreasonable in the exercise of his sovereign will. When Nero pined for the sports of the amphitheatre, he might at any moment call for prisoners to be brought from their dungeons and select two victims, saying, " This one to the lions ; that one to the gladiator's sword." But there is no parallel between that and the divine election. We may not be advised as to the *rationale* of the eternal decree, but it would be impious and preposterous to suggest that there are not good and sufficient reasons behind it.

There is, however, little comfort in claiming these privileges of the moral law. For what is law? "The soul that sinneth, it shall die." And what is justice? Eternal separation from God and goodness. We are sinners, all alike under the penalty of death. To stand upon our rights just here is to court despair. We may have law, we may have justice; but law and justice will land us .in an unbroken and eternal night.

In the story of the pilgrimage to the heavenly city Bunyan says, "As I journeyed I lighted on a certain place where I laid me down to sleep, and as I slept I dreamed. And behold I saw a man clothed in rags standing with his face turned from his own house and a book in his hand and carrying a burden on his back; and as I looked I saw him open the book and read. And as he read he wept and trembled; and being no longer able to contain himself, he brake out into a lamentable cry, saying, 'What shall I do?'"

IV. Fortunately for us we have another right, not natural like the foregoing, but conferred, to wit, the right of appeal from law and justice to the mercy of God. No one among us can presume to stand upon his merits. On Sir Henry Lawrence's tomb at Lucknow is this inscription: "Here lies a man who tried to do his duty. May God have mercy on his soul!" If he tried to do his duty why did he not ask for justice? Because, no matter how earnestly he had striven to live well, he had made a measurable failure of it. Mercy therefore was Sir Henry's only hope. He is a wise man who in like manner, after doing his best and being mindful of his shortcomings, casts himself with an utter abandon on the mercy of his God.

It has been observed that this right of appeal is a conferred right. It is purely of grace. But once conferred it is inalienable. The franchise can never be taken away from us. The covenant of grace is yea and amen. "Him that cometh unto Me"—no matter how scarlet his sins—"I will in no wise cast out."

Observe again, this right is the purchase of the Saviour's blood. But for his atoning work it could not, consistently with justice, have been conferred upon us. As it is written, "What the law could not do, in that it was weak through the flesh, God, sending his own Son in the likeness of sinful flesh and for sin, condemned sin in the flesh, that the righteousness of the law might be fulfilled in us."

And once more, observe that this right is conditioned. It is conditioned upon the exercise of faith in Jesus Christ. A man may do as he pleases about exercising this faith, but in default of it he lives obviously under the law and must take the consequences. Not all are to be refreshed by the water of life, but "whosoever will." A foreigner coming to our country receives the elective franchise on condition of naturalization. In case he does not pass through the formalities necessary to receive it he may live next door to the polls, have a ballot-box in his house, be familiar with all the principles of our Constitution and regarded as a sage in political science; but there is one thing which he cannot possibly do—he cannot vote. So you may be a pew-holder in the church, have a Bible on your table, be able to repeat the Catechism backwards and talk theology like a professor of polemics; but if you do not accept the gospel of Jesus Christ by an appropriating and obedient faith, you never can become a citizen

of the commonwealth of God.   Here is an answer to the
query, "Why are not all saved by the atonement of the
cross ?"

> "Though God be good and free be heaven,
>   No force divine can love compel,
> And though the song of sins forgiven
>   May sound through deepest hell,
> The sweet persuasion of his voice
>   Respects thy sanctity of will.
> He giveth day ; thou hast thy choice
>   To walk in darkness still."

Two closing thoughts. *First.* Salvation is within the
reach of every man.   You may be saved if you will.
When God said, "Ho every one that thirsteth, come ye
to the waters," he meant it.   When he said, "Him that
cometh unto me I will in no wise cast out," he meant it.
Second. You may be lost.   It is easy to fall short of everlasting life.   The grace of God is a slender thread let
down from heaven.   A man may easily push it aside and
pass on.   But in that case eternity will be full of regret.
The most important thing an immortal soul ever does in
this world is to exercise the power of choice with respect
to the spiritual life.   We must choose; God cannot choose
for us.   Each for himself must mark out his own path
through the eternal ages.   God help us to set our faces
heavenward ; and may he minister unto us at·the last, for
Jesus' sake, an abundant entrance into the kingdom of his
grace !

PAUL AT ATHENS.

PREACHED BY DR. BURRELL IN THE MARBLE COLLEGIATE CHURCH.

"Then Paul stood in the midst of Mars' Hill and said:—"
Acts 17:22.

MILTON characterized Athens as the "eye of Greece, mother of arts and eloquence." No man of ordinary taste and culture could stand in the midst of its glories without a feeling of æsthetic enthusiasm. Yet Paul was moved only by an intense pity and indignation. Yonder was the Parthenon, beautified by the skill of Phidias and Praxiteles. Yonder the Areopagus, crowned with its colossal image of Mars; here were the famous schools of philosophy by the Ilissus. On every hand were images of gods and heroes. Pliny says there were three thousands such effigies here. It was a proverb, "There are more gods than men in Athens." The apostle possibly walked down the Street of Hermes when a winged figure adorned the front of every home, or along the Avenue of Tripods, lined on every side with votive offerings given by grateful athletes to the gods who had helped them in the games. Gods everywhere: gods on pedestals, in niches, on the corners of the streets—gods and demigods, good, bad, and indifferent—a wilderness of gods! And the heart of the apostle was moved within him "as he saw the city wholly given to idolatry." At length he

mounted one of the rostrums in the public square and began to speak.   There was no difficulty in getting an
audience, for Athens was a paradise of gossips and saun-
terers.   Its shibboleth was "What's the news?" So they
gathered about him, men and women, priests and philosophers, all sorts and conditions of people.   And he spoke
to them of Jesus and the Resurrection, or as the Greeks
had it, Jesus and Anastasius—a pair of new deities.   He
who introduced a god into Athens was counted a public
benefactor.   The interest of his audience was thus en-
chained at once.   Presently they said, "Let us go to the
Areopagus for a better hearing."   So to Areopagus they
went, and the apostle preached a famous sermon there.

THE PREACHER AND HIS PULPIT.

I. Observe the man.   Renan calls him "the little ugly
Jew."   He was stoop-shouldered, weak-eyed, and a stam-
merer, but it did not take the Athenians long to discover
that there was something in him, and the world, through
all these centuries, has regarded him as one of its famous
men.   No profounder thinker or more skilful dialectician
ever lived.   He said of himself, "They tell me that my
words are weighty, but my bodily presence is weak and
my speech contemptible."   The man's power lay in his
conviction, and "thereby hangs a tale."   In his youth,
while attending the Rabbinical schools, he gave promise
of becoming a leader in his time.   He was a pupil of
Gamaliel, known as "the flower of the law."   All that
good blood and brilliant opportunities could do for him
was done.   In time he became a zealot among his people,

was chosen to an honored place in the Sanhedrin, was distinctly in the line of promotion, and great things were expected of him. Then came the great sun-burst. On his way down to Damascus the Voice, which ever after he revered as his heavenly monitor, spoke to him, and life was never again the same. Thenceforth his will, heart, intellect, and conscience went out towards the things which he had previously hated. The love of Christ constrained him. So thoroughly was his moral nature revolutionized that for the name of Jesus Christ, whom he had previously reviled and persecuted, he cheerfully surrendered all the bright hope of his future, all high ambitions and aspirations—laid everything at the feet of his new Master, saying, "I no longer live, but Christ liveth in me."

II. Observe the pulpit. It was a fateful place. Many a man had here been devoted to death. On this stone platform Demosthenes had stood and uttered forth " breathing thoughts in burning words." Here Socrates had made his apology and was doomed to drink the fatal hemlock. It was an historic platform. Facing it, on a shelf of rock, stood the Temple of the Furies, and over it towered the Temple of Mars. To this place Paul brought such a message as it had never heard before. He spoke as an ambassador from the court of heaven, bringing a message of peace to troubled souls. He stood on the " Rock of Impudence," where criminals were wont to defend their lives. It was not Paul, however, but his religion, that was put on trial that day. And it has been on trial ever since. " The word of the Lord is tried." Christianity has been through the fires of persecution; it has withstood the assaults of criticism ; it has been tested all along the centuries in the histories of nations and men.

We ourselves have put it to the test in the experience of our common life. And everywhere it has withstood the strain. The gods innumerable whom the apostle Paul confronted in Athens have all fallen to their faces on the earth, and "none so poor to do them reverence." Mars has not one worshipper, nor great Athene whose spear and shield glittered in the sun. The gods are gone, all gone. And the philosophies of Athens have gone with them. Zeno, Epicurus, Plato, are scarcely more than names. But the word of the Lord endureth for ever.

III. Observe the audience. Here were priests, doubtless, with the names of their deities worn as frontlets between their eyes. Here were philosophers and students in their classic robes, representing all the various schools by the Ilissus.

(1.) Stoics. These were Pantheists, who spoke of God as "the All," "the Universal Soul," and other terms familiar to us in this day. They thought of man as an exhalation from the all-pervading Force or Soul of the Universe, whose destiny was to be absorbed presently, like a drop of water in the boundless sea.

(2.) Epicureans. These were materialists. They said, "Death ends all." And, inasmuch as life was circumscribed by the narrow horizons of time and sense, what better could they do than make the most of the present hour? Their aphorism was, "Let us eat, drink, and be merry, for to-morrow we die."

(3.) Academicians. These were Agnostics; they dreamed many things, but knew nothing. All their suggestions were advanced with a "perhaps" or "it may be so." And, aside from these philosophers, there were doubtless others who were eager to know about eternal things, earnest, thoughtful, with a great longing to know the truth and to follow it. There were, moreover, the curiosity-mongers and hangers-on; but all alike were immortal men and women, made in God's likeness and travelling on to his judgment-bar. Oh, Paul, preach thy best! If thou believest in the saving power of the Gospel, then, in God's name, proclaim it without fear. Preach as a dying man to dying men, and God help thee!

THE SERMON AND ITS RESULT.

IV. Observe the sermon. Its exordium was exceedingly felicitous. Taking for his theme the inscription upon an altar which he had observed in the market-place, "To the Unknown God," and mindful of the multitudinous shrines, statues, and other tokens of a religious spirit, the apostle began by saying, "Ye men of Athens, I perceive that in all things ye are exceedingly devout." It was a clever compliment at the outset and gained him their good-will. He announces his proposition thus: "God, the unseen, unknown God, him declare I unto you." He then proceeds to show how God, so far from being really unknown, has unveiled himself in many ways. We see him in creation: "He made the world and all things that are therein." We mark his providence: "In him we live and move and have our being." The preacher fortifies himself at this point by a quotation from one of their own poets, Aratus, to wit, "We are also his offspring." We note his goodness also preëminently in his grace. He has made himself known in Jesus Christ, and in him has brought life and immortality to light.

V. Observe the result. Paul's sermon was never finished. The assembly on Mars' Hill was abruptly broken up. But no truth is ever spoken in vain. "For as the rain cometh down and the snow from heaven, and returneth not thither, but watereth the earth and maketh it bring forth and bud, that it may give seed to the sower and bread to the eater, so shall my word be that goeth forth out of my mouth; it shall not return unto me void, but it shall accomplish that which I please, and it shall prosper in the thing whereto I sent it."

(1.) It is written that "some mocked." It was easy for these philosophers to make sport of the stammering little Jew. It was quite in their line to point their finger at his grotesque doctrine of the crucified God. The resurrection and the judgment were preposterous to them. The generation of mockers has not passed away. There may be some now present.

(2.) Others said, "We will hear thee again." But they never did hear him again. No doubt as they sauntered down from Areopagus, like modern congregations, they dissected the preacher. "That was a clever opening," said one, "wherein he complimented our piety." "Very true," said another, "and I like his fervor. How he warmed to his theme when he spoke of the judgment!" A third said, "He is a master of logic. Did you mark his double syllogism, 'We are God's offspring, but we are living souls ; living souls cannot be born of dead matter: ergo, God is not a graven image'? Verily, the man is a dialectician." "Yes, and a master of literature as well. What could have been more appropriate than his quotation from Aratus?" Thus they all agreed that Paul was a man of no common power and quite worthy of another audience. "We will hear him again," they said; but the time never came. Once and again Paul sailed by the port of Athens, but that sermon was never resumed, and the men of Athens never looked into his face again. Oh why do people procrastinate? Why do they await the more convenient season, when the only convenient season is now? Procrastination is in the nature of suicide. Men do not mean to die; they simply put off beginning to live.

> "To-morrow and to-morrow and to-morrow
> Creeps in this petty space from day to day
> Till the last syllable of recorded time ;
> And all our yesterdays have lighted fools
> The way to dusty death."

There is a Russian legend of a man who intended to build a splendid home. The materials were brought and all things ready, but he put off from time to time the laying of the corner-stone, until at length death saved him the trouble, as the legend puts it:

> "And thus in silent waiting stood
> The piles of stones and piles of wood,
> Till Death, who in his vast affairs
> Ne'er puts off things as men do theirs,

> Winked at our hero as he passed.
> 'Your house is finished, sir, at last—
> A narrow house, a house of clay,
> Your mansion for an endless day.'"

(3.) "Howbeit certain ones believed." Among these were Dionysius, who is said to have been afterwards Bishop of Athens, and Damaris, a woman. They listened to Paul's announcement of life and immortality in Jesus Christ. They said, "This is true and it is for me." We are wont to plead earnestly in behalf of our ministers that they may have the gift of tongues. Might it not be well to pray for a while that the people may have the gift of ears? There are some creatures among the lower orders in nature whose auricular organs are so constructed that they can only hear the smaller sounds. They can detect the whisper of zephyrs, the murmur of brooks, the hum of insects; but the roar of the earthquake or the crash of heaven's artillery is nothing to them. In like manner there are some of us who attend only to the smaller sounds that are heard on the sensual levels of life, the call to wealth, to pleasure, to perishable honors, and cannot hear the voice of heaven inviting us to duty, to right living, to life and immortality. Oh for the hearing ear and the understanding heart!

God speaks to every one of us. He calls us to pardon of sin and to peace that passeth understanding. There is life in his word if we will heed it. But if we go our way, like the man who seeth his face in a glass and straightway forgetteth what manner of man he was, it were a thousand-fold better had we never heard it.

AT THE DOOR.

A NEW-YEAR MEDITATION.

PREACHED BY DR. BURRELL, JANUARY 3, 1892.

"Why art thou wroth and why is thy countenance fallen?   If thou doest well, shalt thou not be accepted? and if thou doest not well, sin lieth at the door."   Gen. 4:6, 7.

HERE is the scene.   Two altars; on one of them a lamb consuming in sacrifice, blood streaming down the sides of the altar and smoke ascending towards heaven; beside it a man kneeling with upturned face—a face glorified with the joy of pardon—and lips trembling with praise. On the other altar an oblation from the fields, a sheaf of barley, a basket of pomegranates, olives, clusters of grapes, a bloodless and unaccepted gift; for "without the shedding of blood there is no remission of sin."   By this altar a man standing with a lowering face, hands clenched, eyes flashing with the fires of an ungovernable rage.   He is meditating a dreadful deed; murder is in his heart.   At the instant a Voice speaks to him out of heaven.   Ah! if only he would hear it!   "Why art thou wroth and why is thy countenance fallen?   If thou doest well, shalt thou not be accepted? and if thou doest not well, sin lieth at the door."

At the threshold of the year we look backward and recall many a sad experience.   The shadow of the Death-Angel, mayhap, has fallen across our threshold; hopes have been crushed, ambitions thwarted.   Our neighbor's farm has yielded him a hundred-fold while ours has brought forth naught but briars and thistles. Others' ships have come back laden with treasure while ours have gone down far at sea. Shall we complain then? Shall we murmur at Providence?

> "Father, whate'er of earthly bliss
>   Thy sovereign will denies,
> Accepted at thy throne of grace
>   Let this petition rise :
> Give me a calm, a thankful heart,
>   From every murmur free,
> The blessings of thy grace impart
>   And let me live to thee."

But sorrows and disappointments are not the worst. We have sin and shame to remember. The things which we should have done we have left undone, and the evil that we would not we have done. If our poor efforts at devotion have been like sacrifices unconsumed shall we therefore be wroth with fate? Nay, let us hearken: "Why is thy countenance fallen? If thou doest well, shalt thou not be accepted? and if thou doest not well, *sin lieth at the door.*" The meaning here turns upon a single word. The Hebrew *hattath* is variously rendered, sin, penalty, and sin-offering. The three meanings which are put upon it all have important lessons for us.

I. *Sin boweth at thy door.* Here the figure is that of a slave doing an obsequious obeisance. The meaning is plain. The sins that served us in the old year are ready still to do our bidding. We may follow in the old paths if we will. Our evil habits, passions, and appetites, envy and avarice, evil-thinking and self-gratification, are fawning retainers who now await our further nod and beck.

We are free, if we please, to continue in our sins. Our freedom is an awful thing. As children of the infinite God we have sovereign wills. We speak of our "darling sins." We have loved them, we love them still. They have misled us and deluded us and entrapped us and gotten us into trouble a thousand times, and still we cherish them. Here again with the opening of the year they stand at our elbow, bowing and beckoning like the genii of the Eastern fairy tales, cringing and smiling and pleading to continue in our service. Shall they?

The chances are with them. Our natural bent is along the evil way; our hearts go out towards our besetting sins. It is with our frail nature as it was with Æsop's garden. When his master inquired why the weeds and thistles grew faster than the more useful plants, the rude philosopher, leaning on his spade, answered, "I know not, sir, unless it be that the ground is mother to the weeds and only step-mother to the herbs." So our nature is mother to evil but only step-mother to the good. Wherefore we have need to reinforce its infirmity with the strength of God. To continue in the sins of the former time is to brave the danger of habituation. "His servants ye are to whom ye obey." The sins that come pleading with obsequious proffers of devotion are hiding under their cloaks a writ of bondage and a covenant with hell. In the island of Innisfallen at Killarney are the ruins of the prehistoric Abbey of St. Finian. Through its foundations and about its walls an ivy as large as the trunk of an oak has forced its way. Time was when the vine lifted its modest head from the soil and said, "Let me twine upon thee, O strong abbey. I am but a frail thing; let me cling to thee." And the abbey said, "Thou mayest, surely, if thou wilt shadow me from the hot suns and cover my infirmities with thy pleasant verdure." But as time passed and the vine thrust its fingers into nooks and crannies and displaced stones and mortar, the abbey said, "Thou art clinging too fast; loose thy hold! Thou art sapping my strength." But the ivy laughed, "Not I! not I!" And stone was riven from stone until the structure was in ruins. It is ever dangerous to retain an unholy servitor. Sin grows upon us as time passes. The darling sin, kissed and caressed like an infant, soon reaches a colossal stature and ultimately commands us. It is a shop-worn saying of Pope's,

> " Vice is a monster of so frightful mien
> As, to be hated, needs but to be seen.
> Yet seen too oft, familiar with her face,
> We first endure, then pity, then embrace."

It is in pursuance of the same thought that the apostle James sets forth the genealogy of death: A man is tempted, he says, when he is drawn away by his own desire and enticed; "then when Desire hath conceived it bringeth forth Sin, and Sin when it is finished bringeth forth Death."

II. A second rendering of *hattath* is penalty. "If thou doest not well, *Penalty is crouching at thy door*." The figure here is of a lean tiger awaiting its prey.

The mere suggestion of penalty is repellant to us. We resent it. We cannot avoid the consciousness of sin, but we prefer to waive all consideration of hell. The word grates on ears polite. In these days the air is resonant with love. Why should we hearken to the strident suggestion of retribution or of justice? But while we stand here on the borderland between the years it will be well for us to think for a moment of this lean tiger that crouches at our doors.

We are made under the law of retribution. It is in the constitution of our nature. If there were no voice from heaven, if there were no Bible, if God had never in any wise revealed the truth, we must still believe that penalty follows sin. The law is written in our brain, in our heart, conscience, blood, and sinew, "The soul that sinneth it shall die." *Karma* is a pagan doctrine, but it is a precise fac-simile of retributive justice. All the nations hold to a corresponding truth. The words of Longfellow are an echo from the heathen oracles:

> "The mills of the gods grind slowly,
> But they grind exceeding small;
> Though with patience they stand waiting,
> With exactness grind they all."

Not long ago a murderer was tracked to his hiding-place by the blood-drops which fell here and there along his path. The officers followed the red trail, reached the threshold, climbed the stairway into the attic, and there in the dark of the further corner they found him crouching and trembling. But there was nothing out of the ordinary in that. Sin always leaves a red trail behind it; and the furies come more certainly than the night follows the day.

The part which God takes in the administration of retributive justice is distinctly forensic. He puts his sanction on a just sentence. When Cain fled from the scene of his brother's murder it was not God who laid punishment upon him, though it was to God he cried, "My punishment is greater than I can bear!" It seemed to him that a dreadful unseen something walked beside him, followed after him, touched him. He looked around quickly; nothing was there. He awoke with a start in the night-time all in a clammy sweat; he thought the wraith of Abel was bending over him. It was indeed an intolerable burden that oppressed him. Was God then his pursuer? Nay, as Milton says,

> " Himself was his own dungeon."

God did but suffer justice to have its way. For if it were possible to conceive of the universe and the present order as existing without God, the law of retribution would go right on. The doom of Belshazzar was passed upon him long before the Hand wrote upon his palace-wall, " Thou art weighed in the balance and found wanting." That phosphorescent sentence was but the divine *imprimatur* put upon the holy law.

All this is commonplace—dreadful, but purely commonplace. We know that the tiger crouches, yet we persist in sin. We go hurrying along the broad way despite the beacons kindled on the heights and voices of good angels calling us to pause, until we reach the chasm beyond which lies eternal night. And out of that chasm comes a wail like the soughing of the November wind: *Aion ton aionon*—" For ever and ever !"

III. The third definition of *hattath* gives us this rendering : "*A sin-offering lieth at thy door.*" And here is our most helpful lesson. If in the past we have sinned and come short of the glory of God, why should we weary ourselves in vain lamentation? The lamb for an offering is at our door. We may at this instant be forgiven; we may at this instant enter into the peace of reconciliation with God. The possibility of pardon is at hand. " Say not in thy heart, Who shall ascend into heaven to bring Christ down, or who shall descend into the deep to bring up Christ again? but rather, The word is nigh thee, even in thy mouth and in thy heart, to wit, If thou shalt confess with thy mouth the Lord Jesus and shalt believe in thy heart that God hath raised him from the dead, thou shalt be saved."

If a man sinned in the olden time his first thought was of sacrifice. "Go," cried he, " bring a firstling of the flock, for I have sinned a great sin and must needs expiate it." The lamb was brought to the altar; he saw it slain and placed upon the faggots ; he noted the fire kindling beneath it; he saw the smoke of the oblation rising towards heaven; and then he sang his thanksgiving. In that rising smoke his guilt seemed to be borne away from him. But all this was a meaningless pantomime, an empty dumb show, if it did not point onward to the great atonement which was to be accomplished in fulness of time. The blood streaming down the sides of this altar spoke of the fountain that was to be "filled with blood drawn from Emmanuel's veins."

> "Not all the blood of beasts
>   On Jewish altars slain
> Can give the guilty conscience peace
>   Or take away its stain;
> But Christ, the heavenly Lamb,
>   Takes all our guilt away—
> A sacrifice of nobler name
>   And richer blood than they."

Let us come therefore to the high altar at Golgotha and hold converse with Him.

"Who art thou?" we ask.

"I am the Lamb slain from the foundation of the world. Of me have the prophets spoken from the beginning. It is my blood alone that cleanseth from sin."

"What doest thou here?"

"I am being wounded for thy transgressions and bruised for thine iniquities, that by my stripes thou mayest be healed. By reason of my Godhood there is infinite virtue in the blood which I am pouring forth for thee."

"What then must I do to be saved?"

"Believe, only believe. He that believeth on the Son hath everlasting life. Come now let us reason together: though your sins are as scarlet, they shall be white as snow; though they be red like crimson, they shall be as wool."

Here is inexpressible comfort and encouragement at the opening of the year. A guilty queen walked in her sleep and remembered, and wrung her hands, lamenting, "What's done cannot be undone!" True; what's done, O friend, can never be undone; but it can be forgiven. The sin-offering is at thy door. The penalty may be averted, as it is written, "There is therefore no more condemnation to them that are in Christ Jesus. Who shall lay anything to the charge of God's elect? It is God that justifieth. Who is he that condemneth? It is Christ that died; yea, rather that is risen again, who is even at the right hand of God, who also maketh intercession for us."

What's done can be forgiven; and, moreover, what's done can be forgotten. For he has promised, "I will remember thy sins and iniquities no more." Lethe flows at the foot of Calvary. Therefore, putting our faith in the atoning virtue of the great Sacrifice, let us "forget the things which are behind, and reaching forth unto those things which are before, let us press towards the mark for the prize of the high calling of God in Christ Jesus."

In Bunyan's dream he saw a solitary traveller journeying with a burden on his back. Tears flowed along his cheeks and he groaned by reason of weariness. At length he came to a hill where there was a cross, and at the foot of the cross an open sepulchre; and as he ran and drew near, lo the burden was loosed from his shoulder and it began to fall, and so continued until it rolled into the sepulchre, "and I saw it no more." Then was this traveller glad and grateful. He stood for a while wondering and scarce believing. Then three shining ones appeared and saluted him, "Peace be unto you." One of them said, "Thy sins be forgiven thee;" another gave him a change of raiment; and the third placed in his hand a parchment wherein was written his title to a heavenly mansion. Then the traveller "gave three leaps for joy and went on singing."

Thus have we come to Calvary at the opening of the year. Oh that here our burdens might be loosed and vanish from our sight! Oh that we might hear the voices of the heavenly visitants saying, "Peace be unto you!" Thus leaving the past behind us, let us cheerfully press on towards the duties and responsibilities before us.

I wish you all a happy New Year—a year of prosperity in all things, but most of all in the things pertaining to the kingdom of heaven. I wish you a year of spiritual growth, of faithful service, of close communion with the Master. I wish you a pleasant journey at his side, your hearts burning within you while he opens unto you the Scriptures and reasons with you along the way. And so continually, until, in company with all the Lord's ransomed, we shall come at length to Zion with songs and everlasting joy upon our heads.

LOSING ONE'S LIFE.

PREACHED BY DR. BURRELL, JANUARY 10, 1892.

"For whosoever will save his life shall lose it ; and whosoever will lose his life for my sake shall find it."   Matt. 16:25.

THE key-note of the ministry of Jesus Christ is life. He came to give life and give it more abundantly.   The word is used in a double sense. On the one hand it refers to that higher life which dwells in virtue and usefulness ; on the other, to the lower life of self-gratification which a man shares with his dog that frolics here and there until weary and then counts it the consummation of happiness to lie in the shadow and gnaw a bone.   It is of this latter that the poet Montgomery wrote,

> 'T is not the whole of life to live
> Nor all of death to die.

It is of the former that Bailey sang,

> We live in deeds, not years ; in thoughts, not breaths ;
> In feelings, not in figures on a dial.
> We should count time by heart-throbs.   He most lives
> Who thinks most, feels the noblest, acts the best."

Our Lord knew the higher life.   He was familiar with heaven ; he had breathed the ozone of the celestial realms. He knew also the lower life.   In his thirty years on earth he mingled constantly with men who were dead in trespasses and sins.   Dead people jostled him in the streets ; dead people saluted him on the thoroughfares—men and women whose only life was low and sensual. To breathe and eat and sleep and make merry—this was the sum and substance of it.

The errand of Christ was to bring men and women up from the lower to the higher life. "I am come," he said, "that ye might have life." "I am the Way, the Truth, and the Life." "I am the Bread of Life." "Except ye eat the flesh and drink the blood of the Son of Man ye have no life in you." "God so loved the world that he gave his only-begotten Son, that whosoever believeth in him might have everlasting life." "Ye will not come unto me that ye may have life." "And what shall it profit a man if he gain the whole world and lose his own life? Or what shall a man give in exchange for his life?" "I am the Resurrection and the Life; he that believeth in me, though he were dead, yet shall he live; and he that liveth and believeth in me shall never die."

The law of the higher life is set forth in the passage before us. On four several occasions our Lord announced the principle, "He that saveth his life shall lose it." Once when he was commissioning the twelve (Matt. 10:29-39); again when Peter remonstrated with him against the necessity of his vicarious death (Mark 8:27-37); and again when speaking of the approach of the calamity of Israel (Luke 17:26-33); and once more when the Greeks came to him as the vanguard of the Gentile world (John 12:23-26). On each of these occasions our Lord enunciated with the utmost distinctness and solemnity this law by which we proceed from death to glorious immortality: "Whosoever shall save his life shall lose it; and whosoever shall lose his life for my sake shall find it."

I. *What is it to save one's life?* Jesus lived in an age when the multitudes were doing it. The shibboleth was *Dum vivimus, vivamus*—"There is nothing better for a man than that he eat and drink and make merry!" This was the highest good, the sum total of life, and the people were making the most of it.

I have stood on Mount Tom when the blue heavens seemed so vast and glorious that men and things below were scarcely in the reckoning. The farmers who were swinging their scythes in the fields seemed like pigmies. The horses trudging along the highways were no larger than ants. From an open carriage came sounds of laughter—how far away it seemed! How like Liliputians were they all! So from his high outlook our Lord saw multitudes living within the narrow horizons of the senses, toiling for shining dust or chasing thistledown; souls, godlike and immortal, who

> For ever hastening to the grave,
> Stooped downward as they ran.

Some were striving for wealth—getting, hoarding, spending—as sordidly and recklessly as if this life were all. Some were intent on pleasure, gratifying the senses with delights that perish with the using, crowning themselves with chaplets that would fade at nightfall. And some were pursuing honor, as multitudes are still pursuing it. The number of those who expect to occupy high places of authority is very small, but those who seek preferment or emolument of one sort or another—lovers of popularity, votaries of social position, solicitants of stars and garters, aspirants after preëminence—these are legion. And the realization of their hopes is, in comparison with higher things, as the mote in the sunbeam or as the small dust of the balance. These are the pursuits that make up the lower life ; these are the things for which men and women agonize by day and dream uneasy dreams all night. There are people who go about our streets and alleys gathering rags and scraps of paper and bits of broken glass. This is their livelihood. " It's a poor living," we say. Alas, those who live upon the lower levels are rag-pickers all! And such as look down upon them from the heavenly heights and mark them mingle in low and base pursuits must in their hearts compassionate them. " A poor living indeed," they say, " a wretched life at its best !" Is it worthy of us, indeed, to amass the best this world can give us? Are the flotsam and jetsam worth the saving?

II. *But what is it now to lose one's life*—to lose it for noble ends ? Jesus knew. He came from heaven to earth to cast away his life for the welfare of our ruined race. He surrendered all for us ; not otherwise was it possible for him to rescue us. He said distinctly, " The Son of Man must needs be delivered up and crucified "— *must needs be.* And with the purpose of making this necessity clear to his bewildered and remonstrating disciples he said, " Except a grain of corn fall into the ground and die, it abideth alone ; but if it die it bringeth forth much fruit." Here is the great principle of life proceeding out of death, of conquest born of self-sacrifice. The farmer who stints his seed-corn is a foolish man. He that soweth sparingly shall reap sparingly. Scatter the wheat, O friend, whether in your own field or God's, if you care for a golden harvest and loaded wains and bursting bins. This is the word of the Master to all earnest men and women, "If any will come after me, let him deny himself and take up his cross and follow me."

"*Let him deny himself.*" Here is the first step towards the higher life. The Chinese tell of an old-time potter who vainly sought to put a certain tint upon his vases, until at last in desperation he cast himself into his furnace; then, when the kiln of pottery was taken out, lo the exquisite color was upon it! It is a true parable. The fairest thing in our universe is character; and character never puts on its utmost beauty until self is wholly surrendered to secure it.

"*And let him take up his cross.*" The cross is a symbol of altruism. Self-denial is negative; altruism is positive. We save others by sacrificing ourselves. This truth finds its preëminent illustration in the story of Golgotha. "If thou be the Christ," they cried, "save thyself; come down from the cross!" But he could not. "He saved others," they tauntingly shouted; "himself he cannot save!" Alas, it was true! A moral necessity was upon him. If he would save the ruined race, himself he could not save. And the same constraint is upon us. The cross has vast significance. It means distinctively the taking up of a painful service in behalf of our fellow-men. We serve others and rescue the perishing just as we enter into fellowship with our Saviour's death; and so doing we pass out of the lower life into the higher, out of the sordid world of self-gratification into the kingdom of God. It is thus that we become partakers of the divine nature. Thus the apostle said, "I am crucified with Christ; nevertheless I live; yet not I, but Christ liveth in me."

"*And let him follow me.*" To follow Jesus is to step in bloody footprints that lead ofttimes to the haunts of sin and shame, mayhap to Golgotha, but always at last into the spiritual and eternal life. The prayer of our Master was, "Father, glorify thyself!" His life was devoted to the glorification of God. To follow Christ is to give God the uppermost place. He must dominate all our powers and rule in all our tasks and pleasures; as the sky over-arches the earth, so must the thought of the Infinite One canopy the soul of him who follows after the only-begotten Son of God.

To live thus is to be worthy of our manhood. We were created in the image and after the likeness of God. The consummation of all worthy purpose is to return to him. To leave this out of the reckoning is to be unworthy of our birthright. When Themistocles was asked by one of his soldiers why he gathered none of the golden chains and other spoil which the enemy had thrown away in their flight, he answered, "Thou mayest, for thou art not Themistocles." A man has made a great stride towards the noblest possibilities of his nature when he has rightly conceived the thought of his divine birth and has heard God's voice calling him.

III. *What is it to find one's life for ever*, or, as elsewhere, to preserve it unto life eternal? What is that? I wish I knew. I wish I could elucidate it. How easy to say "life eternal," but how impossible to grasp even a modicum of the meaning of it.

We begin this higher life here and now. We do not wait for a heavenly summons in order to enter the kingdom of God. The sense of pardon, a good conscience, the fellowship of the Spirit, the hope of glory—these make the beginnings of heaven on earth.

> Celestial fruits on earthly ground
> From faith and love do grow.

"The life is more than meat," said the Master, "and the body is more than raiment. Why therefore should ye be anxious as to what ye shall eat or what ye shall drink or wherewithal ye shall be clothed? Seek ye first the kingdom of God and his righteousness, and all these things shall be added unto you." To get above the fret and worry, the sordid cares of those who have no life beyond that of the madding crowd, to have God's peace abiding in one's heart—this is to dwell in the higher life, this is to be, here and now, in the kingdom of God.

But hereafter—what must it be hereafter? The life everlasting! To have our names written in the book of Life, to receive a crown of Life, to drink from the river of Life, to eat of the tree of Life which is in the midst of the paradise of God—it is not possible for us to understand the delectable things which are concealed in these metaphors. The pilgrim in the allegory who had escaped from the City of Destruction and saw Heaven in the distance, ran with all his might, despite the voices of his friends and kinsmen, and as he ran he thrust his fingers in his ears and cried, "Life! Life! Eternal Life!"

The picture of "The Temptation of Jesus in the Wilderness," by Ary Scheffer, is criticised by many on the ground that, like Milton in " Paradise Lost," he has made Satan the most imposing figure. This however is so only to the superficial view. Christ, as you will remember, stands on a barren spur of the mountain. Just below him is the tempter, a commanding presence, strong in every nerve and sinew. He has just directed the thought of Jesus to the kingdoms of this world and offered them all for a single act of homage. He seems to say, " I know thy purpose. Thou hast come to conquer the world by dying for it. But why shouldst thou endure the anguish of the cross? I am the Prince of this world and am prepared to abdicate my power on one condition. All these kingdoms shall be thine if thou wilt fall down and worship me!" Above him stands the calm figure of Jesus, his face marked by the assurance of divine power and authority. With a simple wave of his hand he dismisses the alluring thought. At such a price the kingdoms of this world cannot tempt him; he puts them all away. He waves the world aside and wins it! Thus may we attain to the highest by putting the lowest from us. Thus may we attain unto life by bidding our lower natures die the death. Thus may we spurn the world to enter the kingdom of God.

Here is the great problem after all, the problem that confronts every earnest soul, " What shall it profit a man if he gain the whole world and lose his life? Or what shall a man give in exchange for his life?" He that believeth on the Son hath life. And he that liveth and believeth in him—oh blessed, blessed immortality!—shall never die.

THE
BRAZEN SERPENT.

PREACHED BY DR. BURRELL, JANUARY 17, 1892.

" And as Moses lifted up the serpent in the wilderness, even so must
the Son of Man be lifted up; that whosoever believeth in him
should not perish, but have eternal life." John 3:14, 15.

ONE night in Easter week a man sat in an upper chamber in the city of Jerusalem. It was late and he was alone. The lamp on his wall burned dimly. He was plainly clad and his hands were calloused with toil. It was plain to be seen that he was a man of the people. An open scroll lay before him, but he was not reading it. There was a far-away look in his eyes. He was communing with heaven, hearing distant voices — the hallelujahs of the kingdom. There was a step on the outer stairway, and a moment later a visitor entered. He wore a garment falling to his feet, a broad phylactery on his forearm, and a frontlet between his eyes whereon was written, "Hear, O Israel, the Lord our God is one Lord!" He was an old Sanhedrist, one of the inner circle of Jewish wise men. What was he doing here? He closed the door quickly, glanced backward to assure himself that he was not followed, advanced, and made the customary salutation. The other arose, and bowing low, answered, "Peace be unto you."

It was a notable meeting. And in the interview that followed there were wonders upon wonders. Our first surprise is at the very threshold. For it is passing strange that Nicodemus should have been received at all. Thereby we know that our Lord is willing to welcome the humblest and worst of us. This man was a moral coward, else he would not have come to Jesus under cover of the night.

He feared the pointed finger, dreaded to have it known that he had visited the Nazarene teacher. Thrice only in the Scriptures is Nicodemus named, and always with this qualification, "The same came to Jesus by night." We may meet him some time in the kingdom; but if we do, the angel who introduces us will be likely to say, "This is Rabbi Nicodemus, the same who came to Jesus by night." Despite his cowardice, however, the Lord graciously received him. His motive was of the lowest; he was probably scourged thither by an uneasy conscience, by his fear of the torments which follow sin. All this was sufficiently selfish, yet the Lord did not reject him. Wherefore we conclude that there is a welcome for all, even unto the uttermost. The promise is, " Him that cometh unto me I will in no wise cast out." Let no one hesitate to fling himself upon the heart of this Jesus; his hands beckon, his mercy is for all.

Not only was Nicodemus admitted to an audience that night, but to him were revealed some of the deepest and sublimest of truths. One of these was *Regeneration*. On entering he saluted the Nazarene prophet with a graceful compliment, " Master, we know that thou art a teacher come from God;" but under this formal greeting, deep down in his heart, was a throbbing desire to know the way of everlasting life. Skilled in the art of forensic dissimulation, he gave no outward token of this longing; but the Lord saw it. At a glance he saw the case of Nicodemus through and through. And giving no heed to his courtesy, he proceeded straightway to the matter in hand: " I know the purpose of thy heart; I know thine aspiration after a nobler and a better life. Verily, verily I say unto thee, except a man be born again he shall not see the kingdom of God." The Rabbi was bewildered. He was familiar with the learning of the rabbinical schools and the speculations of philosophy, but this being born again was all mystery to him. Thus to-day there are multitudes of learned men, professional men of broad culture and liberal education, who can scan their Virgils and quote from Aristotle, but know next to nothing about spiritual things. They are blind as bats with reference to those great problems which reach out unto the eternal world. Thus it is written, "The natural man receiveth not the things of the Spirit of God, because they are spiritually discerned." There was hope for Nicodemus, however, inasmuch as he frankly confessed his ignorance. "How can these things be?" he exclaimed. The Lord must teach him as if he were a lad in a kindergarten. It was a gusty night; the wind whistling through the narrow streets furnishes the object-lesson. "The wind bloweth where it listeth, and thou hearest the sound thereof but canst not tell whence it cometh or whither it goeth: so is every one that is born of the Spirit." The blowing of the wind is an undeniable fact despite the mystery attendant upon it: so also is the "'gain-birth." We mark its tokens in the transformation of character as distinctly as we hear and feel the blowing of the wind. We may not understand, but as frank and sensible people we must needs acknowledge it.

The other truth revealed to Nicodemus in this interview was that of *Redemption*. The Lord having pierced this Rabbi's soul with the sharp dogma of regeneration, now brings the balm of redemption to mollify his wound: "For God so loved the world that he gave his only-begotten Son, that whosoever believeth in him should not perish, but have everlasting life." Yet here again Nicodemus was amazed. All this was so contrary to his accustomed way of thinking, so opposed to rabbinical notions and the tradition of the elders. He had been wont to reason along the lines of retribution; sowing and reaping made up his philosophy of justice : "The soul that sinneth it shall die." It was not strange that he stumbled now at the thought of the sinner's going scot free, at the innocent suffering for the guilty, at the saving virtue of faith. The Lord again found his object-lesson at hand. "Do you remember," said he, "how Moses lifted up the serpent in the wilderness?" It was an old story: the Hebrew people were all familiar with it.

The thing happened towards the close of the wilderness journey. For thirty-eight years and more the children of Israel had been going round about on their way to the Promised Land. It was a short journey in fact, and a few months should have accomplished it. But sins are clogs and fetters to a pilgrim in the heavenward way. God must needs discipline these people and rid them of their infirmities before they can enter in and possess the goodly land. So round and round they went, "compassing Edom," over the scorching sands and under the blazing suns. They were not able to enter in because of their unbelief. Their murmurings and idolatries kept them out. Now here they were again upon the border. They could climb the mountain and look over upon their inheritance. Behind them were the broad, barren stretches of the wilderness; before them, sweet fields all dressed in living green and rivers of delight. "To-morrow," they said, "we will cross the river." But that night King Arad with his barbaric hordes came out against them. They called upon God in their extremity and he made bare his arm in their behalf. Then burying their dead they set forth. But the roads were steep and rugged, and "they were discouraged because of the way." Their women and children were worn out, and wearily trudging along the difficult paths they fell again into their besetting sin and began to murmur, "Why have ye brought us up hither?" They loathed their blessings and reproached God. What could be done with this stiff-necked people? This was their twelfth murmuring; it must be punished. The fiery serpents came, crawling from the coppices, hissing along the paths, stinging with their venomous fangs. Cries of anguish were heard everywhere. Multitudes were sick unto death. Then Moses in answer to his intercessory supplication was bidden to raise the brazen effigy upon a pole in the midst of the encampment; and the proclamation was issued, "Look and live."

Do you believe the story? Our Lord evidently believed it and wished Nicodemus to believe it. But then it must be remembered that He was not as familiar with the facts of Scripture as some of our modern wise men. We have been recently told that we must not be surprised to find limitations put upon the knowledge of Christ. This is going a step farther than to deny the inerrancy of the Scriptures. But whatever our learned critics may think, it is plain that Jesus accepted the truth of the old narrative, and the Church universal, despite the caveat of irreverent criticism, yields a cordial assent to it. "These things," says Paul, "happened unto our fathers for types." (1 Cor. 10: 11, margin.) There must, therefore, be helpful suggestions here for us.

I. Our first lesson is about *sin*. Sin is virus. The tempter is "that old serpent." In his first approach to the human race he came in serpentine form. And his influence was deadly as a serpent's fang. Sin courses through our blood like venom—from heart to brain, to feet, to finger-tips. The sinner is poisoned through and through. The whole head is sick and the whole heart faint. Isa. 1 : 5.

There is no cure in our *materia medica* for the serpent's bite. In vain did the Israelites search for an antidote. Their herbs and nostrums and incantations were in vain. The world has been groping through the ages for some remedy for sin. Mythology and philosophy are but tokens of the vain quest. Here is the problem: What shall I do to be saved? How shall God be just and yet the justifier of the ungodly? Or how shall a man be just with God?

Sin is mortal. The deadliest thing in the world is a cobra's bite. The eye of the victim grows dull and glassy, his flesh cold and blue to his fingers; in an hour his body is laid out for its burial. We cannot separate sin from its penalty. Sin is death. The soul that sinneth it shall die.

II. Our second lesson is of *the Saviour*. Here is a striking similitude.

(1.) The brazen effigy for the healing of the Israelites was in the likeness of their malady. A tablet might have been raised upon the pole with the name "Adonai" upon it. Would not that have answered just as well? No, it must be a brazen serpent, for it is intended to prefigure that Christ who must assume the form of sinful flesh in order to deliver the world from sin. As it is written, "He who knew no sin was made sin for us, that we might become the righteousness of God in him." And again, "He hath redeemed us from the curse, being made a curse for us; as it is written, Cursed is every one that hangeth on a tree." And again, "What the law could not do in that it was weak through the flesh, God sending his own Son in the likeness of sinful flesh and for sin, condemned sin in the flesh; that the righteousness of the law might be fulfilled in us, who walk not after the flesh, but after the Spirit."

(2.) But while this effigy was made in the similitude of a serpent, there was no venom in it. Of all the vipers that crept and hissed throughout the camp, there was not one that did not have poison under its tongue. This serpent alone was harmless. In like manner Christ, who assumed a sinful form and came for our deliverance, was "holy, harmless, and undefiled," the only sinless man on earth. "There was no guile in his lips." Who shall lay anything to his charge? "I find no fault in him at all."

(3.) But this harmless effigy had power, like a mad-stone, to draw the virus from every wound. Our Lord upon his cross has a like power to save. Our sin is laid by imputation upon him, that he in turn may cast about us, by the imputation of his righteousness, a garment of fine linen, clean and white. He is the sinless One; and yet, hanging yonder as our substitute before the offended law, he becomes in our behalf the very chief of sinners. The world's burden is laid upon him. He assumes the curse of the race. The blood upon his brow seems like a frontlet bearing this word, "Accursed!" The priests and Pharisees passing by wagged their heads and cried, "Cursed is every one that hangeth on a tree!" The earth, rumbling in the deep darkness, utters forth his doom, "Accursed!" His own anguished cry, "*Eloi, Eloi, lama sabachthani!*" betrays his conviction that the curse of the perishing multitude is rolled upon him. It is by virtue of this imputation that he, being made in the likeness of sin, can draw the venom from the world's mortal wound. "He bare our sins—bare them and bare them away—in his own body on the tree."

III. *The Great Salvation.* "I, if I be lifted up, will draw all men unto me."

This "lifting up" meant death. So the Jews always

understood it. Only by the death of Jesus could he give us entrance into life. His blood cleanseth. In an assembly of so-called "Liberal Christians" the question arose, "Why is it that all the evangelical bodies of believers are making rapid and manifest progress while we alone go backwards?" Various answers were given. At length one of the delegates was moved to say, "Brethren, we must not expect to receive great accessions from among the people so long as we reject the doctrine of the blood. We have no blood in our religion." A most notable and significant confession. No blood in their religion! God help them then, and God pity their followers; for without the shedding of blood there is no remission of sin.

It is because our Lord was thus "lifted up" on his cross, tasting death for every man, that salvation can be offered to all. If any man on earth is a universalist, I more. Christ's life, death, and resurrection are for all. He is the light that lighteth every man that cometh into the world. By his atoning work every sinner is brought within the charmed circle of a possible salvation. Not that all are saved. Would to God they were! But all are made salvable. The responsibility of life or death is thrown upon them. There is none that cannot be saved. "Ho, every one that thirsteth, come ye to the waters!" "The Spirit and the Bride say, Come; and let him that heareth say, Come; and let him that is athirst come; and whosoever will, let him take the water of life freely."

The sole condition affixed to eternal life is belief in Christ. "He that believeth shall be saved." Only believe! Look and live! No doubt there were many in Israel who, notwithstanding the proffer of life, perished and were buried in the desert sand. There were some who put their dependence upon such human help as was at their command; and they died. There were some who said, "We are likely to recover in any case; there is no need of alarm;" and they died. There were some who could not understand how there was healing power in a brazen serpent on a pole: "It is mere superstition, and we decline to have anything to do with it;" and they died. There were some who had passed the stage of anguish and were in torpor when bidden to look; they were comfortable and did not wish to be disturbed; and they died. But others, multitudes of others, hearing the invitation, looked towards the brazen effigy and lived. There are hundreds on hundreds of excuses that may be offered by the unbeliever for refusing to believe in Christ; but they all mean rejection; and his is the only name given under heaven whereby we must be saved. "He that believeth in the Lord Jesus Christ shall be saved; he that believeth not shall be damned." He shall die in his sins as certainly as the serpent-bitten in the wilderness who would not look and live.

Faith is a simple thing, but it is "the coupling of destiny;" it links the soul with the mercy of God. There is a legend of Bishop Forannau that, fleeing from his enemies, he with twelve companions came to the seashore. There, being at their wits' end, they found two flotsam logs. These they pushed out upon the waves and cast themselves upon them. The logs formed themselves into the shape of a cross and were borne away by favorable winds to the Flemish shore. Thus Forannau and his twelve were saved. The fable teaches that no man ever yet trusted himself to the cross and was not saved. No man ever looked to Jesus and died in his sins.

> Look! look! look and live!
> There is life for a look at the crucified One,
> There is life at this moment for thee.

MAKING HASTE.

PREACHED BY DR. BURRELL, JANUARY 24, 1892.

"He that believeth shall not make haste." Isa. 28:16.

THIS "making haste" is one of our generic sins. We are all in a hurry. A wise man among the ancients, on being asked what panacea he would suggest for the evils of human life, gave this answer: "Patience; all things come right to those who wait." Among the attributes of a symmetrical character, as given by the apostle Peter, to wit, " Faith, virtue, knowledge, temperance, patience, godliness, brotherly-kindness, and charity," we are accustomed to think of patience as the least attractive and most commonplace of all. She is the scullery maid in the sisterhood of graces. But in the final outcome this Cinderella will be at the palace, clothed in royal apparel and wedded to the king's son.

The reason why we lack patience is because we have so little faith. We believe in God as a far-off entity; but how faintly do we grasp our intimate and cordial relations with him. We believe in ourselves in a manner, but not half in ourselves as divinely born and destined to a heavenly inheritance. We believe in such wealth as the sordid multitudes are striving for, but how little in the inestimable riches of the grace of God. We believe in getting the most of pleasure out of these passing hours; but if we could realize what those pleasures are which "are at the right hand of God for evermore," what manner of persons we would be! We live in a narrow, sensuous circle, bounded by the reach of our finger-tips. Oh for a larger faith in God, in the possibilities of this life, and in those eternal verities which reach out unto future ages! He that believeth in these shall cease all worry and fretfulness and rest content in God. " My soul, wait thou only upon God, for my expectation is from him."

.I. At the outset we are over eager to meet the tasks and responsibilities of earnest life. Our sons and daughters can scarcely wait to be through their schooling. One of the most painful disappointments that ever came to me was when I first met Dr. Taylor on old Andover Hill. I had gone there to Phillips Academy for a little final polishing in preparation for college. He looked my scant accomplishments over and said, " My boy, you need two years of earnest study." Then seeing how my countenance fell, he added, " There 's no hurry. Do n't fret; the world will wait for you." It was a true saying. The world waits for everybody who is earnestly preparing to take part in its important affairs. But our boys and girls can with difficulty be made to believe it. The outlook seems interminable ; four years at college and three more of professional study! But it pays to get ready and to get ready well. The issues involved are so momentous that none should presume to meet them until he has bound his girdle about his loins.

Our Lord himself was an apprentice in a carpenter shop. He made ploughs and harrows and mended the furniture of the village folk. He knew that the world was dying for want of his redemptive offices. He heard the foot-fall of the innumerable multitude as they passed by heedless of duty and unmindful of the great spiritual truths: he knew they were going, lock-step, down to eternal death. A soul was passing into eternity every second and he was aware of it; yet he went on mending ploughs and harrows, and taking an interest in the commonplace affairs of his townsmen. Thus he grew in stature and wisdom. He learned his lessons line by line and precept by precept at the rabbinical school, and in fulness of time he entered on his work well prepared for it.

II. In our secular pursuits we are all too much given to worry and precipitation. This is preëminently an American sin. A young man sets out in the practice of law. He waits for clients, but no clients come. He cannot bide his time. He casts his eye upon the political arena and sees men struggling there for the mastery. He strips to the waist and enters for the prize. He wins it : a local office. Then promotion, and at length a seat in our national councils. Is this success? One thing is certain; he has failed as an attorney-at-law ; whether he has succeeded otherwise remains to be seen. There is a last chapter in every life. The saddest sight along the sea is the hulk of an old vessel, water-logged, abandoned, and useless. The corresponding sight in common life is a political hulk, high and dry upon the shore, friendless and of no apparent use.

A young man enters commercial life to find that weighing sugar and measuring cambric by the yard are slow work. Is there not a shorter road to wealth? Ay. Presently he puts his little capital into speculation or into loans at exorbitant interest. He may thus accelerate his purpose, but is this success? At the time of the Chicago fire I knew men who lost the accumulations of a lifetime by opening their vaults too soon. Had they waited they might have saved all their bonds and mortgages ; but turning the key in the white-hot locks, there was a puff of flame, a heap of ashes, and everything was gone. How many a man has been ruined by such over-eagerness. The best livelihood and most satisfying in the long run is that gotten by what Robert Burns has called "gin-house prudence and grubbing industry." All things come right to those who wait.

III. So also with respect to spiritual things. It is not well even to come to Christ precipitately. He himself said to a multitude who were following him, "If any man will come after me, let him deny himself, take up his cross, and follow me." Pointing to an unfinished tower by the roadside, he bade the people mark it well as indicating the folly of undertaking a very important work without pausing to count the cost. "This man," he said, "began to build and was not able to finish." The Christian life involves all our most momentous interests here and hereafter. It is not to be entered upon thoughtlessly, therefore, nor in haste, but wisely and with deliberation.

Let it be understood, however, that deliberation is one thing and delay another. A man may do a thing with the utmost thoughtfulness and yet do it instantly and in the nick of time. The blacksmith when he draws the red iron from the forge, lifts his hammer with the utmost deliberation, measuring the necessary force and the distance to be traversed by the blow, doing nothing in haste and yet striking instantly; for he must needs strike while the iron is hot. We deceive ourselves oftentimes, when facing great spiritual responsibilities, in thinking that we are waiting for more light or for deeper convictions, when in fact we are merely putting off the duty which presses vitally upon us. With respect to our surrender to the demands of Christ, we have all weighed the question well. and over and over and over again. It has been before us ever since we learned of Jesus at our mother's knees. No new facts enter into the problem No new developments with respect to the solution of the question are to be looked for. The only thing that remains is to do what we know to be manly and right and to do that instantly. The man who acts on impulse is sure to blunder seriously, but the man who lets his opportunity go by default, doing despite his heart and conscience day after day and year by year, is guilty of one continuous and disastrous blunder. It was a frontier philosopher who said, " Be sure you 're right, then go ahead :" but neither Paul nor Plato could have marked out a wiser rule of life.

IV. Still further, with respect to spiritual growth. We are ofttimes disheartened because we seem only to creep, whereas we would "run up the heavenly way." We forget that character is slow growth—first the blade, then the ear, then the full corn in the ear. There must be time in grace, as in nature, for God's rain and sunshine. The sturdy oak that defies the storm and whirlwind is the product of a hundred years. The fungus under its shadow springs up in a single night, but a rude breath kills it. True Christian character, the stalwart stuff that martyrs and confessors are made of, is a gradual development. Mere pious sentiment, the stuff that Pharisaism is made of—the stock in trade of the unco-guid—cometh up as a flower. How we envy the dear saintly grandmother who sits in the chimney-corner with her Bible before her, God's peace that passeth all understanding filling her heart, and her dim eyes full of visions of the heavenly life! She seems to have quite subdued all sin and passion and to have entered into the inner place of the Lord's pavilion. No bondage of sin, no warring of spirit and flesh, no doubts or misgivings; she simply rests in God. How came she to this large measure of sanctification? By the very path that we are treading now, by years of patient continuance in well-doing. Take heart, O young disci-

ple of Christ! The pilgrim's progress to the land of Beu-
lah is the journey of a life. All the invention of these
bustling times has devised no plan of expediting our pilgrimage to heaven.

> We go the way the prophets went,
> The way that leads from banishment,
> The King's highway of holiness.

An Alpine tourist set out at early morning to climb
the Matterhorn. The air was bracing and he pressed on
with springing steps. Presently he passed a peasant
going on with steady strides, and to himself he said,
" Slow fellows, these, hereabouts;" and on he hastened.
But the path was steep and rugged. Ere noon his steps
lagged and he reclined to rest under an overhanging crag.
Then along came the peasant with that steady, swinging
gait and passed on before him. It is but another version
of the Hare and the Tortoise, a lesson which holds true
in spiritual as in secular life. It pays to be patient. It
pays to plod. Faith is our alpenstock, beloved; let us
lean hard upon it.

The man who thoroughly believes in God can afford
to be patient. He knows that all things are working together for his good. He is assured of good times coming.
He can bear up under trouble, not because his nerves are
unsensitive, but because he is confident that his afflictions
are but for a moment, and that they are destined to work
for him a far more and exceeding weight of glory. He
never surrenders to fate. He bears up bravely and waits.
There was true philosophy in the words of the little maid
who, being asked to define patience, said, " It means,
Bide a wee and dinna weary." Time rights all things.
The years roll on for ever, and almost before we are aware
we shall awake in the resurrection morning. A little

while! What is this that he saith? "Why art thou cast down, O my soul, and why art thou disquieted within me? Hope thou in God; for I shall yet praise him, who is the health of my countenance and my God."

V. We note a similar restlessness in Christian service. We are all too eager to accomplish the great thing. We forget that spiritual success is best achieved by always doing the next thing. The apostles, if left to themselves after our Lord's ascension, might have proceeded at once to the conquest of the world; and had they done so dismal failure would have awaited them. But they remembered his word, "Tarry ye at Jerusalem until ye be endued with power." They waited, not restlessly or indolently, but upon their knees, and the enduement came; then they went forth to accomplish great things for God. Let us look to our preparation. Have we tarried for our enduement? Have we suffered the Lord to adequately prepare us for work?

Then we are so impatient as to results. I know a lad who planted beans beside his mother's door, hoping that vines would creep up over it. But alas, he could not wait; again and again he dug them up to see if they were sprouting. We are all doing something of the sort in our larger tasks. How many mothers have been praying for wayward sons since the days when they held them in their arms, and the days and years have come and gone and still no answer! Is God's ear heavy that he cannot hear? Hath he forgotten to be gracious? No. O petitioner at Heaven's gate, lean hard upon thy staff of promise: "He that goeth forth and weepeth, bearing precious seed, shall doubtless come again with rejoicing, bearing his sheaves with him." Our duty is to scatter seed. Its germination and springing are not by the will of flesh nor by the will of man, but of God.

Adoniram Judson wrought and prayed year after year with a consuming passion for souls, yet saw not one converted. Where was the fault? Nowhere. God was merely biding his time. At length the Pentecostal blessing came. There were thousands who began asking as with one voice, "What shall we do?" And the wilderness blossomed as the rose. Let us be patient. The harvest will ripen, but it may ripen on our graves. Our faith should be willing to have it so. Remember the words of the Lord Jesus how he said, "Men ought always to pray and not to faint." John dreaming in Patmos saw golden vials full of odors, which he tells us were the prayers of the saints. Not one of them is forgotten before God.

VI. Further, as to the great Apocalypse. We wait for our Lord's appearing. Maranatha! The Lord cometh! He shall so come as ye have seen him go up into heaven. His word was, "Behold, I come quickly!" Nearly two thousand years have passed since then; but what of that? A thousand years are with him as a single day. It was therefore only as the day before yesterday that he promised it. "He that shall come will come and will make no tarrying." It will be in the fulness of time. As the bud opens, as the chrysalis bursts, as the sun rises, so shall he appear in the fulness of time. Meanwhile let us love his appearing and be preparing for it.

> He 's faithful that hath promised; he 'll surely come again.
> He 'll keep his tryst wi' me; at what hour I dinna ken.
> But he bids me still to wait an' ready aye to be
> To gang at ony moment to my ain countree.
>
> So I 'm watching aye, an' singin' o' my hame as I wait,
> For the soun'ing o' his footfa' this side the shining gate.
> God gie his grace to ilk ane wha listens noo to me
> That we a' may gang in gladness to our ain countree.

THEREFORE GET WISDOM.

PREACHED BY DR. BURRELL, JANUARY 31, 1892.

"Wisdom is the principal thing; therefore get wisdom." Prov. 4:7.

THE desire of knowledge is common to all human kind. Dr. Johnson said, "A man would scarcely be willing to learn needlework; but if he could arrive at it without the painful process of acquisition, he would e'en be glad to know how to mend his wife's ruffle." All knowledge is worth the having—the three R's, the arts and sciences and philosophy, the polite accomplishments, everything in the encyclopædia—but far more desirable and infinitely above all is the knowledge of spiritual things. To this is given the name wisdom. Of this apprehension of truths in the higher province it is said, "Wisdom is not to be valued with the gold of Ophir. Wisdom is the principal thing; therefore get wisdom; and with all thy getting, get understanding;" that is, understanding with respect to these verities of the eternal world.

We are confronted by great problems which it behooves us, as far as possible, to solve. Here are some of them: "If a man die, shall he live again;" or "does death end all?" "How shall a man be just with God;" the sinner who has rebelled against the holy law of Jehovah, how shall he be reconciled with Him? What shall it profit a man if he gain the whole world and lose his own life; or what shall a man give in exchange for his life? These and kindred questions are worthy of the most strenuous endeavor on the part of every earnest man.

I. *It is possible to get wisdom*, to arrive at a measurable solution of these tremendous problems, to apprehend more or less of spiritual truth.

We are living in an age of weak convictions, of guesses as distinguished from beliefs, of opinions rather than established views. The most popular phase of thought in these times is known as Agnosticism. The word itself is significant. It is the Greek equivalent of the Latin *ignorance*. A Greek agnostic would therefore in plain Latin be an ignoramus. Agnosticism asserts the unknowableness of everything super-sensible. It is Know-nothingism in religion. It shuts a man up within the narrow province of the senses. It forbids him to go beyond the reach of his finger-tips. The original agnostic was Pyrrho of Elis. He was the universal skeptic, the cosmopolitan ignoramus, whose philosophy was merely an interrogation point. He regarded a perfect suspense of judgment as the highest accomplishment. He made ignorance to be the pillow of the soul. He said, " We know nothing, not even that we do know nothing." The modern father of Agnosticism was Comte, who said in substance, " We are cognizant of impressions, but we cannot know whether they correspond to anything real. Our ideas may be mere phantasms ; it is impossible to determine whether there is anything behind them. We ourselves may be only as shadows walking in a dream." One of the modern apostles of agnosticism is Matthew Arnold, who defines God to be that Force in the universe, outside of man, that makes for righteousness. A Force? What is an impersonal Force to a soul in trouble? What use have we, as earnest men and women, for this armless, eyeless, heartless Spectre of a God? Another of the apostles of this strange philosophy is Herbert Spencer, whose rhetoric is marvellous as an illustration of the art of going round about and concealing thought. Here is his definition of life: " Life is a definite combination of heterogeneous changes both simultaneous and successive in correspondence with external coexistences and sequences." And another of the apostles of this philosophy of spiritual ignorance is Maudesley, who questions even the reality of thought. What is mind? Phosphorus. What is thought? The product of atomic friction. The process is like this: " An electric force runs

along a pulpy cord called a nerve until it reaches a pulpy
substance called the brain, and the result is an idea."
Thus real things are dissipated into thin air; materialism
and idealism are combined into one; Gnosticism becomes
Agnosticism; Science becomes Nescience; and knowledge is made synonymous with ignorance. Our most
arrogant thinkers to-day are those who insist that neither
they nor anybody else can know anything at all beyond
the province of the senses—just as the old-time mendicant friars were said to be prouder of the holes in their
garments than princes were of their purple and fine linen.

> The truest characters of ignorance
> Are pride and vanity and arrogance,
> As blind men use to bear their noses higher
> Than those who have their eyes and sight entire.

In contravention of this way of thinking we hold that
it is possible to know respecting spiritual things. We
have the faculty wherewith to apprehend them. This faculty or *spiritual* sense is the link binding us to God.
There is an instrument called a spectroscope which is sensitive to certain chemical effects, so that being turned upon
one of the heavenly bodies millions of miles away it will
detect nitrogen or sodium there. In like manner our spiritual sense is sensitive to spiritual forces. It can apprehend God and heaven and righteousness. We have this
faculty as a divine inheritance; it belongs to us by reason
of our divine birth. God made us akin with himself, in
his own likeness and after his image, breathing into our
nostrils the breath of life, so that we became living souls.
At this point we are distinguished from all the lower
orders of being. A fox calculates the width of the brook
which it purposes to leap—an eagle reasons with respect
to the distance from which it must swoop sheer downward
upon its prey. But there is no creature among the lower
orders that can apprehend a moral truth or commune with
God.

Then, moreover, the spiritual things which we desire
to apprehend lie within our sphere of vision. God is not
far from any one of us. Heaven is not a country in remote space. "Say not who shall ascend into heaven to
bring him down, or who shall descend into the deep to

bring him up, for lo the word is nigh thee, even in thy heart and in thy mouth." An Indian hearing the rolling thunder overhead says, "The Great Spirit is yonder;" feeling the breath of the wind upon his cheek he reverently says, "The Great Spirit is round about me;" marking the pulsation of his heart or quite as plainly the quick response of his conscience to a moral suggestion, he says, laying his hand upon his breast, "The Great Spirit is here," which is precisely what the Master meant when he said, "The kingdom of God is within you." Thus we are in the midst of the great problems. God is the ubiquitous One. We are environed by spiritual facts. Eternity stretches out here at my feet, an ocean vast and shoreless. Heaven and hell are worlds at my right and left hand, between which I walk to the great unknown. And these worlds are separated from me by a gossamer veil so thin that the sting of an insect may rend it or the hand of death draw it aside at any moment. Thus we are sons and daughters of the Infinite, walking in the midst of infinite things.

I do not say that we can exhaust all or any spiritual truth. Indeed there is no moral verity of which man can say, "I count myself to have apprehended it." We cannot take into our lungs the entire atmosphere which envelops the earth fifty miles deep, but we can inhale one breath, and that will meet the necessities of life. We may not drink the ocean at a gulp; but, athirst on our journey, we may dip into the brook and drink enough out of the palm to satisfy our thirst. We may not have the earth, whether we want it or not; but we may have a little garden-plot in which to raise a few roses to make life sweeter and better. A mouse lived in a cheese-box until its provender was quite exhausted, and then, climbing up and looking over the edge, it cried in amazement, "I never dreamed the world was so large!" We are living here in like manner, shut up in the close environment of sense; but one of these days we shall climb up and look over, and, O beloved, a great surprise awaits us! As yet we have formed no conception, can form no conception, of the vast, interminable stretches of spiritual and eternal truth.

II. *It is our magnificent privilege and prerogative to inform ourselves concerning these things.*

> The mind of man is this world's true dimension ;
> And knowledge is the measure of his mind.
> And thus the mind in its vast comprehension
> Contains more worlds than all the world can find.

We were not made to "grovel here below, fond of these trifling toys." We are divine and immortal. The things which most concern us are those that eye cannot see and hands cannot handle. The things which are seen are temporal, but the unseen are eternal. In reaching out for spiritual truth we give distinct evidence of our descent from God.

Old Kaiser Wilhelm of Germany, being in one of the rural districts of his empire, took occasion to visit the common schools. While interrogating a little child, he said, holding up a coin, "My dear, to what kingdom does this belong ?" She answered, "To the mineral kingdom, Sire." And, holding up an orange, "To what kingdom does this belong ?" "To the vegetable kingdom." Then, laying his hand upon his breast, he said, "And, my dear, to what kingdom do I belong ?" She paused a moment and answered, "Your Majesty, you belong to the kingdom of God."

The lowest attitude which men can assume towards truth is that of credulity. Here dwell the superstitious folk, dupes, fetich-worshippers, the people who nail horse-shoes to the mast, tie an amulet about their necks, object to sitting at table in a company of thirteen ; the people who take everything on hearsay, who attach an awesome dignity to the ministerial office and believe what their pastor tells them without ever applying the acid test of heart and conscience. Like that collier in Wales who, being asked what the people of his parish believed, answered, "Why truly, sir, we believe as the preacher does," and being further asked, "What does the preacher believe ?" answered, "Why, sir, he believes as we do," and questioned once more, "What do you and your preacher believe ?" replied, "Why surely we both believe the very same."

A step higher and we reach the doubters. Doubt is

nobler than credulity. A skeptic is a better man than an unthinking bigot, just as an active mind is better than a torpid one. Doubt, genuine doubt, is a good thing; not as an end, mark you, for so it is deadly, but as a means to an end. To be sure your skeptic is not a learned man; for true learning implies conviction. He is a half-educated man; and a little learning is ever a dangerous thing. He is like the blind man whose eyes being partially opened, said, "I see men as trees walking." The probability is that many people are mistaken as to their being doubters. Their doubt is unbelief, confirmed and ultimate. Men often call themselves honest doubters when they are pure and simple infidels, contentedly dwelling in rejection of the truth. Doubt, genuine doubt, is not a thing to abide in, only a bit of ground large enough for a footprint, on which a man may step and straightway move on. Doubt is always something to move away from. If you are a doubter, move on. It is dangerous to pause a moment. In God's name move on! Doubt may be tested by a man's agonizing desire to be relieved of it. The man who honestly doubts as to Jesus Christ will not sleep to-night until he has solved the great question and accepted or rejected Christ as the only-begotten Son of God. There are two kinds of doubt as there are two twilights: one growing darker and darker, the shadows gathering, moon and stars vanishing, leaving naught but silence and solitude; the other leading on to light and gladness, brighter and brighter until the shadows flee away and the day breaks.

One more step and we have reached the highest terrace of human character, to wit: belief. Here dwell the people who say, *Credo*. There is an impression that faith is an unsubstantial thing which has no evidence behind it. On the contrary, the best definition ever given of faith is this: "Faith is the substance of things hoped for, the evidence of things not seen." It is substance resting on evidence; the substance of spiritual things resting on evidence which appeals to the moral sense. The just shall live by such faith. The man who gave that definition was himself a living illustration of the power of faith. He suffered, and in his pain he was upheld by the hope of a better time coming. Paul was precisely what his faith made him.

And indeed the character of any man is measured by his creed.   Pope wrote,

> For modes of faith let graceless zealots fight;
> His faith cannot be wrong whose life is right.

But let us transpose and read the other way—

> For modes of life let righteous pedants fight;
> His life cannot be wrong whose faith is right.

There is no such thing as inconsistency.   A man lives up to what he believes: not always to what he says he believes, but to what he does believe in his inmost heart. As a man thinketh in his heart so is he.

III. It is our bounden duty, therefore, to have sound convictions as to spiritual truth.   We have no right to allow the great problems to go by default.   If there is a God, it behooves us to know it.   If my soul is a bundle of powers under control of a sovereign will, it is incumbent upon me to know it.   If eternity is real, stretching out beyond me like a boundless ocean, it behooves me to ask with the utmost solemnity, Whither?   If sin has defiled my whole nature, if the law has sent forth its retributive sentence, "The soul that sinneth it shall die," and if God has provided a means of salvation through the sacrifice of his well-beloved Son, then I am not worthy of my manhood unless I accept the situation and make the very best of it.

But how shall we know?   How shall we get this wisdom?   Not by the scientific method.   God never yet became a Q. E. D.

Here, however, is the secret.   In James 1 : 5 is a great promise: "If any one of you lack wisdom, let him ask of God, who giveth to all men liberally, and upbraideth not; and it shall be given unto him."   God is light; open the windows and let God shine in.   The fear of the Lord is the beginning of wisdom.   Bow down at the mercy-seat and ask him to illuminate the dark chambers of your soul. The natural man receiveth not the things of the Spirit of God, for they are foolishness unto him; neither can he know them, for they are spiritually discerned.   "Canst thou by searching find out God?"   The monks of four hundred years ago might have seen Jupiter's moons, had they only been willing to look through Galileo's telescope, but they would not. They insisted on seeing nothing beyond the reach of their naked eyes, so they fell short of their opportunity and the world moved on without them. Prayer is our telescope through which we look at spiritual things, discerning the realities which are afar off. No man, unaided, ever yet found out God or theology. Therefore, O man, to your knees! Commune with heaven, reason with the Infinite, turn your eyes towards the things which are unseen and eternal! Get wisdom from God!

But at the best we shall only touch the outer borders. A blind boy who had come under the influence of one of our missionaries in India was fond of repeating, "I know that my Redeemer liveth, and in my flesh I shall see God, whom I shall see for myself and mine eyes shall behold, and not another's." In his last moments, rolling his dim eyes, he exclaimed, "I see, Copaul sees. Tell the missionary that the blind boy sees the King in his beauty!"

Here we know in part and see as in a glass darkly; but there we shall see face to face and know even as we are known. No more mists and vapors; no more shadows on the soul. Reality! Reality! Blessed be God for the promise of the break of day!

AN

INCREDIBLE RUMOR.

PREACHED BY DR. BURRELL, FEBRUARY 7, 1892.

"Who hath believed our report? and to whom is the arm of the Lord revealed?" Isa. 53:1. "But though he had done so many miracles before them, yet they believed not on him; that the saying of Esaias the prophet might be fulfilled, which he spake, Lord, who hath believed our report? and to whom hath the arm of the Lord been revealed?" John 12:37, 38. "But they have not all obeyed the gospel. For Esaias saith, Lord, who hath believed our report?" Rom. 10:16.

ABOUT 700 B. C. there was a great revival in Israel. It followed the dark reign of Ahaz. He had fostered idolatry in its grossest forms. The flames of human sacrifice, kindled on all the high places round about Jerusalem, cast a lurid glare upon the pillars of the neglected temple. The schools of the prophets were filled with wizards and necromancers. The king forced his own children to pass through the idolatrous fires; the people bowed down and kissed their hands to the winged horses of the sun. But there was one man who remained faithful to the religion of the true God. He prayed for the nation and called upon all to repent and return to God. And at length he saw the reward of his faithfulness. The blessing came upon Israel as grateful as the morning dew. The songs of pure worship were heard again in the temple and the people bowed at the altars of Jehovah. This return to truth and righteousness was, however, merely temporary. It was as the flashing of Northern Lights;

the returning darkness was deeper than ever.   King and people went back to their abominations, and the prophet disappeared in the gloom of the gathering night, uttering this sad lament, " Who hath believed our report? and to whom is the arm of the Lord revealed?"   In vain had he preached truth and righteousness.   In vain had he prophesied the coming of the Holy One.   On the eyes of the stiff-necked people a thick film of blindness had gathered. They could not see ; they would not hear.   In vain was God's arm made bare for their redemption, as a workman rolls back his sleeve for the undertaking of a mighty task. He would have delivered them : he would have gloriously redeemed them ; but they would not believe it.

Seven hundred years went by, and around the spur of Mount Olivet passed a procession on its way to the Holy City.   " Hosanna ! Hosanna to the Son of David !" cried those that went before and those that followed after.   Jesus entered the temple, and from the porch where Isaiah had vainly besought the people to repent and believe he preached the glorious gospel.   But in him there was no form nor comeliness that men should desire him.   He seemed to them as a root out of a dry ground.   He was despised and rejected.   The heart of the people was in no wise changed, as Esaias had written, " Who hath believed our report? and to whom is God's arm revealed?"

When all was over and the glorious work had been verified by the Saviour's triumph over death, Paul, writing to the people of Rome, bids them believe that their salvation is near ; he would have them rejoice in the good news of deliverance from sin.   " How beautiful upon the mountains," he exclaims, "are the feet of him that bringeth good tidings, that publisheth peace !"   Yet still the message was rejected, and the apostle finds utterance for his disappointment in the prophet's words, " Who hath believed our report? and to whom is the arm of the Lord revealed ?"

And here am I, eighteen hundred years after, preaching the same gospel.   Has human nature changed in the meantime ?   Nay, human nature is the one constant factor in history.   There are multitudes who still reject the offer of redemption in Jesus Christ.   The truth is unto some a savor of life unto life ; but to the many, alas! it is a savor of death unto death.

What is this report which the people so persistently reject? It is the story of God's intervention in behalf of our ruined race. He so loved the world that he gave his only-begotten Son to redeem it. It is a message of joy unspeakable and full of glory. How is it then that any should reject it? Ruskin says, " Pride is at the bottom of all our blunders." The greatest blunder that a human soul can ever make is to refuse the proffer of salvation in Jesus Christ. And pride is at the bottom of it.

I. Pride of intellect. We all know something, and none knows over-much. " A little learning is a dangerous thing." The temptation is to reject everything which does not fall within the grasp of reason. In fact, however, the wisdom of man is foolishness with God. The moment that we approach anything divine, we are beyond our depth. Observe some of the fundamental facts of the gospel over which we stumble because they baffle us.

(1.) The Manger. "Great is the mystery of godliness ; God made manifest in the flesh : the angels desire to look into it." Not for a moment must it be supposed that a finite mind can comprehend the mystery of the Incarnation. If a man were to enter here with a tin cup, a foot rule, and a pair of steelyards, and tell us that he meant therewith to measure the ocean, compass the earth, and weigh the clouds of heaven, we should know that he had gone daft. It were greater folly still for any man to think himself capable of solving this preëminent spiritual mystery. That, however, is absolutely no reason at all why we should reject it.

(2.) The Cross. How can the innocent suffer for the guilty? How can the infinite God bear the sins of his creatures? How can justice be satisfied by vicarious pain? These and kindred questions crowd thick and fast upon us. But the mystery of God's vicarious death in our behalf is really no more incredible than the lower but like mystery of a mother's love. And a mother's love is the commonest thing in the world. A child born out of her travail pains, carried on her weary arms, and feeding upon her life, tears away from her restraining care at length, plunges into sin, and breaks her heart. To insist then upon puncturing that heart and analyzing its blood, finding there so much of serum, so much of coagulum, with the proper proportion of iron and phosphorus, would be no more preposterous than for God's children to undertake, by what is called the scientific method, to fathom the doctrine of his redemptive love and vicarious pain for us.

(3.) The Open Sepulchre. He that was dead is alive again. This also is repugnant to our reason. How can the dead live? And yet life out of death, the mystery of mysteries, is all around us and ever forcing itself upon us. I stand in a ploughed field where the farmer has scattered the seed and never think of asking, "Can this death beneath my feet. return to life?" I know it will. But I stand in Greenwood where the dead are lying all about me, and despite the universal analogy of nature, I cry aloud, "O God, can these dead live?" And the Lord answers, "The trumpet shall sound and the dead shall rise." Then shall be brought to pass the saying that is written, "Death is swallowed up in victory. O death, where is thy sting? O grave, where is thy victory?"

We must expect mystery in the spiritual province. How indeed, could it be otherwise when God himself is the fundamental and greatest mystery? Canst thou by searching find him out? How little the definitions of God mean to us. He is "that circle whose centre is everywhere and whose circumference is nowhere." This means only that he is infinitely beyond us. We may know that he is and that he is the rewarder of them that diligently seek him; but there we pause. All God's works are like himself, mysterious. Here is the line of differentiation between our work and his. I may understand a steam-engine and possibly be able to take it apart and explain its wheels and pistons and cylinders; but the moment I undertake to deal with a snowflake, a dewdrop, or an electric flash, I am at my wits' end. Man can fathom what man has done or can do; but it is the glory of God to conceal a matter. His works are past finding out. We veil our faces before him.

II. Moral pride. The worst of us thinks moderately well of himself. Pass through the corridors of The Tombs and ask the criminals there to pass judgment on their own cases, and the chances are that every one will pronounce himself a pretty fair sort of man. No religion can commend itself to the average man which antagonizes this confidence in personal merit. We are not all in The Tombs, but we are all "concluded (literally, imprisoned) under sin." There is no difference; we have all sinned and come short of the glory of God.

(1.) The suggestion of sin is abhorrent to us. It disturbs our equanimity; it troubles our sleep. We are reasonably comfortable until Jesus Christ comes our way and brings accusation against us. His own entire life was a protest against sin. His preaching was a two-edged sword, dividing asunder the soul and spirit of a guilty man. His death was a terrific outcry against the horror of sin. No man wants to be shaken thus out of his ease. Christ tears away the turf from our assumption of virtue and exposes a grave-full of "dead men's bones and uncleanness." Little wonder that a sinner will have none of it.

(2.) We do not like the notion of repentance. Herod, being disturbed by John the Baptist's cry, "Repent ye! Repent ye!" cast him into Machærus, fed him on bread and water, and ultimately beheaded him, only to be haunted by his wraith walking up and down and crying still, "Repent! Repent!" We all would kill John the Baptist could we catch him. For he ever goes before the gospel with his weird cry and troubles the soul that the Good Physician may heal it.

(3.) The doctrine of Free Grace is repugnant to us. The gospel says, If you are ever saved it must be without money and without price. Our pride revolts. We want to be doing. Every merit-maker on earth—the moralist, the Brahman devotee measuring his length along the weary way to the Ganges, the humble payer of Peter's pence—is doing his utmost to earn salvation. We would cheerfully pay; but Crœsus himself could not, with all his generous possessions, buy one of the clusters from the King's vineyard. "Ho, every one that thirsteth, come ye to the waters; and he that hath no money, come, buy and eat; yea, come buy wine and milk without money and without price." We would be glad to suffer if suffering could expiate the mislived past; but we cannot. Christ has suffered once for all. No penance can save us; no sacrifice can avail.

> Once for all. O sinner, receive it!
> -Once for all. O brother, believe it!
> Cursed by the Law and bruised by the Fall,
> Christ hath redeemed us once for all.

What then remains? How shall a sinner be saved? By simply accepting the proffer of pardon and life. He that believeth shall be saved. Faith is the appropriating hand. Is this all? Ay; and it is the slightness of it that offends us. All our pride rises up within us. We will not be saved *gratis*. We will not be thus beholden to God. A proud soul will pay its own reckoning. It will not be humbled like a mendicant. But it must. It must take life for nothing or it will never take it at all. We must come to Christ as Constantine came to the cross on Calvary, taking off his crown and purple robes and making himself of no reputation before that effigy of divine mercy. We must become nothing in the presence of Christ, to the end that Christ may become everything to us.

There are two concluding thoughts.

(1.) The report that God has loved us and given himself for us is true. This *is* the news, the gōd-spel, the glorious gospel of the blessed God. Whether men believe it or not does not affect the truth. God bared his omnipotent arm on Calvary to work redemption for us. His own word stands voucher for the rumor. The hearts and consciences of a great multitude of saints redeemed answer Yea and Amen to it. On one of Bradlaugh's journeys through Cornwall he delivered an infidel address to a large assemblage of miners. At the close of the address he gave the customary opportunity to any who might wish to question or reply to him. Possibly he thought some callow youth would take up the gauntlet and be easily disposed of. But an old woman, wearing an antique bonnet, with a basket on her arm, came forward to the platform. She said, " Sir, I paid thrippence to hear ye tell us of something better than the gospel of Christ. This was what your placard promised, that you would show us 'something better than the gospel.' But ye have not done it. Let me tell you what this gospel has done for me. I was left a widow thirty years ago with ten children to care for. I trusted in Christ, and he helped me. All my little ones have grown up to be respected and beloved. I was often sore pressed and the flour was low in the barrel, but my Lord ever helped me. Many a time my heart was near breaking for my boys and girls, but he raised me up. And now I am old and poor and decrepit, but happy as a morning lark, and looking for, the city which hath foundations, whose builder and maker is God. Sir, ye have cheated me of my thrippence. Ye have not told me of anything that can be compared with the gospel of my Lord." The infidel rubbed his hands and smilingly said to his audience, " Really this good woman is so happy in her delusion that it would be a pity to undeceive her." " No, no," she said, " that will never do, and your laughing does not alter the case. I have given you proof of the gospel, and what have you answered? Naught but a sneer, a patronizing fling—weapons from the armory of folly that a man like yourself should be ashamed of. Sir, ye have cheated me of my thrippence and ye are not an honest man." Thus it is written, God hath chosen the foolish things of the world to confound the wise, and the weak things of the world to confound the things which are mighty. Our gospel has been tried in ten thousand times ten thousand cases similar to this, and found to be gloriously, gloriously true.

(2.) And if it were not true, still let us cherish it. If it be only a fond delusion, let us in any case continue in it. If but a dream, let no rude hand or unkind voice awake us. If there is no God, no Almighty Friend to care for this world and its suffering creatures, still let us dream of a kind Providence and murmur in our sleep, " Abba, Father." If death is really the end of all and our future is no better than that of the beasts that perish, let us dream nevertheless that we, being made in the divine likeness, are to live for ever; and in our sleep let us still see visions of the heavenly city with its pearly gates and golden streets and the ineffable glory shining over it.   If they which have fallen asleep in Christ are perished, if our parting with dear ones who have gone before us into the unknown was not *Auf Wiedersehen*, but *Farewell for ever*, still let me dream that one day I shall have them again, that I shall touch their dear hands and kiss their lips in the glad day of the reunions in our Father's house.   In the name of all that is kindly and gracious, leave me to my fond delusions ; let me still and ever dream on.

But the gospel is true.   This is no cunningly devised table.   We speak that we do know and testify that we have seen.   God's arm has been made bare for us.   With yonder cross he has beaten down, as with Thor's hammer, the gates of hell.   Here life and immortality are brought to light.   This is a faithful saying, worthy of all acceptation, that Christ Jesus came into the world to save sinners. He that believeth shall live.   Rescue is at hand.   The sound of the bugle is heard upon the hills.   Let us throw open the great gates of our hearts that God with his great salvation may enter in.

THE

TREASURES OF THE BIBLE AS A BOOK AMONG BOOKS.

PREACHED BY DR. BURRELL, FEBRUARY 14, 1892.

Therefore every scribe which is instructed unto the kingdom of heaven is like unto a man which is an householder, which bringeth forth out of his treasure things new and old." Matt. 13:52.

HERE is a brief parable. The door into the meaning of the parabolic teachings of Jesus turns upon the hinges of Oriental custom. Were it not for this fact it might be impossible to interpret them. The customs of the Orient have remained substantially unchanged to this day as if to assist us in apprehending the truth. The farmer still goes out with a forked stick over his shoulder to plough his field; Ruth still gleans after the reapers; Rebecca still leads her flock to the well and lets down the waterpot upon her hand to give the wayfarer to drink; Lazarus still sits at the gate waiting for his plate of crumbs; the indolent still stand with folded hands in the marketplace the bridesmaids still carry their lamps along the dark streets, and the cry is heard, " Behold the bridegroom cometh !"

As to the reference in this particular parable : a traveller has come to an Oriental home at eventide and is being entertained.   His host, desirous of showing his importance, brings out his wealth and spreads it before him.   There were no banks or other places of safe deposit in those days.   Treasure was buried in the ground or kept in a recess in the wall.   The householder here goes to his treasury and bring out things new and old : antique coins ; necklaces worn by princes of long ago ; golden shields bearing the dint of old-time battles ; precious stones plucked from the crowns of captive kings ; the loot of the campaigns of ages.   All these are spread before the eyes of his wondering guest.   Now, says Jesus, the scribe is the custodian of God's treasury.   The key is at his girdle.   His business is to bring forth the wealth of Scripture, new truths and old truths, to dazzle the eyes. The preacher is the scribe.   It is his special function to expound the divine Word.

There is a coterie of select wise men in our time who arrogate to themselves this distinct prerogative.   They will have no trespassing.   Over the gateway of the Scriptures they have placed this *caveat*, " N. B. This preserve is for the use of duly accredited Biblical Critics.   No trespassing. *Cave canem.*   Ministers of the gospel in particular are warned off.   By order of *The Erudite Junto*." But ministers of the gospel are not to be so easily repelled.   It is their particular business to know the Scriptures and their special duty to expound them. A Biblical Critic is, to the minister of the gospel, as the apothecary's apprentice to the physician. The 'prentice makes the pills and lotions, knows their constituent parts, and possibly feels himself a master of the Materia Medica; but it will probably be conceded that the physician, whose business is not merely to know what the pills and lotions are made of, but how to apply them to the necessities of physical life, is somewhat the wiser of the two. Certainly the young knight of the pestle has his place, but in the practical uses of the pharmacopœia the physician is master of the situation. So the minister of the gospel, despite the admonition of the learned Critics, must insist upon his prerogative in the exposition of the Word. It is his place to know not merely those Scriptural infinitesimals which men discover with the microscope, the jot and the tittle, but to know what the Scriptures are good for. It is claimed, therefore, in behalf of ministers of the gospel, that they are incomparably better qualified than any other class of scholars whatsoever to speak advisedly regarding the Word of God.

We have to do just now with the Scriptures as a Book among books. Erase the name of Jehovah from its title page—were that possible—and regard it for the nonce as merely a volume in the world's library. In which case we shall find that no book in all the world's literature is for a moment or in any particular to be compared with it. This is the preëminent classic, with respect to which there is practical unanimity among thoughtful men.   In Froude's life of Bunyan he says that amid the enforced silence and solitude of Bedford jail the prisoner had only two books and one of these was the Bible, of which he adds significantly, The Bible is a literature in itself, the richest and rarest in human thought, so that he who masters it is a liberally educated man.

Let us now visit this treasury and bring forth some of the things, new and old, which commend it as worthy to be called the Word of God.

I. The Poetry of the Bible.   One third of the Old Testament is in poetic form.   The earliest of all—and probably the oldest scrap of poetry in existence—is the Song of the Sword in Genesis 4 : 23, 24.   It seems to be commemorative of some blood-shedding in that early time :

> Adah and Zillah, hear my voice;
> Ye wives of Lamech, hearken to my speech !
> I have slain a man for wounding me,
> A young man for smiting me.
> If Cain was seven times avenged,
> Then Lamech seventy-seven-fold.

Alas, that ever since those primitive times the world has been singing the Sword Song !

The sweetest hymn of the springtime is that of Solomon.   All the poets have sung the vernal beauties and the renewal of life, but never one so sweetly as this :

> My beloved spake and said unto me,
> Rise up, my love, my fair one, and come away .
> For lo, the winter is past,

The rain is over and gone :
The flowers appear on the earth ;
The time of the singing of birds is come,
And the voice of the turtle is heard in our land
The fig-tree ripeneth her green figs,
And the vines are in blossom,
They give forth their fragrance.
Arise, my love, my fair one, and come away !

The most stirring of battle songs is that of Deborah. The "Marseillaise," "God save the Queen," and the "Battle Hymn of the Republic" are flat, stale, and unprofitable beside it. She summons the princes of Israel and the people to the fray. We hear the footfall of the multitude rushing towards the high places of the field. The stars in their courses are marshalled to fight against Sisera. The river Kishon, that mighty river, sweeps past in tumult, bearing the terror-stricken enemy in rout towards the sea. And above the hoarse artillery of heaven, the roar of the torrents, the shriek of the dying, we hear the song of the prophetess inspiring the victors and invoking maledictions upon those who lingered among the bleating flocks :

Curse ye Meroz,
Curse ye bitterly the inhabitants thereof ;
Because they came not to the help of the Lord,
To the help of the Lord against the mighty !
Through the window looks
The mother of Sisera.
Why lingers his cart in coming ?

Why tarry the wheels of his chariot?
Thus let them perish,
All thine enemies, O Jehovah!
O my soul,
Thou hast trodden down strength.

Of this memorable battle song it may be said, as Carlyle wrote of Burns' "Scots wha hae wi' Wallace bled," that it should be sung with the voice of the whirlwind.

And where is there anything like Habakkuk's vision from the watch-tower? He sees the Almighty marching through history:

God came from Teman,
And the Holy One from Mount Paran;
His glory covered the heavens
And the earth was full of his praise!

Before him goes the pestilence and burning coals are under his feet; on either side the hills are bowing and the mountains are scattering in affright. The ocean utters his voice and lifts his hands on high. Sun and moon stand still in their habitations at the flash of his speeding arrows and the shining of his spear. With flail in hand he strides through the ages and generations threshing the nations in his wrath.

The New Testament opens with the song of the angels: To you is born this day a Saviour, which is Christ the Lord. Glory to God in the highest, and on earth peace, good-will towards men!

Is there anything sublimer than that anywhere? Yes,

the last song of the Book, the adoration of the angels: Worthy art thou to receive honor and power and riches and wisdom and strength and glory and blessing for ever and ever. Amen.

Where are the singers in literature? We call them inspired—Virgil and Homer and burning Sappho, Goethe and Schiller, Milton and Shakespeare—but how they dwindle beside the bards of Scripture! They are as twittering swallows in a field of morning larks. Never have poets sung like those who dipped their pens in "Siloa's brook that flows fast by the oracle of God."

II. Let us visit the treasury again and bring forth some of its wealth of Eloquence. We begin with Judah's plea for his brethren at the Egyptian court, probably the oldest display of oratory in existence. He was a stranger in a strange land, arraigned with his brethren on a criminal charge. The possibility of death confronted them. Over them brooded the memory of a dreadful secret sin. It was under such conditions that he presented his argument, earnest and pathetic almost unto death. "His fancy plays with rare delicacy around the venerable form of that patriarch who in the distant home is waiting for Benjamin, and whose very life is bound up in the life of the child. For Benjamin and that aged father he supplicates with tearful fervency: 'And it shall come to pass that when we come to thy servant, my father, and he seeth that the lad is not with us, he shall die. We shall bring down his gray hairs with sorrow to the grave!'"

The plea of Aaron for the emancipation of Israel has no parallel in history. Day after day, sixteen times successively, he comes before the tyrant Pharaoh wielding the rod of Jehovah and in his name demanding that the chains of the people shall be broken. How puny seem the forms of Wilberforce and Lloyd Garrison in the presence of this mighty liberator! "Thus saith Jehovah, Let my people go." The river of Egypt rolls with blood, reptiles infest its soil, the sun is veiled in darkness, and the pestilence stalks abroad, the harvests are beaten down by angry tempests, and the wail of death goes up at midnight from every home! Then the people march forth; three millions of slaves delivered by the irresistible voice of a devoted man.

The time would fail me to tell of Nathan and his parable of The Little Ewe Lamb, or of John the Baptist, taught in the wilderness to cry, "Repent ye, repent ye, for the kingdom of heaven is at hand!" or of Stephen courting death in his eager passion to unveil the sin of the people in crucifying God's well-beloved Son; or of Peter at Pentecost, preaching so mightily that three thousand souls were brought sobbing penitently before the feet of Christ; or of Paul on Mars' Hill, setting forth the doctrine of human rights in words that were the foregleam of all subsequent manifestoes in behalf of civil and ecclesiastical freedom: "God hath made of one blood all nations of men for to dwell on the face of the earth."

The crowning eloquence of the Scriptures is that of the Master. The common people heard him gladly. He spake as one having authority. They wondered at the gracious words which proceeded out of his mouth. A Roman guard being sent to take him, listened, were captivated, and returned without their prisoner. " Why have ye not brought him ?" their masters demanded. It was a strange answer they gave, these men of battle, proof against sentiment, hardened to all merciless tasks, " Never man spake like this man !"

III. We go again to the treasury and bring forth some of its Historical wealth. Here we have the only authentic record running back to the infancy of time. All other chronicles are fragmentary. Cæsar and Xenophon wrote episodes; but here are the universal annals. This is a deep river, flowing backward in its course past the ruined cities of antiquity, in tortuous windings whose roar and thunder are as the confused noise of battle, through the quiet pastures of peace, through the solitudes of the primeval ages, past the confusion of tongues, the deluge, the creation of man, past that remote period when the earth was without form and void, onward still past the floating nebulæ, and still beyond to the ineffable glory. Its source is beneath the heavenly throne, as it is written, " In the beginning, God."

And this Scriptural chronicle is entirely trustworthy. It has stood the test of adverse criticism for long centuries, and has come out of the ordeal without the smell of fire upon it. In these last days the archæologists, digging among the ruins of ancient cities, have unearthed many confirmations of Holy Writ. Voices have come from mummy crypts and buried forums and sculptured obelisks saying Yea and Amen to it.

The cradle of the race was in the Mesopotamian Valley. Thence came the nations, the religions, and the political organizations of the world. But of the primitive civilizations of that Valley next to nothing was known until about forty years ago, when a royal library was found dating back to 640 B. C., written in the cuneiform character. Here are text-books of every sort. Here are tablets commemorating the deeds of sovereigns who reigned 2000 B. C. Here is the name of Nimrod, the mighty hunter before the Lord. Out of the mist of the primitive civilization thus disclosed rise the towers of old Babylon. We find here an account of the deluge and a tradition of the fall. Here is the story of the raid of the four kings and of many other occurrences which had previously rested upon the sole authority of the Scriptures. Thus voices from the tombs are continually and more and more declaring the historical authority of this Word of God.

IV. Let us glance at the Scientific wealth of the Bible. We are aware that the science of the Scriptures has been persistently assailed in these last days. It is a common thing to hear it said, " The Bible was not intended to be a scientific book," giving the impression that it makes little difference whether the science of the Scriptures is trustworthy or not. This, however, is not a matter of small moment. If the book is not veracious in respect to science, what ground have we for committing ourselves to its spiritual guidance? A minister who proves himself unreliable in secular matters, whose opinions cannot be trusted anywhere except in religion, would not for a moment pass unchallenged as a spiritual counsellor. The question is not whether the Bible was intended to be a scientific book or not, but whether the Bible is true. It is not true unless it is reliable every way. If it cannot be trusted in other respects, where is the ground for relying upon it in matters pertaining to truth and morals?

Observe that the Old Testament Scriptures abound everywhere in scientific allusions. They treat of biology, ethnology, astronomy, geology, zoölogy, indeed of every department of natural science. You would have to tear the Book to tatters if you were to take all references to science out of it. But these statements have not yet been successfully impugned. All the substantial discoveries of science—observe, I do not say dreams and hypotheses— are continually indorsing and verifying them. It is not to be denied that multitudes of undevout scientists are clamoring against them. But the Bible has withstood the criticism of centuries, and this will not affect it.

V. The Ethics of the Scriptures. By universal consent the Bible is the standard of universal morals. We take our stand between Sinai and Olivet, the two mountains of the Law and the Gospel, and find here the source of the world's jurisprudence and the sanctions of all civil and social courtesy.

Here also is a portrait gallery of worthies in whom the precepts of morality have found their best illustration,

Enoch, Abraham, David, Elijah, Ruth the virtuous, the Marys, Paul, and the Sons of Thunder. What a roll-call of mighty and virtuous ones could be gotten from these pages! Yet they are all "concluded under sin," and all join in the confession that they "come short of the glory of God." There is one among them, however, whose face shines as the sun shineth in his strength. Over him we write, "The Wonderful," and under him, "Verily this was a righteous man." Oh how it helps all struggling men and women to have so glorious an ideal! In him we behold duty, holiness, manhood, character. He is the only one who ever lived on earth of whom it could be said, He was as good as the law. In him all graces were combined, as all colors blend in the white solar ray—the golden glory of the sunrise, the deep blue of the heavens, the emerald of the sea. Thus Christ combines all virtues and excellencies and stands forth in history as the Ideal Man.

VI. Once more let us bring forth from the storehouse its wealth of Doctrine. For the Scriptures are of pre-eminent value with respect to spiritual truth.

There are some things which our souls are aching to know. We can get along without science, we can live without the lower forms of knowledge, but we must somehow be advised respecting the problems touching our eternal destiny. Is there a God? And are we immortal? Shall we stand before him in judgment, and live for ever in weal or woe? Is there a heaven? Is there a hell? Can a man be delivered from the shame and anguish of his sin? These are questions that will not down. They demand an answer at the hands of every earnest man.

These are the things embraced in that old question, "What is truth?" The Academy by the Ilissus, the painted porch of Zeno, the garden of Epicurus, represented vain efforts to answer it. Canst thou by wisdom find out God? The despair of the world found expression on the curled lip of Pilate when he satirically asked, "What is truth?" But it has pleased God to make known in the Scriptures the things which the unaided reason of man could never have arrived at.

(1.) They reveal God. They reveal him as I AM THAT I AM. He is "the Lord God, merciful and gracious, slow to anger and plenteous in mercy." He is Jehovah Tsidkenu, our guide and helper. He is—best of all—our Father in heaven. Nowhere but in the Scriptures can we thus perceive him.

(2.) The Bible also reveals the true nature of man. He was created in God's likeness and after his image, a soul living and destined to live for ever. He fell from his high estate and Ichabod was written on his brow—"The glory hath departed." But blessed possibilities still open up before him. All is not lost.

(3.) The Bible makes known the great at-onement between God and man. It points to the cross as the point whereat God can be just and the justifier of the ungodly. It bids us believe that God himself, taking flesh upon him, bore our sins in his own body on the tree, that whosoever believeth in him shall not perish, but have everlasting life. Other books have poems, but no other sings the song of salvation and gives the troubled soul a peace that floweth like a river. Other books have eloquence, but no other enables us to behold God himself stretching out his pierced hands and pleading with men to turn and live. Other books have history, but no other tells the story of divine love reaching from the remote councils of eternity to the consummation on Calvary, "the old, old story of Jesus and his love." Other books have science, but no other can give the soul a definite assurance with respect to spiritual life, so that it may say, "I know whom I have believed and am persuaded that he is able to keep that which I have committed to him against that day." Other books set forth philosophy, but no other makes us wise with respect to those great doctrines which centre in the living God.

This, therefore, is the book to live by, the one book that makes the future bright and brings heaven near. Other systems of philosophy are like ships which carry their lights at the stern, "casting a lurid glare on the white wake of receding foam, warning of no peril and lighting to no anchorage." This book carries a searchlight at the masthead, showing the dangers on every side and throwing a splendor on the waters clear to heaven's gate.

And this is the book to die by. I would that you might have known my friend Parmentier, an old Huguenot, dim-eyed, pain-stricken, bent with years, friendless and penniless. In his humble hut he had three things to comfort him: the flowers that grew in the little garden before his door (how they flourished under his loving care!), the birds—a score of singing birds that hung in the sunshine of his solitary window—to whom he talked as little girls talk with their dolls, and his Bible, well thumbed and greatly beloved. The last time I saw him, we bent together over the fourteenth chapter of St. John, and the last words we read were these, " Peace I leave with you, my peace I give unto you: not as the world giveth, give I unto you. Let not your heart be troubled, neither let it be afraid." The blessed Book is resting on the coverlet of many a death-bed to-day. Its truth is the strong staff of the dying as they pass on to the city of God.

Remember then, beloved, the word of the Master, how he said, " Search the Scriptures." Search them as for hid treasure. And blessed is the man who finds here the secret of eternal life.

> This is the field where hidden lies
> The pearl of price unknown;
> That merchant is divinely wise
> Who makes that pearl his own.

When we were children we were led by fairy guides into subterranean caves, where vaulted roofs and fretted walls sparkled with jewels and precious stones. Thus, to the reader whose eyes are opened by the touch of the Spirit, do the Scriptures glow with the unspeakable riches of truth. But amid their sparkling splendors there is none so bright as Christ himself. He is the Kohinoor, the crown-diamond among them all.

It is possible to search the Scriptures without finding life. It is possible to know them by heart without having a heart interest in the salvation which they proclaim. It is possible to be critically familiar with every jot and tittle of the written page, yet blind as a mole at noonday to the living truth. The gracious Redeemer with hands outstretched and face aglow with goodness walks in the midst of these oracles; but alas, if our eyes are so holden that we fail to recognize him! Oh that we all may find the Incarnate Word in the written Word of God!

SUNRISE.

PREACHED BY DR. BURRELL, FEBRUARY 21, 1892.

"Then spake Jesus again unto them, saying, I am the light of the world: he that followeth me shall not walk in darkness, but shall have the light of life." John 8:12.

GOD is light, "essential, original, unapproachable." God is light and in him is no darkness at all. Christ is the manifestation of God. He is the brightness of the Father's glory, and as such also is light. He was prefigured in the golden candlestick that threw its radiance upon the ceremonies of the Holy Place. He was set forth in the Shechinah, the luminous cloud that led the children of Israel on their journey to the promised land. His advent was prophesied as the coming of the morning: "But unto you that fear my name shall the Sun of Righteousness arise with healing in his wings." Mal. 4: 2.

We shall the better understand these words, "I am the light of the world," if we review the circumstances under which they were spoken. It was at the Feast of Tabernacles. The ministry of Jesus was drawing to a close. He had much to do and the time was short. "I must work while it is day," said he, "for the night cometh." His home during the feast was with his friends at the suburban town of Bethany. It was his custom to rise early in the morning, walk into Jerusalem, and spend the day there in preaching and working miracles. His enemies, who had pursued him long, were now closing in upon him. In vain thus far had they set gins and snares for his feet; but on this particular morning fate seemed to favor them.

The Lord, having " prevented the day," was in the temple porch preaching to the early worshippers, when an interruption occurred.   A boisterous company, led by certain rabbis, dragged through the gate and into his presence a wretched woman who had been taken in the act of adultery, probably in one of the pilgrim tents.   They threw her down upon the marble pavement, crying, " Moses in the law saith that such shall be stoned, but what sayest thou ?"   Here was a dilemma.   If he said, Let the law have its course, his gospel of mercy was flung to the winds. If he said, Let her go scot free, he would lay himself open to the charge of heresy against the Jewish law.   There she lay, poor guilty thing, her hair dishevelled, her garments torn, cowering and hiding her crimson face in her hands.   There they stood, arrogant churchmen, silently awaiting his word.   He stooped and wrote upon the dust of the pavement.   It was his only written sermon.   They followed his finger as it traced the words, " Let him that is without sin cast the first stone at her."   And one by one those gray-bearded priests and rabbis, conscience-stricken, turned and crept away ; so that when Jesus arose and looked about him, lo, they all were gone, and he was alone with his little congregation and the sinful woman in their midst.   By this time, as we venture to surmise, the twilight was lifting and the day began to break.   The sun slowly appeared above the eastern crags of Gilead, and far towards the west the sky threw back a golden glow. It was perhaps at this moment that Jesus said, " I am the light of the world ; he that followeth me shall not walk in darkness, but shall have the light of life."

We mark here certain notable points of similitude between the natural sun and Christ as the luminary of the spiritual world.

I. *The Sun is the great revealer.*   At its rising the

darkness was withdrawn like a folded curtain. The mists rose from the Tyropœon Valley and in tortuous wreaths and columns vanished out of sight. The shadows from under the brows of the overhanging crags came forth and pursued each other, like silent spectres, across the hills. The smoke rose in dense masses from the heaps of sacrificial offal burning in the ravine of Hinnom. The beasts gat them away together and hid themselves in dens; and the earth everywhere, like an opened scroll, was disclosed to view.

Thus Christ unveils the soul. It was because he threw a white light into the hearts of those proud Pharisees that they silently betook themselves out of his sight. The old priest, Simeon, who held the infant Jesus in his arms and sang, "Now lettest thou thy servant depart in peace," prophesied that this child would be "a light unto the people," and that by him "the thoughts of many hearts should be revealed." He brings us into the solitude where, as in some gallery of horrors, we look about us and behold our sins: our envyings and jealousies, avarice and sordidness and utter selfishness, our offences against our fellow-men and our disloyalties towards God; they stand out before us as vividly as the handwriting on Belshazzar's palace wall. Thus he is a discloser of the secret thoughts and imaginations of the heart.

And in this he is an offence to the natural heart. It is scarcely to be expected that we should like the exposé. It is written, "This is the condemnation, that light is come into the world, and men love darkness rather than light, because their deeds are evil." Sin ever seeks the cover of the night. In the reign of Charles II. a man named Heming received a contract for lighting the streets of London with lamps hung at every tenth door on all moonless nights from Michaelmas to Lady's Day. Macaulay says that Heming's lanterns wrought more effectively than any revolution in the interest of public morality.

The hardest of prayers to offer is that of David, "Search me, O God, and know my heart; try me and know my thoughts." None but a man of moral courage can offer it. Some go so far as to wish,

> Oh wad some power the giftie gie us
> To see oursels as ithers see us;

but the mere thought of gazing upon our corrupt natures with the clear eyes, not of "ithers," but of God, may justly overwhelm us.

II. *The Sun is the great extinguisher.* That morning the moon grew dim at his coming, the stars shone more and more faintly, until the last lingering spark of heaven faded from view. In the porch of the temple was the great candelabrum, reputed to be fifty cubits high, magnificently adorned with sparkling stones and surmounted with lamps that cast their glow throughout the city. At the rising of the sun these lights grew dim and cast a shadow on the temple floor.

> Night's candles were burned out, and jocund Day
> Stood tiptoe on the misty mountain-tops.

In like manner all lesser lights are quenched in the glory of the Sun of Righteousness. The moralist walks proudly in the feeble glow of his personal merit until Christ comes his way, and then he sees himself unworthy. Lo, all his righteousnesses are as filthy rags. The formalist wearing his broad phylacteries walks erect in the glow of the altar-candles until Christ comes his way, and then he sees himself as a Laodicean impostor, " wretched and miserable and poor and blind and naked." No earthly light can live in the shining of His face.

Here is the reason why all false religions and philosophies have died or are smitten with death. Where are the gods of the Pantheon, great Jupiter with his hand full of thunder-bolts; Thor, smiting with his hammer the gates of Jotunheim; Ammon, crowned with the solar disk? All gone, and none so poor to do them reverence. Where are the schools of philosophy that stood by the banks of the Ilissus? Who follows Plato now, or Zeno or Epicurus? Their names are but a suggestion of shadows fleeing before the sun. But the gospel of Jesus shines with ever-increasing splendor, shines brighter and brighter unto the perfect day.

III. *The Sun is the great beautifier.* It was a scene of wonder that spread before the eyes of those who were gathered in the temple porch that morning. In the valley of the Kedron lay dewy pastures and oliveyards. On the slopes of the surrounding hills were purple vineyards, with here and there the tents of devout pilgrims gleaming in the sun. Far to the north were snow-capped mountains, and away to the west the mists rising from the Mediterranean, and over all the blue firmament that ever showeth the handiwork of God.

So Christ brings out the best and noblest in human life and character. He transforms the sinner into a saint. There was Jerry McAuley, the river thief, whose life was in a round of sordid and vicious pleasures. Christ came to him and the sun rose upon the darkness. He was a new man in Christ Jesus. Old things were passed away and all things became new. The things that he had loved, he hated now. New hopes and aspirations and purposes came to him. He found his delight in doing for others and in serving the Lord. I was in Jerry McAuley's mission a little while ago and heard a woman's testimony to the gracious influence of his memory. She had been a woman of the town. "But now," she said, while tears ran down her cheeks, "oh I love every board in this floor, I love every nail in these walls; for here I found the Saviour. Whether my heart is changed I scarcely know, but there is a change somewhere. All things seem transformed. I do believe that now I love the things which are pure and lovely and of good report." Such is the influence of the gospel of Christ. It touches the melancholy heart and fills it with gladness. It cultivates the graces; faith, hope, and charity burst into bloom like flowers in a garden open to the east. The trees of the field seem clapping their hands for joy. Instead of the thorn comes up the fir-tree and instead of the brier comes up the myrtle-tree. The wilderness and the solitary place are glad because of Him. Christ's coming into a human life is like the morning of the first creative day.

> "God said, 'Let there be light!'
> Grim darkness felt his might and fled away.
> Then startled seas and mountains cold
> Shone forth, all bright with blue and gold,
> And cried, ''T is day! 'T is day!'"

IV. *The Sun is the great quickener and invigorater.* When Jesus walked from Bethany, in the early dusk, all was so silent that the fox startled from the roadside made itself heard; and as He climbed the marble steps of the temple his solitary footfall echoed among the great arches. But as the morning drew nigh the world gave tokens of life. The smoke rose curling above the homes of the city. The people issued from their doors and could be seen greeting each other in the narrow streets. Down by the gates there were signs of chaffering; the booths were open, the hum of traffic had commenced; the city was awake. So the soul bestirs itself at the word of the Master, and life that had been passed in dreams and visions is henceforth real and earnest. "I am come that you might have life," said he, "and that you might have it more abundantly."

The forces of the material world have their source and centre in the sun. George Stephenson, seeing a railway train in motion, said to his friend Dr. Buckland, "Tell me, what drives it?" "One of your great engines," was the answer. "But what drives the engine?" "Steam." "Ay, but what drives the steam?" "The sun," said Dr. Buckland; "the light that was absorbed by the decaying life of the carboniferous age, stored away for centuries upon centuries, is now liberated and set at work."

So do the moral forces find their centre in Jesus Christ. He walked but for a little while on earth, a brief ministry of thirty years, and went his way. But he still lives among us. His life and character furnish the world's spiritual energy. He dwells among us, a living, loving, striving, helpful, glorious Christ.

> We may not climb the heavenly steeps
>   To bring the Lord Christ down;
> We may not search the lowest deeps,
>   For him no depths can drown;
> But warm, sweet, tender, even yet
>   A present help is he;
> For faith has still its Olivet
>   And love its Galilee.
> The healing of his seamless dress
>   Is by our beds of pain;
> We touch him in life's throng and press
>   And we are whole again.

Is there one in this company who has grown cold-hearted—one who espoused Him long ago but has neglected duty and forgotten the pleasant paths? What is needed? Only to let the sun shine in. When Alexander the Great visited Diogenes he asked, "Is there anything I can do for you?" It was in his power to give crowns and fortunes; but the old cynic had no desire for them. "Nothing," he answered, "but to stand out of my light." And indeed in our Christian life this is the supreme need, to have everything put away from between us and the shining face of our Lord. There is nothing so full of healing as a sun-bath. One thing only can separate between us and our Lord; that is sin. A single thread of a spider's weaving, if it lie across the glass of a telescope, may hide from view the brightest planet in the firmament. So is it with a sinful habit; it hides the Sun. Therefore let us put away the sin that doth so easily beset us and bask in the shining of his face.

Is there one here who has not received Him? Oh there is a sweet delight in store for you! Come out of the dusk and twilight; come into the morning! In the polar regions where the sun is below the horizon six months of the year, the return of the springtime is heralded with great joy. The people, weary of the gloom and loneliness, betake themselves to the mountain-tops and watch for the first appearing of the light; and when, at last, they behold the flush upon the forehead of the king of day, they cry aloud, "O beautiful sun! O beautiful sun!" There is a like pleasure for all who will suffer the heavenly grace to shine upon them. And this is your privilege now. It is for you to say whether or no the day shall break and the shadows flee away.

My last word is the benediction of the morning: The Lord bless you and keep you; the Lord make his face to shine upon you and be gracious unto you; the Lord lift up upon you the light of his countenance and give you peace. Amen.

THE

BRIGHT LIGHT IN THE CLOUD.

PREACHED BY DR. BURRELL, FEBRUARY 28, 1892.

"And the men see not the bright light in the cloud." Job 37:21.

THE book of Job is a dramatic poem. The central figure is an Arab sheikh who dwelt in the land of Uz. He was possessed of enormous wealth for those days: seven thousand sheep, three thousand camels, five hundred yoke of oxen, five hundred she asses, and "a very great household" or retinue. The guards at his door were able to defend him against all but adversity. His home was a happy one. He had a lovely wife—despite all that has been said against her—and seven sons and three daughters. He was in possession, also, of perfect physical health, a blessing which no man thoroughly appreciates until he has lost it. And, best of all, Job was an upright man, who feared God and eschewed evil.

The next of the *dramatis personæ* is Satan. He is represented as appearing at heaven's gate, where the Lord greets him, "Whence comest thou?" and he answers, "From going to and fro in the earth and from walking up and down in it." No rest for his feet; no rest so long as there is one righteous man to be tempted, so long as there is a possibility of dragging one more into evil. And Satan said, "Doth Job fear God for naught? Is his piety disinterested? Nay, nay. Thou hast put a hedge about him so that he cannot be tried—a hedge about his house and about his cattle and his flocks; but

let me touch what he hath and he will curse thee!"   And
the Lord gave Satan power to tempt him.   The same
happens in the case of every man.   No character is possible without trial.   Blessed is he that endureth temptation, for when he is tried he shall receive the crown of
life.   Our Lord himself was led out into the wilderness to
be tempted of the devil.   The servant is not greater than
his Lord.

Then came the succession of trials.   To begin with,
poverty.   In a sudden foray all Job's property was lost;
he was left penniless, naked as when he came into the
world.   But the malignant purpose of the tempter was
thwarted, for in his calamity he said, " The Lord gave and
the Lord hath taken away.   Blessed be the name of the
Lord."

Then bereavement.   A messenger came announcing
that his children had been swept away in sudden death.
All gone!   In the morning he had parted with them at
the door, wishing them a happy day ; now the poor comfort was left him of holding their lifeless hands and
smoothing the damp hair from their cold foreheads.   The
tempter stood by to hear him curse this evil providence;
but he said again, " Blessed be the name of the Lord."

Then sickness.   A painful and loathsome form of lep-
rosy was laid upon him, and he took him a potsherd to
scrape himself withal and sat down among the ashes.   It
was then that his wife said, " Curse God and die."   Not
that she was a shrew ; her heart was broken under these
repeated troubles.   Poor soul, it was little wonder that
her patience gave out.   But he said unto her, " What,
shall we receive good and not evil at the hands of God?
Blessed be his name!"

Next among the *dramatis personæ* are the comforters,
Bildad, Eliphaz, and Zophar, old friends and neighbors.

And they lifted up their eyes afar off and knew him not, so greatly was he changed; and they rent their mantles and sprinkled dust upon their heads.   For a while they sat down with him upon the ground in silence, and when at last they spoke it was to present a wrong view of providence.   Miserable comforters were they all.   Their thought was that God deals out adversity in strict requital, *quid pro quo*, an eye for an eye, a tooth for a tooth, each sin finding its own punishment in this present life.   If therefore Job had not been a great sinner these calamities could never have befallen him.   Little wonder that he resented this false philosophy.   It *is* a false philosophy. St. Augustine wisely said that if no sin were punished in this present time we would believe in no providence, but if every sin were punished here we would believe in no judgment hereafter.

Then Elihu arose; he had modestly waited for the others because they were his elders.   His conception of providence was the true one.   God disciplines his children through suffering; he makes all things work together for the good of those who love him.   No chastening for the present seemeth to be joyous but rather grievous: nevertheless afterwards it yieldeth the peaceable fruit of righteousness unto them which are exercised thereby.   Elihu despairs, however, of commending this view of providence and expresses a fervent desire that God would appear and make himself known.

Then God appears, the last of the *dramatis personæ*. He comes in the whirlwind; and out of the cloud, sweeping through the heavens, he proclaims his majesty: "Gird up now thy loins like a man, for I will demand of thee and answer thou me!"

The cloud is God's pavilion.   It is the appropriate medium through which the Infinite reveals himself to man.   In the nature of the case it is not possible to have a revelation without a corresponding adumbration of Him. He is like the natural sun, which cannot be seen without a dimness intervening between it and the naked eye.

At Sinai God appeared in a cloud.   He led his children through the wilderness in the Shechinah, a pillar of cloud which was called " The Glory of the Lord."   At the dedication of Solomon's temple he manifested his presence in a luminous cloud that came forth from the Holiest of All and filled the house "so that the priests were not able to minister by reason of it."   The birth of Jesus was announced to the shepherds from the Shechinah; as it is written, " The Glory of the Lord shone round about them."   On the Mount of Transfiguration, where the Redeemer showed his Godhood for an instant to his disciples, " they feared as they entered into the cloud."   At his ascension a cloud received him out of the sight of his disciples; and he shall so come as they saw him go, in the clouds of heaven and the holy angels with him.

This is God's way of revealing himself: he must needs obscure his glory in manifesting it.   The complaint of Elihu is that men behold the cloud but not the bright light within it.

I. As to God's Personality.   No man hath seen him at any time.   Canst thou by searching find him out?   To know him is the summit of human aspiration.   This is life eternal, to know God and Jesus Christ who is the manifestation of God.

It is an easy matter to utter His name; but who can apprehend the tremendous truth suggested in that little word of three letters! Infinitude is embraced in it. When Simonides was intrusted by King Hiero with the duty of defining God, he returned at the close of the day to ask for further time.   A week, a month, a year passed by, and then he reported, "The more I think of him the more he is unknown to me." There have been campaigns of controversy, centuries of research, libraries of theology, and still here we are asking, What is God? The cloud bewilders us.

But one thing we know: God is love. This is the bright light. Whatever else we fail to grasp, this we may fully apprehend. If Jesus Christ had done no more, as Madame de Gasparin said, than to reveal the divine Fatherhood, that would have compensated for his incarnation. He taught us to say, "Our Father which art in heaven." We are received, not by the spirit of bondage again to fear, but by the spirit of adoption whereby we cry, Abba, Father!

II. As to God's Character. His attributes of truth, justice, holiness are the habitation of his throne. In the year that King Uzziah died the prophet saw Him "high and lifted up upon his throne, and his train filled the temple. Above it stood the seraphim, each of them having six wings; with twain he covered his face, and with twain he covered his feet, and with twain he did fly. And one cried to another, Holy, holy, holy is the Lord of hosts. Then he said, Woe is me, for I am undone, because I am a man of unclean lips and mine eyes have seen the King!" The thought of the divine holiness appalls us, for we are defiled and by our sins infinitely separated from him.

But, again, love is the bright light. The Cross stands in the midst of the divine holiness. The cross is pre-eminently the manifestation of the divine love. At the moment when Jesus died the veil of the temple was rent in sunder, and a new and living way was opened up for sinners into the Holiest of All. " *Procul, procul este, profani !*" cried the pagan priests. Depart, O sinful ones! But out of the cloud that envelopes the Cross of Jesus there proceeds a voice, " Come unto me, all ye that labor and are heavy laden, and I will give you rest."

III. As to the divine Decrees, or God's dealings with us from the eternal ages. The very suggestion offends us. Yet we must be aware that God would not be God if he had not foreknown and foreordained whatsoever cometh to pass. It is vain, however, to undertake to simplify the doctrine. At the door of the Puritan Church at Plymouth, after a long Sabbath service spent in discussing " freewill, fixed fate, foreknowledge absolute," an old man stood with his staff in his hand stirring the depths of a stagnant pool. On being asked what he was doing, he said, " Searching for the eternal decrees." All the efforts of the Christian Church during these centuries to simplify the great mystery have been but a muddying of the waters. We fall back upon the Scriptural statement, " Whom God foreknew he also did predestinate; whom he did predestinate, them he also called; whom he called, them he also justified; and whom he justified, them he also glorified."

But here again love is the bright light. God's decrees are founded in his mercy. Election has never kept one out of heaven, but has brought an innumerable multitude into it. Two lads were looking at a picture of Elijah ascending to heaven in a fiery chariot. One of them said, " Would n't you be afraid to ride that way?" The other replied, " No, not if God drove." We look calmly upon the mystery of the divine foreordination and rest assured that the God of all the earth does right. We are not afraid. His name is Love.

IV. As to divine Providence. Here surely clouds and darkness are round about him. Pain, sorrow, and disappointment are our common portion. We are born to trouble as the clouds to fly upwards. We are all burden-bearers. Why must it be? Oh the mystery of it!

> God moves in a mysterious way
> His wonders to perform."

The poet Cowper who wrote that impressive hymn had resolved to drown himself in the river Ouse. His burden was greater than he could bear. His soul was shrouded in melancholy; life was not worth living. He hired a cabman to drive him along the country road to the river, three miles away. But the driver lost the way, and Cowper sitting within had time to reflect. The old days came back to him; the mother's face, the village church, the promises of God's blessed Word, they came to him with new significance now: "Weeping may endure for a night, but joy cometh in the morning;" "These light afflictions, which endure but for a moment, shall work for us a far more exceeding and eternal weight of glory;" "I am persuaded that the sufferings of this present time are not worthy to be compared with the glory which shall be revealed in us." Presently he leaned out of the window and bade the cabman carry him home, and there he wrote,

> God moves in a mysterious way
> His wonders to perform;
> He plants his footsteps in the sea
> And rides upon the storm.
>
> Ye fearful saints, fresh courage take;
> The clouds ye so much dread
> Are big with mercy, and shall break
> In blessings on your head.
>
> Judge not the Lord by feeble sense,
> But trust him for his grace;
> Behind a frowning providence
> He hides a smiling face.

So, here again, love is the bright light. All God's dealings with us are illumined by the thought that he does

not willingly afflict us.   He is making all things work together for our good.

Not long ago in the Chinese quarter at San Francisco,
under one of the theatres, I saw a child of six years with
her mother in a narrow room with Joss-gods all around
them.   For a coin the little one sang to us.   It was a
strange place for a gush of heaven's melody.   This is
what she sang :

> Jesus loves me ; this I know,
> For the Bible tells me so.

Oh that we might all carry away with us this morning
the assurance of our Father's love !   Christ is its supreme
manifestation.   He loves us !   He loves us !   Whatever
darkness may gather, this is the bright light.

> Yes, Jesus loves me ;
> Yes, Jesus loves me ;
> The Bible tells me so.

CHRIST AND THE BIBLE;

HOW THEY STAND OR FALL TOGETHER.

"Had ye believed Moses ye would have believed me, for he wrote of
   me; but if ye believe not his writings how shall ye believe my
   words?" John 5:46.

THE two storm-centres in our religious history are
Christ and the Bible. All notable controversies have
gathered about these. As to Jesus, who is he? Is he
what he claimed to be, the only-begotten Son of the Father, or a mere trickster and dissembler? The strife of
centuries has turned upon this and kindred queries; for
it has been understood all along that if Christ could be
disposed of Christianity would go to. pieces. And when
the controversy has not been respecting Christ it has one
way or another centred in the Bible. What is this old
Book? Is it what it claims to be, God-breathed, or is it
above the ordinary only by reason of certain venerable
associations? Are there any clear characteristics which
lift it quite out of the category of other books? Can it
be received with absolute confidence as an infallible rule
of faith and practice; or are those who so regard it no
better than a sort of fetich-worshippers? Is it the Truth,
or does it merely contain it? What think ye? Christ
and the Bible, these are the two controversial centres of
our religion—as they ought to be—and these two are
really and substantially one. The porch of Solomon's
temple was upheld by two mighty brazen pillars, the
names of which were *Jachin* or strength, and *Boaz* or
continuance. A Jew going up to the temple, faint and

heavy-hearted, felt his strength and confidence renewed by the sight of those pillars with their capitals of lily-work. Thus Christ and the Bible uphold our blessed religion. While they remain it is safe. And they shall abide for ever; the mouth of the Lord hath spoken it.

It is significant that Christ and the Bible are each called the Word of God. How indeed could God reveal himself to men otherwise than by his Word? He was know in nature, but not clearly or intimately. It would be difficult for a man to look so far "through nature up to nature's God" as to be able to say "Abba, Father!" He would be much more likely, standing amid the bewildering glories of the earth and overarching heavens, to cry aloud in desperate desire, "O God, if thou art, or wheresoever thou art, speak to me! speak to me!"

And God has spoken. His Word has come to us. As it is written, "In the beginning was the Word, and the Word was with God and the Word was God; and the Word was made flesh and dwelt among us." Language is the medium of our acquaintance with each other. You know what sort of person I am, the trend of my thought and purpose, by what I am saying. Thus God's incarnate Word is his way of making us acquainted with himself. Our Lord and Saviour is, as it were, God's articulate Speech addressed to men. He revealed the Father fully. This he could do because he was himself the express image of the Father. In him dwelt the fulness of the Godhead bodily.. On one occasion Philip said to Jesus, "Show us the Father, and it sufficeth us;" and Jesus answered, "Have I been so long time with you and yet hast thou not known me, Philip? He that hath seen me hath seen the Father. How sayest thou then, Show us the Father? Believest thou not that I am in the Father and the Father in me?"

But this incarnate Word was not enough. God must speak further and otherwise if he would reveal himself to all mankind. For Jesus was hemmed in by a narrow environment of time and space. His ministry lasted only three years, during which he traversed, to and fro, a small portion of an inconsiderable province in a remote corner of the earth. Shall the gracious offices of the only-begotten Son of God be confined to healing a few sick folk and preaching to some thousands of stiff-necked and unregenerate Jews? Nay, all nations and centuries are groaning and travailling for him. The Word must traverse the world. The Sun of Righteousness must go forth as a bridegroom out of his chamber and rejoice as a strong man to run a race. This He does in the written Word, which is the reflex of himself, his universal and perpetual shining forth. Christ is made known through the Scriptures to all tribes and generations of the human race. They, therefore, rightly share with him the honor of the title "Word of God."

The pages of Scripture, like the leaves of the tree of life, are "for the healing of the nations." They have fluttered forth upon the four winds of heaven bearing the tidings of redemption to those who sit in darkness and the shadow of death. If Jesus Christ is to reign universally it is because, under the present Dispensation of the Spirit, the propaganda is being successfully carried on through the instrumentality of the written Word. We are expressly told that "the sword of the Spirit is the Word of God." Thus the Bible is the complement and counterpart of Christ. The incarnate and the written Word are one— the binomial Word of God.

And they stand or fall together.

We hear much in these times about a Christocentric religion ; as if indeed it had ever been called in question that Christ is the only foundation, that he is first, last, midst, and all in all.   The word Christocentric has a very attractive look and a mellifluous sound; but there is reason to fear that under certain conditions it may be made to serve Christ himself an ill turn.   If it be used to emphasize the need of a profounder regard for Christ and the *entire Christian system*, then let us cordially assent to it; but if it be employed in any quarter as a cloak for rejecting Christ's teaching as to Holy Writ, then good Lord deliver us!   We may be sure that Christ himself would be the very first to repudiate a Bibleless gospel, no matter what sweet adjective might be attached to it.   Mere protestations of loyalty to Christ must go for nothing, particularly in a controversy like this respecting the divine Oracles, unless a man can prove his loyalty by an unswerving and unreserved adherence to the doctrine of Christ.   "Not every one that saith unto me, Lord! Lord! shall enter into the kingdom, but he that doeth the will of my Father which is in heaven."

> A man may cry "Christ, Christ,"
>   With no more piety than other people;
> A daw 's not counted a religious bird
>   Because it keeps a-cawing from a steeple.

This, then, is the question which we now approach: *Can we throw over the Bible and still retain Christ?*

I. *Let us observe what the Bible has to say about Christ.*

To begin with, it is something more than a mere biography of him.   To say that its purpose is to outline the scheme of salvation, in its narrow sense, furnishes a taking phrase but not a complete statement of fact.   There are very many things in Scripture which have no direct bearing on the way to escape hell-fire and reach the joys of heaven. And whatever the Book contains, whether theological, ethical, or scientific, is true, absolutely true. Thus it is written, " All Scripture, given by inspiration of God, is profitable for doctrine, for reproof, for correction, for instruction in righteousness, that the man of God may be perfect, thoroughly furnished unto every good work," i. e., that he may have a well-rounded and symmetrical furnishing for life every way.

It is true, however, that the golden thread running through all the Scriptures is Christological. Their theme is Christ. This is true of both the Law and the Prophets.* (1.) The moral Law as delivered from Sinai is a schoolmaster to lead sinners to Christ. The ceremonial Law in all its rites and symbols pointed to him. Its local centre was the Tabernacle, which, from the brazen altar at its door to the Ark of the Covenant in the Holiest of All, was everywhere typical of Christ. Its temporal centre was the great Day of Atonement, when every occurrence, from the robing of the priest in white to the sending away of the scapegoat to Azazel, was eloquent of Christ. (2.) The same may be affirmed of the prophets. The beginning of prophecy was the protevangel in Eden, " The seed of woman shall bruise the serpent's head." As years passed on and men forgot God and lapsed into the abominations of the heathen, Abram was called out of Ur of the Chaldees, called and " chosen " to preserve monotheism and hand it down through the generations until the coming of Christ. To him was the promise given, " I will bless thee, and make thy name great ; and in thee shall all the families of the earth be blessed," a promise to which Jesus himself ascribed a distinct Messianic import. The Psalms of David are so full of Christ

* The common title of the Scriptures among the Jews was, " The Law and the Prophets."

that they furnish much of the material for our Christian hymn-books. Isaiah for a similar reason is called "the evangelical prophet." He foretells Christ as a child, a teacher, a wonderworker, a man of sorrows, a vicarious sacrifice, dying, triumphing over death, and evermore living as the Mediator and Advocate of penitent souls. Daniel saw the great world-powers rising and flourishing and passing away to make room for the universal dominion of the Son of Man. The last of the prophets, Malachi, in the gathering gloom of that Egyptian darkness of four hundred years which intervened between the two Economies, waved his torch, crying, "The night cometh, but be of good courage, the Sun of Righteousness shall arise with healing in his wings!" Thus Christ is everywhere in Law and Prophecy like the theme of an oratorio; so that it would be obviously impossible to keep the Bible and let Christ go.

II. *What, now, has Christ to say about the Bible?* He was familiar with it. He learned it *memoriter* when a lad, and received it as his "infallible rule of faith and practice"—so received it without any twisting of language or qualification or mental reservation. In each of his three temptations in the wilderness he used it as an effective foil against the adversary. When urged to change the stones into bread to satisfy his hunger he answered, "Nay, I cannot! For I remember what my dear mother taught me out of the Book, 'Man shall not live by bread alone, but by every word that proceedeth from the mouth of God.'" And when urged to cast himself down from a pinnacle of the temple, thus showing his Godhood by his superiority to natural laws, he answered again, "Nay, I cannot! For I remember what my Bible says, 'Thou shalt not tempt the Lord thy God.'" And when urged finally to avoid the agony of the cross and accept the world's sovereignty in return for a single act of homage rendered to its *de facto* prince, he answered again, "I cannot! For the Book says, 'Thou shalt worship the Lord thy God, and him only shalt thou serve.'" Thus in every case the Bible was his stand-by. "It is written" was enough for him. And blessed is every one of his followers who can defend himself in like manner with the sword of the Spirit.

(1.) But now to be more specific: Christ declares the Scriptures to be true. He does not scruple to call them "truth." He does not say that they contain, but that they are, the word of God. Thus in his sacerdotal prayer in behalf of his disciples he pleads, "Sanctify them by thy truth; thy word is truth." A follower of Christ ought to be willing to follow him in his indorsement of the Scriptures no less than in faithful service. He affixed his seal to the story of the Deluge, saying, "As it was in the days of Noah, so shall the coming of the Son of Man be: they were eating and drinking, marrying and giving in marriage, and the flood came and swept them all away." He believed in the old story of the destruction of the Cities of the Plain by fire and brimstone from heaven, in the healing efficacy of the brazen serpent, in the turning of Lot's wife into a pillar of salt, and in Jonah in the whale's belly. He gave an explicit assent to those Old Testament "fables" which are so abhorrent to many of the learned critics of these days. He was probably as well advised as most of our Biblical exegetes respecting the real facts bearing upon the question of inerrancy, and knowing all he did not hesitate to indorse the entire trustworthiness of the most vulnerable portions of Holy Writ.

And then observe his eloquent silence respecting all those alleged errors and discrepancies which so vex the souls of certain of our learned folk. Did he know that these blunders were to be found in the sacred pages?

How is it that he uttered no word against the Mosaic cosmogony?   How is it that he did not denounce those imprecatory Psalms which are too horrible to be read in some of our modern pulpits?   How is it that he did not expose the falsity of those prophecies concerning himself which have never been fulfilled and never can be because their time has gone by?   Surely it is not too much to suppose that Jesus was an honest man.   He seems to have been a fervent hater of shams and impostures, lying frontlets and phylacteries, false traditions of the elders, and deceptions of every sort.   Is it possible that his eyes were not so clear in this particular as those of our recent Biblical scholars?   Or was his soul not so sensitive with regard to those dreadful things in Scripture?   We are in a dilemma.   Was he unscrupulous or merely ignorant?   Must we put the most severe limitations upon his knowledge, assuming that he knew no better than to let these errors pass unchallenged, or must we impugn his ingenuousness? In either case we could scarcely receive him as our Saviour and spiritual Guide.

(2.) Let us further mark how Christ adventures his entire work on the verification of Scripture.   At the very outset of his ministry he went into the synagogue at Nazareth and opened the scroll at the place where it is written, " The Spirit of the Lord God is upon me ; because he hath anointed me to preach good tidings unto the meek, to bind up the broken-hearted, to proclaim liberty to the captives and the opening of the prison to them that are bound, to proclaim the acceptable year of the Lord and the day of vengeance of our God; to comfort all that mourn, to give unto them beauty for ashes, the oil of joy for mourning, the garment of praise for the spirit of heaviness ;" and having read this passage, he said to his audience, " This day is this Scripture fulfilled in your ears."

During the three years that followed he hypothecated the truth of his teaching and the genuineness of his work in all particulars on the sanction of Holy Writ. And after his resurrection, while walking with certain of his disciples along the way to Emmaus, he "began with Moses and opened the whole Scriptures concerning himself." It would be interesting to know the substance of that expository sermon. We may be quite sure that he unfolded the meaning of ancient rites and symbols as well as of Messianic prediction in the light of the things which had recently happened at Jerusalem. We may be equally sure that he carefully avoided any suggestion of the fact which has recently been discovered, that "the great body of the Messianic prediction has not only never been fulfilled, but cannot now be fulfilled, for the reason that its own time has passed for ever." What he did say seems to have been of directly contrary import. It was directly in line with his previous utterance, "Not one jot or tittle shall pass away until all be fulfilled." Thus Christ planted himself on the absolute truth of Scripture and adventured his whole ministry upon it; and what was good enough for our Lord and Master ought to be sufficient for us. He stood as a constant witness to their unqualified truth, ever turning to them as a Court of Last Appeal in verification of his divine nature and mediatorial work, saying, "Search the Scriptures, for in them ye think ye have eternal life, and they are they which testify of me."

III. I do not see, therefore, how it is possible to detach the Written from the Incarnate Word. They must stand or fall together. Christ is interwoven with the very fibres of the Book, and it is everywhere loyal to him. They are both revelations of the same God.

Attention is here called to *a striking parallel* in the following particulars :

First : Christ and the Scriptures are both alike called The Truth and The Word of God.

Second : They are both theanthropic: that is, the divine and human are inextricably blended in their fabric. Christ was conceived by the Holy Ghost and born of the Virgin Mary; but in partaking of his mother's humanity he in no wise inherited her sin. In like manner the Holy Ghost wrought upon certain men to produce the Scriptures; as it is written, "Holy men wrote as they were moved by the Holy Ghost;" and in this case also the product was free from human imperfection. No doubt the features of Jesus bore a distinct likeness to those of his mother; just as the pages of Holy Writ are marked by the mental characteristics of their human penmen; but in neither case does this resemblance prevent that absolute faultlessness or inerrancy which belongs to any word of God.

Third : It is only in the original that either the Incarnate or Written Word can be called "inerrant." With respect to the Scriptures the Higher Critics are accustomed to say, "What is the use of affirming inerrancy of an 'original autograph' which is not in existence? The theory that there were no errors in the original text is sheer assumption, upon which no mind can rest with certainty. We must take the Scriptures as we have them, without reference to an hypothetical original which no man living has ever seen." But it is a poor rule which cannot be made to work both ways. No living man has ever seen Jesus Christ. There is no accurate portrait of him in existence, certainly not if the Scriptures are errant. Every representation of him in the life and character of his disciples is full of imperfections. Nevertheless we do believe that the original Christ, who for a brief period of thirty years lived among men and then vanished from sight, was "holy, harmless, and undefiled," just as the Scriptures were in the original autograph as it left the pens of those holy men who wrote as they were moved by the Spirit of God.

Fourth: Notwithstanding the errors in transmission, the Word of God in both cases remains in such substantial perfection as to be effective in the accomplishment of its work. A special providence has kept before the eyes of all generations the image of an immaculate Christ. A special providence has, likewise, so guarded the transcription of the Written Word as that we may confidently hold it to be an infallible rule of faith and practice. Neither the Incarnate nor the Written Word, as we have them, can lead a soul astray, but will infallibly direct "unto every good work" and lead at last to heaven's gate.

The Ark of the Covenant, which was the centre of the cultus of the old economy, was a complex type of the Written and Incarnate Word. In it were the tables of the Law which were the nucleus of the Scriptures or "Book of the Law." Over it was the Shechinah, the luminous cloud in which Christ as "the Angel of the Covenant" was wont to manifest his presence. It was understood that the welfare of Israel was involved in the destinies of that Ark of the Covenant. It was carried eventually into the battle at Ebenezer as a forlorn hope. The old priest Eli sat by the gate awaiting the result. And there ran a man of Benjamin out of the army with his clothes rent and earth upon his head; and when he came, lo, Eli sat by the wayside watching, for his heart was troubled for the Ark of God. And he said, "What is there done, my son?" And the messenger answered, "Israel is fled before the Philistines, and there hath also been a great slaughter among the people, and thy two sons Hophni and Phinehas are slain, *and the Ark of God is taken !"*   And it came to pass when he made mention of the Ark of God that Eli fell from off the seat backward and died.   Woe worth the day when Christ and the Bible shall lose their place in the forefront of the Christian Church !   But it shall not be.   The veracity of the living God stands pledged to the perpetuity of his Word.   All flesh is as grass, and the glory of man as the flower of grass ; the grass withereth and the flower thereof passeth away, but the Word of the Lord endureth for ever.   The mouth of the Lord hath spoken it.

THE

FAITH OF AN INFIDEL.

PREACHED BY DR. BURRELL, MARCH 13, 1892.

"Hast thou faith?" Romans 14:22.

FAITH is reliance on evidence as to things not lying within the province of the senses. Observe, it is reliance on evidence, not taking things on hearsay. St. Paul says, "Faith is the substance of things hoped for, the evidence of things not seen;" or, as given in the new version, "The assurance of things hoped for, the proving of things not seen."

The province of faith is the entire universe of the unseen. Our belief in all abstract truths is founded on faith. Our position as to all the great problems that take hold on eternity is conditioned on faith. How small and narrowly circumscribed is the province of the senses. I look about me from the highest mountain-top and fifty miles away on every side terminates the visible world, while 25,000 miles farther every way lie hills and valleys and oceans that I apprehend solely by faith.

It is the universal faculty. We live, move, and have our being by it. In the morning we rise and go forth, like Abraham when he looked westward from the bank of the Euphrates, into a country that we know not. No man has ever been there; none has ever returned to tell about it. Yet we go untrembling to meet its duties and responsibilities. All through the day we walk among innumerable dangers; but we are not afraid, because we have an assurance of divine protection. And at night we lay ourselves upon our beds and venture forth fearlessly into another *terra incognita*, the world of darkness. Thus we live continually by faith, by a fearless reliance on things not within the province of the senses.

A step further. Unbelief and belief are alike founded on faith. In other words, belief and unbelief differ only in leading to opposite conclusions. I say I believe in the story of ancient Troy; you say you disbelieve it, i. e., you believe the story to be a fabrication. I say I believe in civil service reform; you say you do not, i. e., you believe in the maxim, "To the victor belong the spoils." Moreover unbelief is frequently associated with an almost incredible credulity. The infidel, in his eagerness to cast off the old wives' fables of religion, finds himself accepting without a murmur no end of preposterous averments: like that Scotch mother whose son returned from a sea voyage and told her among other things how he and his comrades had found on the shore of the Red Sea a golden wheel from one of the chariots in Pharaoh's army, and how, as they sailed along, they saw fish flying through the air. "Sandie, Sandie," she exclaimed, "I can believe what ye tell o' the chariot-wheel, but ye maunna be deceivin' your auld mither wi' tales o' flyin' fish!"

Here is our proposition: *It requires more faith to reject the fundamental doctrines of the Christian religion than to accept them.*

First. Let us take the doctrine of God. We believe in a God who created all things out of nothing, and that he upholds them by the word of his power. You do not. Let us see then what is the substance and measure of your faith in this particular.

(1.) You must believe in effects without causes, and in

doing so you set yourself squarely against the experience and observation of the ages. An effect without a cause was never seen. Not a grain of sand can be shown to have come into existence of itself. No life was ever self-produced. All attempts to discover a case of spontaneous generation, from the ancient scientists through Hæckel to this day, have been utterly vain. If but a single fungus, or one animalcule, could be shown in evidence, you might have some ground for your belief; but as matters stand you are believing without any evidence whatever. You are rejecting the cardinal axiom, " Out of nothing nothing comes," and we cannot follow you.

(2.) Moreover, to reject God, you must believe in design without a designer. And here again the like cannot be shown. All things in the world around us appear to be fitted to their places in the universal order and adjusted to their uses : the eye for seeing, the ear for hearing, the eagle's wing for piercing the air, the throat of the nightingale for melody. You call this a mere happening? If a geographical globe were standing here and I should say, " This miniature of the world, showing its seas and continents, mountains, rivers, and lakes, was never planned, but merely happened so," you would laugh at me ; yet you say substantially that thing of the world itself, with its real continents and seas, its appropriate furnishings, and its myriad forms of life.

(3.) Still further, you believe in law without a lawgiver. Can you discover anywhere an analogy of this? If I were to tell a half-witted boy that the Ordinances of the City of New York made themselves, he would smile and shake his head incredulously. Yet you believe that the laws with which the universe is invested, laws that keep the rolling orbs of heaven in their orbits so that they move on for centuries without jar or jostle, laws that control the forces of nature so that summer and winter, seed-time and har-vest never fail, laws that can be traced through all the avenues of material existence, governing men and beasts, the fowls of the air and the fishes of the sea—you believe that these did not originate in the brain of a lawgiver, but made themselves! We cannot follow you so far. Our faith is not equal to the demand you make upon it.

Second. Let us take the doctrine of Immortality. We believe that man was created after the divine likeness, that God breathed His own breath into his nostrils, and that he can no more die than God himself can cease to be. We believe that this life is not the real life, but only the threshold whereon we stand waiting and knocking until the death angel shall open, saying, " Pass in and live for ever." You believe that death ends all.

(1.) In order to believe that way you must reject the testimony of your own intuition. For we may reason as we will and speculate as we will, there is a spirit in man which starts up and in the face of all skepticism cries, " I shall live and not die!" The thought of the annihilation of the soul is pure and simple assumption; there is not one jot or tittle of evidence to sustain it. When you see upon an untenanted house the sign, " To Let," do you leap at once to the conclusion that the family that formerly occu-pied it have all died and been buried? I protest, there would be no more folly in that than in saying over the mortal remains of a man, " His soul has ceased to be."

(2.) Not only so; you must reject the testimony of all ages and nations. For it is a well certified fact that from the foundation of the world the human race has believed in immortality. The Egyptians mummied their dead in the expectation that soul and body were to be reunited in after days. The Greeks placed an obolus under the tongue of the departed to pay their ferriage across the dark river to the better land.   The Indians bury with their chiefs the bow and arrows and blanket for use in the happy hunting-grounds.   The Arabs tie a fleet camel beside the grave of their sheikh that he may be able to ride in haste to the blooming plains of heaven.   Do you say that this consensus is wrong?   It is the infidel against the world.

(3.) Furthermore, in rejecting the doctrine of immortality you throw over the best results of science. Let me remind you of the conservation of energy.   You cannot annihilate force; it is a constant quantity.   The force which is expended when I raise a sledge-hammer and let it fall upon an anvil passes into the anvil in the form of molecular motion or heat.   If I send a current of electricity along a wire to a point where the wire is so small that it cannot transmit the whole quantity, a part goes on and the remainder is—wasted?   Oh no; changed into its equivalent of another force; and this is the *rationale* of the Edison electric light.   No energy is lost.   But the most powerful mechanism in all the universe is the soul of man.   What do you propose to do with that?   Annihilate it?   You believe that the physical energies of John Milton were indestructible, that the muscle of his right arm was immortal; but his soul, the soul that soared aloft to kindle its undazzled eyes at the full midday beam, that moved the world to wonder and admiration, that touched and moulded the social and political institutions of his time, was quenched like the flame of a candle, that it absolutely and for ever ceased to be?   To what lengths of credulity is your philosophy leading you!   O infidel, great is thy faith!

Third. Let us look at another of the fundamental doctrines of our religion, the Incarnation.   We believe that in fulness of time God sent forth his only-begotten Son upon a divine crusade for the deliverance of ruined men.

In order to the accomplishment of his beneficent purpose this Son was clothed in flesh; he was both God and man in one person. We admit the mystery. "Great is the mystery of godliness; God manifest in flesh, the angels desire to look into it!" Nevertheless it requires a less strain upon the faculty of faith to receive than to reject it. We are in the presence of a problem which all thoughtful men must somehow solve. "What think ye of Christ?" is the question. There are difficulties in the way of forming any opinion whatever concerning him; yet an opinion we must have. As Dr. Samuel Johnson said in another case, "A man must believe in either a *plenum* or a *vacuum*; it is hard to accept either; yet unless I wish to be regarded as a fool, I must have an opinion." So in respect to Christ, the necessity of a decision is upon us. What think ye of him? He must have been either God, or man, or both God and man.

(1.) Was he God only? So the Docetists held. They said his humanity was spectral. He was God seeming to be man, a divine Ghost walking the earth. But that opinion is not worth considering. It died and was buried long centuries ago.

(2.) Was he man only? If so he must have been either a good man or a bad one. You cannot believe that he was simply a good man. He claimed to be more. He spoke of himself as incarnate God. He said, "I and my Father are one." He bade the people believe that he had all power given him in heaven and on earth. He arrogated to himself every one of the divine attributes. He allowed himself to be worshipped. Peter said, "Thou art the son of the living God," and Thomas cried, "My Lord and my God!" and he did not reprove them. He was accused of making himself equal with God and made no retraction. He was finally crucified "for making himself equal with God." And you call him a good man! He was either what he claimed to be or else he was an arrant and shameless impostor, who was justly sentenced to die on the accursed tree. Yet it is equally difficult to believe him a bad man; for none could lay anything to his charge. No guile was found in his lips. He lived so uprightly that his betrayer was forced to say, "I have betrayed innocent blood!" his Roman judge, "I find no fault in this man," and the centurion who superintended his execution, "Verily, this was a righteous man." He spent his life in doing good, he preached the Sermon on the Mount, he gave to the world moral precepts that have been the safeguards of society and the dependence of just government since the beginning of the Christian era. This Jesus of Nazareth simply a man, and a bad one at that! Oh no; it is impossible to entertain the thought. You cannot believe it.

(3.) But you must believe something about him. There He stands, the Problem of the ages. I see no way out of the dilemma except to admit that he was God-man. The simple logic of the doctrine is that of Anselm's: if he is to be a Saviour he must be man that he may suffer, and God that he may suffer enough to make atonement for all his people's sins.

These are some of our grounds for saying that it lays a greater burden upon our faith to reject than to accept the fundamental truths of Christianity. The same course of reasoning might be applied to other doctrines. The fact is, the gospel of Jesus Christ is preëminently reasonable. It is a gospel of common sense. We are not asked to accept anything which is incredible or which cannot stand the most exacting test of brain and conscience and heart. "Prove all things," is the injunction, "hold fast that which is good." We are invited to confer with Jehovah, face to face, concerning the great doctrine of atonement. "Come now, saith the Lord, and let us reason together: though your sins be as scarlet, they shall be as white as snow; though they be red like crimson, they shall be as wool." If it be objected that the innocent cannot suffer for the guilty, we reply that the innocent are suffering for the guilty all around us. We are all bearing one another's burdens. The very heart of sympathy is vicarious pain. To say that our Father shall not sacrifice himself for us is to rule him out of the category of rational beings and to repudiate our kinship with him. The noblest thing possible to our human nature is self-denial; we should expect to find something in the divine nature corresponding to it. To empty himself in our behalf is just what our Heavenly Father should be expected to do. To say that "He so loved the world that he gave his only-begotten Son, that whosoever believeth in him should not perish, but have everlasting life," is to call him the most natural and best of fathers. So far from being unreasonable, it is just like God.

So, looking at the Christian religion from any standpoint whatsoever, it seems easier to accept than to reject it. I pray you therefore, men and women, earnest and thoughtful, travelling on to the eternal world, think on these things. It is written of the simple, "He believeth every word," but of the prudent, "He looketh well to his going." Let us look well to our going and believe only the truth. If the things which are preached in the name of the Lord Jesus seem wise and reasonable, wait no longer, but bow in glad assent to this glorious gospel of the blessed God.

THE
GREAT LODESTONE.

PREACHED BY DR. BURRELL, MARCH 20, 1892.

" And I, if I be lifted up from the earth, will draw all men unto me."
John 12:32.

No living man can explain the peculiar properties of
the native oxid of iron.   It has been invested with a curious interest from time immemorial.   It was originally
called the Magnesian stone from the place where it was
found in Asia Minor.   We call it the lodestone or the
magnet.   In the absence of any satisfactory explanation
of its phenomena all sorts of magical virtues were ascribed
to it.   It was supposed to heal diseases; it was used also
as a love philter.   The alchemists and conjurers made
much of it.   But while no one could explain it, one thing
was admitted on all hands, to wit, its power of attraction.
Sir Isaac Newton had a lodestone in a seal-ring, weighing
only three grains, which was capable of holding up seven
hundred and fifty grains of iron.   In the spiritual world
the antitype or counterpart of the lodestone is Christ
crucified.   Here, also, is much of mystery.   A simple
lad can ask more questions in an hour concerning the
great doctrines which centre in the cross than the wisest
theologian can answer in a lifetime.   But one thing is
beyond controversy, namely, its power of attraction.   David Hume was frank to admit that the Christian religion
had wielded an influence among men and nations which

passed his comprehension. Gibbon, also an unbeliever, made a similar admission. How the story of a crucified Nazarene should have been the great enlightening and evangelizing influence from the beginning until now is indeed a mystery; but the fact remains, and it is precisely what Christ announced, "I, if I be lifted up from the earth, will draw all men unto me."

As one approaches the harbor of Queenstown, skirting the southern coast of Ireland, he sees upon one of the highest hills a graveyard and in the midst a white cross towering aloft, whereon a white Christ faces the west with his hands outstretched, as if to say, "Look unto me, all ye ends of the earth, and be ye saved!" It is an apologue of history. This is the mighty influence which, all along the centuries, has been appealing to men and nations. Other religions have one after another been stricken with decay and death: but the gospel like a rising sun shines brighter and brighter, and the red cross banner is being advanced to the farthest headlands of the earth. The vision of Isaiah is in process of fulfilment; the ships of Tarshish, rams of Nebaioth, dromedaries of Midian, doves flying to their windows, all mean that the mighty Lodestone is doing its work. Our crucified and risen Lord is drawing all men unto him.

I. One cause of the attractiveness of the Christian religion is its preëminent reasonableness. We are not asked to believe anything here which does not commend itself to brain and conscience and heart. When Nahash the Ammonite came up against Jabesh-Gilead and its inhabitants proposed to capitulate, he answered, "On this condition will I make a covenant with you, that I may thrust out all your right eyes." It is a mistake to think that any such condition is laid upon those who approach the gospel of Christ. It proposes on the one hand an ethical system to which our nature intuitively assents. No one has ever been found who could successfully impugn the integrity of the Decalogue and the Sermon on the Mount. All men and nations agree that "the statutes of the Lord are right." On the other hand the gospel proposes a system of doctrines which are equally consonant with reason. It touches the great problems of the spiritual life in such a manner as to rationalize them all. In particular the doctrine of the atonement, which was called by Luther the "Article of a Standing or a Falling Church," is presented not as a mere dictum but rather as a pathetic appeal to thoughtful acquiescence. "This is a faithful saying and *worthy of all acceptation* that Christ Jesus came into the world to save sinners." The vicarious pain of our Lord and Saviour is but a following out of the analogy of all human sympathy. The self-sacrifice of Jehovah as set forth on Golgotha is merely the consummation of that self-sacrifice which is universally regarded as the highest point of human character. It is just what a thoughtful man would expect to find in God. We are, indeed, asked to receive the truths of the gospel by faith; but faith is ever buttressed by reason. "Come now, saith the Lord, *let us reason together;* though your sins be as scarlet they shall be as white as snow; though they be red like crimson they shall be as wool."

II. Moreover, the attractive power of the gospel is largely due to its delightsomeness. The church of Jesus Christ is recruited from the multitude of young men and young women, such as naturally object to entering upon a life which has nothing of enjoyment to offer them. It would be vain to entice them with a melancholy gospel. Blessed be God, we need not! No doubt there are some Christians who so profoundly realize the solemnity of life that they view all things through blue glasses.

> "They wear long faces, just as if their Maker,
> The Lord of goodness, were an undertaker."

The truth remains, however, that the gospel is full of gladness. The Lord himself struck the key-note when he went down to the marriage at Cana and took part in the festivities, changing the water into wine. We invite the young, therefore, to set out upon the Christian life because it is the life of real pleasure. To represent it otherwise would be to misrepresent it. Go down to the wharves and hear the sailors as they hoist anchor for an ocean voyage. They cry in unison, "Heave yo! heave yo!" and there is a rhymic inspiration in the word. To set forth otherwise would be to cloud the voyage with an evil omen. In like manner we are asked to begin the Christian life with an assurance that despite all its duties and responsibilities, its self-denials and cross-bearings, it is full of unspeakable delight. We are servants of One at whose right hand are pleasures for evermore.

Why shall not we rejoice whose sins are pardoned? Our God is the God of salvation. We were in Egypt, but our chains are broken. No more unrequited toil in Pharaoh's brick-yards! No more groaning under the whip of scorpions in the hand of a hard task-master! The Lord our God hath brought us up out of the land of Egypt out of the house of bondage.

> "I 've reached the land of corn and wine,
> And all its riches freely mine;
> Here shines undimmed one blissful day,
> For all my night has passed away."

Why shall not we rejoice who are retained in the service of the King of kings? Of all earth's creatures the most insensate and unconcerned is the beetle. It toils on the dusty highway, shut up in a little world of its own and heedless of all momentous things transpiring around it. The king with pomp and circumstance may pass that way, but what cares Scarabæus? He hears not the rumble of the royal chariot. Armies come marching over the dusty thoroughfare, to death or glory, but Scarabæus gives no heed. In his narrow world, blind and deaf to vaster things in the universe, he plods sordidly on, until one day a soldier's foot or the wheel of a chariot reduces him to his native dust. There are human lives like that— lives spent in the narrow round of selfish care and pleasure, heedless of those momentous issues which should enchain the interest of every immortal soul, blind to earth's sublimest possibilities and deaf to the songs of heaven, until death comes; then the body returns to the earth as it was and the soul to God who gave it. The glory of the Christian life, however, is that it turns our attention to matters of eternal import. We have lot and part with God himself in the great work of the building up of the kingdom of righteousness on earth. Ours is the joy of service. We are co-laborers with God.

III. The attractiveness of the gospel lies, furthermore, in its helpfulness. For life is not all a merry-go-round. There are tasks to be performed and crosses to be borne. And therein God is our helper. He does not give us our religion and then leave us. He gives us a religion and himself along with it. "Lo, I am with you alway, even unto the end."

He is with us helpfully in our common tasks. In the story of the "Watchmaker of Geneva" occurs a paragraph like this: "The tool slipped and his work was spoiled. He laid it aside and repeated the attempt, and again unsuccessfully. A momentary expression of trouble came over his face, an impatient word escaped him. Then he closed his eyes, his lips moved, his trouble was gone, and he resumed his work." This is an experience common to all. We are bunglers at the best; "the tool slips" constantly. But oh what strength is gotten from a moment's interview with Christ! He is never far from any one of us. The closing of our eyes is like the shutting of the closet-door which leaves us alone with him.

His help is vouchsafed also in our struggle against sin. Every true man is conscious of the " war in his members," the conflict for mastery between his higher and lower nature. Each has his own, his darling sins, his vicious propensities. We wrestle not against flesh and blood, but against principalities, against powers, against the rulers of the darkness of this world, against spiritual wickedness in high places. Who is sufficient for these things? When David went forth to encounter Goliath his well-meaning friends buckled Saul's armor upon him. But the helmet slipped over his eyes, the mail-coat rattled upon him, and the sword trailed along the ground. "Loose me," he said, "and let me go forth in the strength which God shall give me." And presently he hurled his challenge across the valley, " Thou comest to me with sword and buckler, but I come to thee in the name of the Lord of Hosts." That way lies victory. The man who meets his evil passions with a firm reliance on divine help is sure of ultimate triumph. Of myself I can do nothing; I can do all things through Christ which strengtheneth me.

IV. Once more, the gospel attracts by reason of its hopefulness. We believe in life and immortality. Our threescore years on earth are not our lifetime, but only the beginning of it. We are spending our school-days here, preparing for eternal tasks and responsibilities. The true philosophy is that which pushes back the horizons infinitely. To spend our energies in the pursuit of things which perish with the using is to fall vastly short of our destiny. All true men are children of Abraham, who lived by faith. It is written that when he was called to go unto a country which he should afterwards receive for an inheritance, "he went out not knowing whither he went." Thenceforward he had no abiding-place, but lived in constant expectancy. Whether he pitched his tent by the banks of the Euphrates, under the oaks of Mamre, or on the slopes of Hebron, it was always as a wayfarer listening for the voice that should bid him strike tent at daybreak and move on. We too are pilgrims and sojourners, ever looking for a better country, even a heavenly, and for a city which hath foundations, whose builder and maker is God. We live therefore not in the present, but in the future. Our conversation is in heaven. Our life is hid with Christ in God. It matters little, therefore, what happens so long as the outlook is fair. "Our light affliction is but for a moment." By way of the cross we journey to the crown. We climb the rough paths to the stars.

These are some of the reasons why the gospel has attracted us and is attracting the multitudes of men. But however we may observe the elements of this attractive power, the Lodestone itself is a mystery still. The cross is foolishness to the Greek and to the Jew a stumbling-block, and thus it always will be. But to those who seek salvation by faith it is the wisdom and the power of God.

At one time when Dr. Chamberlain was at Hyderabad, he was advised that if he continued to preach the gospel it must be at the peril of his life. In the morning when he came, as his custom was, to the market-place, he found himself surrounded by an angry mob. They had torn up the paving-stones and stood ready to slay him. By an artifice he succeeded in getting them to listen to a story. He began with the Child in the manger, told of his marvellous life, how he healed the sick, opened the blind eyes, wiped away the lepers' spots, how he spake as never man spake concerning the great truths of the eternal life, how he lived so purely that no man could lay anything to his charge; he told of his calm demeanor before his judges, and finally of the hours of mortal anguish on the cross. As he proceeded he saw his hearers going to the street and dropping the paving-stones. There were tears in their eyes. "This is my story," said he; "stone me if you will." But they were willing to listen now; and from that time onward he was never hindered in his preaching. Oh there is a wonderful power in the old story of Calvary! The marvel is that it does not touch all consciences and break all hearts. It has in it the secret of an endless life.

If these things are so, beloved, if the religion of Christ is reasonable, enjoyable, helpful, and hopeful, if it gladdens and saves and satisfies, surely, surely this is the religion for you and me.

"THE JERICHO ROAD."

PREACHED BY DR. BURRELL, MARCH 27, 1892.

"Then said Jesus unto him, Go, and do thou likewise."
Luke 10:37.

THE probability is that the lawyer who is here represented as "standing up and tempting" Jesus was not maliciously inclined. He was a dialectician and desired to test the mettle of the Nazarene prophet. The question he propounded, "What shall I do to inherit eternal life?" was a common one in the controversy of those days. Two answers were possible; *first*, Keep the law. The man who obeys the law shall live by it; but, by the same token, to disobey the law is to die under it. *Second*, Accept the gospel. If any man sin, we have an advocate with the Father, even Jesus Christ the righteous. The only work of merit possible to the sinner in the sight' of Almighty God is acceptance of the proffer of grace; as it is written, This is the work of God, that ye believe in him whom God hath sent. And, He that believeth in the Lord Jesus Christ shall be saved.

In answer to the lawyer's question the Lord directed his attention to the Scripture written on his frontlet and the phylactery: "What readest thou?" On those leathern bands was inscribed the compendium of the law, to wit, "Thou shalt love the Lord thy God with all thy heart and mind and soul and strength; and Thou shalt love thy neighbor as thyself." Jesus said, "This do and thou shalt live." But the lawyer was not satisfied. There was something in Christ's answer that convicted him. He was baffled and confused; and wishing to justify himself, he asked, "But who is my neighbor?" Then the Lord related this story of the Waylaid Traveller, in which, as you perceive, he deftly turned the tables on his questioner and answered not his query Who is my neighbor? but the vastly broader one which lies at the centre of all philanthropy, *Whose neighbor am I?*

This is generally regarded as a parable, but without apparent reason. There is every indication that it is the relation of an actual occurrence. Had there been a daily newspaper in Jerusalem at that period, the incident would have been announced in flaming headlines, " Violence on the Jericho Road. A Traveller Waylaid and Robbed— Beaten and Left for Dead." The road from Jericho to Jerusalem, a distance of twenty-one miles, is still called " The Bloody Way." It runs through an ancient river-bed. The surrounding country is likened to an ocean congealed in some mighty tempest. There are caves, ravines, inaccessible cliffs, lurking-places for banditti on every side. Modern travellers going that way hire a special guard and take every possible precaution. The man of whom Jesus speaks foolishly set out alone and unprotected. The thing he should have expected befell him!

Here is an apologue of life. We need not go far to find the " Jericho Road." Sin is the robber chief, the Ali-Baba, leading on a furious band of passions and unholy ambitions — highwaymen all. Life runs through their lonely country. There is a cutpurse in every fastness. Oh how many are wounded and robbed! How many left for dead! — despoiled of manhood, of self-respect and a good conscience, maimed by their unholy passions, shot through the head by rationalism or through the breast by convivial vices. We have all heard the arrows whizzing past, been struck by the stones hurtling down upon us from the overhanging cliffs.

What have we, as Christians, to do about it? How does it concern us as followers of Christ? Much, every way.

First, it behooves us to do our utmost towards the improvement of the Bloody Way; to make life as safe as possible for the innocent and unwary. And the place to begin, for us, is New York city.

A good deal is being said at this moment about the wickedness of New York city. Not to enter into particulars, it is safe to admit that our Metropolis is not as righteous as the New Jerusalem. It requires no great stretch of the imagination to conjure up a better lot of politicians than ours, or to conceive a more Utopian condition of things generally. At the entrance of our harbor stands "Liberty Enlightening the World." If on some dark night she could descend from her pedestal, land at the Battery, and pursue her way along our streets, it is much to be feared that next morning we should see her facing this way and lifting a menacing finger. As she passed Wall Street she would probably cast a sidelong glance that way. At City Hall she would pause with a look of mingled surprise and indignation. She would note with horror the frequent red lights which mark the points whereat our thoroughfares open into Gehenna. Her soul would be stirred by the sound of rattling dice and loud laughter from the upper rooms along the way. If, under the impression that our stalwart policemen are guardians of the peace, she should call their attention to some of these lawless sights and sounds, her bewilderment would only be increased by the smiling information that she and not they must vindicate the law. She would shrink with alarm from the rudeness of belated revellers on their devious way homeward, and would withdraw her garments with loathing from the touch of the woman "whose feet take hold on hell."   The tokens of vice entrenched and unmolested in splendid mansions would add to her dismay.   At the corner of Fifth Avenue and Fiftieth Street her eyes would flame at sight of a monument reared in commemoration of the most brazen and colossal robbery ever known in municipal affairs.   It is an open question whether, after thus familiarizing herself with New York by night, she would return to her pedestal at all, or, if we found her there at daybreak, it would certainly be with her torch inverted or under an extinguisher, as if to suggest that New York under its present conditions is scarcely the proper centre from which to enlighten the world.

If, however, New York is to be made a better city, it must come about largely through the instrumentality of the Church.   And her ministers must lead the way.   It should gladden the hearts of all good citizens that the pulpit has recently made itself heard in fearless and vigorous denunciation of civil corruption.   We preach a gospel which touches life at every point of its circumference.   No living man can utter a caveat or say that we may anathematize sin up to the threshold of politics, but must pause there.   God alone has authority over his ambassadors in this matter, and his word is, "Cry aloud, spare not, and show the people their sin."

But the ministers must not be left to bear the burden alone.   That way lies failure.   The responsibility of reform rests upon the shoulders of every lover of truth and righteousness.   No right thinking man is absolved from the duty of this hour.   "How easy it would be to reform the nation if every one would look to his own reformation." There are Christians enough in New York to dislodge all organized wickedness and drive the rascals out. But everything depends upon united effort. *Eendracht maakt macht.* If we are to succeed it will be in the line of Wesley's motto, "All at it, always at it, altogether at it."

Nevertheless, after all good people have done their utmost the ravages of evil will continue. The wounded will still need to be helped and cared for at the inn. This also is the business of God's people. The bitter cry of the lost and abandoned comes to us from every side. The men and women who haunt the rendezvous of vice and reel along our streets were once innocent children in their mothers' arms, boys and girls playing among the hollyhocks and sweet-williams in the gardens of the old country homes. They started for the city under the rainbow arch of promise to make their fortunes. But the arrows have pierced them, the banditti have beaten and robbed them. What shall be done? Who will be neighbor to them? The tramps, the gamin, the outcasts, the drabs, the drunkards, the criminals, all immortal souls made in God's image, soiled, dragged in the mire, despoiled of their divine inheritance—who will succor and lift them up?

The Church is a great organized benevolence. Its very name, *ecclesia*, suggests its vocation. It is called out of the world to uplift the fallen and to deliver the lost. No other association on earth has a like commission. The State, if true to its functions, puts up lights along the dark windings of the Bloody Road and furnishes safeguards to the wayfarer; but it does not reform the guilty, restore the fallen, or redeem the lost. This is the business of the Church of Jesus Christ; and only such as are in cordial sympathy with him in his divine purpose of deliverance can engage in it.

It is written that when this traveller fell among thieves, "by chance there came down a certain priest that way, who saw him and passed by on the other side." This priest was a doctrinaire. While he walked he was buried in thought. The groans of the poor fellow who was weltering in his own blood fell upon his ears; he lifted his eyes, looked that way, and passed on. The suffering multitudes have little or nothing to hope for from cold philosophy. A creed is essential to an earnest life, but a truth on parchment is no better than a homœopathic pellet before it has been drenched in the mother-tincture. A sword hanging on a nail is a vain thing; it needs a heart behind it and a strong arm to wield it. Faith without works is dead; its feet are cold, its eyes are glassy, its heart is still, its hands are folded over its breast.

And likewise a Levite came that way, looked on him, and passed by on the other side. He was a ceremonialist. It was his business to look after the pomp and circumstance of worship. No doubt he was hastening to reach Jerusalem for an appointed service; and when he saw this poor fellow he said in his heart, "I am sorry, but if I touch him I shall be defiled. Moreover, the sun reminds me that I shall be late for worship." It was plain that he could do nothing. There is a class of high-churchmen who make the outward form of more importance than the inward life; who exalt the church spire above the Cross. Such pietists are not the stuff that reformers and philanthropists are made of.

Then came the good Samaritan; "and when he saw him, he had compassion on him, and bound up his wounds and brought him to the inn and took care of him." Here is the Christian. He has a creed and a form of devotion, but above all a heart beating responsive to his Master's love for the children of men. Our Lord himself was the

universal neighbor. He came to seek and to save the
lost.

> He saw us plunged in deep despair
> And flew to our relief.

He touched the leper, beckoned to the crazy demoniac,
talked with the abandoned woman of the hope of better
things. There was healing in the hem of his garment;
there was comfort in the kindly glance of his eye. None
of the great masters has been able to portray the beauty
of his face. They have painted him with eyes uplifted in
devotion or with hands crossed over a bleeding heart.
Ah! if some painter could have caught the gracious look
upon his face while he passed through the porches of
Bethesda, laying a gentle hand upon the suffering, speaking a helpful word to all!

To be a Christian is to be following in the footsteps of
Christ. It is to go about as Peter and John did, saying
to the troubled and helpless, " In the name of Jesus Christ
of Nazareth, rise up and walk !"

> He prayeth best who loveth best
> All things both great and small :
> For the dear Lord who loveth us,
> He made and loveth all.

Of the multitudes of the suffering ones whom we meet,
not one has wholly lost the semblance of manhood or the
possibility of restoration. On the shield of the Humane
Society of London a little girl is represented as trying to
revive a dying fire by breathing upon it; and above are
the words *Forsitan scintilla*, " Perhaps a spark !" Oh,
beloved, there are no lost souls on earth. None are lost
until the great doors of the midnight world have clanged
behind them. Let us bend over the fallen, feel their pulse,
watch for tokens of returning life, never give them up !

I call upon you all, good men and women, to join in the rescue. Help the next sufferer whom you meet. Seek opportunities of kindness. I have heard of a Christian woman who, moved by a desire to do good, took her place beside the prison door, resolved to help the first who should issue forth. The one that came had lost almost the semblance of humanity—a poor, abandoned, shame-stricken wretch. They confronted each other for a moment in silence, then this woman put her hand upon her shoulder, looked into her face, and without a word kissed her poor faded cheek. Thereat she cried out, " My God ! don't do that ! Don't do that ! Nobody's done that since mother died !" The spark was quickened. In every man and woman there is left something of nobility and with it a remnant of hope.

> Down in the human heart,
> Crushed by the Tempter,
> Feelings lie buried that grace can restore;
> Touched by a loving heart,
> Wakened by kindness,
> Chords that were broken will vibrate once more.

This is the work to which we are summoned as follow-ers of Christ. Let us rejoice that we are called to be saved, but much more that we are called to administer salvation to others. The word of the Master is, " Come unto me, all ye that labor and are heavy laden, and I will give you rest." But he has another word of invitation which should touch us deeply to-day : " Arise and *follow me*. Join me in the deliverance of suffering souls. Come with me along the Bloody Way, to help those whom sin has waylaid, robbed, and left for dead !" Come, brethren, and let us henceforth, like Christ himself, be neighbor to every man.

HOW
JESUS KEPT THE SABBATH.

PREACHED BY DR. BURRELL, APRIL 3, 1892.

"And they watched him, whether he would heal him on the Sabbath
day, that they might accuse him." Mark 3:2.

OUR Lord, driven out of Jerusalem, had come to Ca-
pernaum, and was henceforth to make his headquarters
there. His enemies pursued him. On this occasion
while he preached in the synagogue there were spies
present watching him. They saw the man with the withered hand and knew that Jesus would probably heal him ;
and if he did so it would be a technical violation of the
Sabbath law. He knew what was in their hearts, and he
saith unto them, " Is it lawful to do good on the Sabbath
day or to do evil ? to save life or to kill ?" But they held
their peace. " What man among you," he continued, " it
he hath a sheep fallen into a pit on the Sabbath day, will
not lay hold upon it and lift it out ? But how much better is a man than a sheep !" His logic was good, but the
traditions were against him. When he healed the withered hand he gave his enemies a distinct ground for accusation, and the shadow of the cross grew darker over him.

Christ is our exemplar in everything. We can make
no mistake in following him. *Imitatio Christi* is the secret of right living. Let us also, therefore, watch him, not
with hostile eyes like those of his Jewish pursuers, but with

the reverent purpose of shaping our conduct after his. His manner of Sabbath observance will furnish us with a safe rule for the keeping of the holy day.

I. Observe, to begin with, he rested from secular tasks. His carpenter-shop was closed. It is safe to say that money would not have tempted him to take down his saw or plane unless for a work of absolute necessity. The most rudimental precept as to the Sabbath has reference to the duty of physical rest. " Six days shalt thou labor and do all thy work; but the seventh day is the Sabbath of the Lord thy God ; in it thou shalt not do any work." And the sanction of the Sabbath, as here given, is manifestly permanent, inasmuch as it rests upon the divine example : " For in six days the Lord made heaven and earth, the sea and all that in them is, and rested the seventh day : *wherefore* the Lord blessed the Sabbath day and hallowed it." When that "for " and that " wherefore " shall lose their logical significance, or when it shall cease to be an historical fact that God rested after his six days of creative work, it will be time to speak about the abrogation of the Sabbath law.

The necessity of devoting one-seventh of our time to physical rest is written not only in Holy Scripture, but in the human constitution. During the Reign of Terror in France it was ordained that every tenth day should be set apart for this purpose. A fine was imposed for the keeping of the Sabbath, the object being to utterly eradicate this with every other religious observance. It was found, however, that the divine law would tolerate no such infringement. One-tenth was not the right proportion. The nation broke down under it and was obliged to restore the sanctions of the Lord's day.

It is stated that three million one hundred and forty-five thousand of our American people are at work every

Sabbath; one in ten of our wage-earners; a representative of every sixth family in the land. A portion of this labor is no doubt necessary. It is safe to say, however, that two million of these workmen might, without perceptible inconvenience in any quarter, be released from their unnatural bondage. Our Government is the chief sinner. In New York city the postal service goes on about as usual during the Lord's day. Hundreds of clerks and carriers are kept on duty. So also at Philadelphia and in every important city. If this be urged as a business necessity, it is enough to answer that London, the great centre of universal commerce, with its five millions of people, manages to get along without a Sunday delivery or collection of mails. In this matter we are needlessly defying God. In 1828 petitions from twenty-one States of the Union were sent to the Postmaster General calling for a cessation of the Sunday postal service. His reply was a complex illustration of impiety and demagogical impertinence. " So long," said he, " as the silver river flows and the green grass grows and the oceanic tides rise and fall on the first day of the week, so long shall the mails of this republic be circulated on that day." It is to be hoped that he spoke for himself alone, for no nation could deliver itself in that manner without provoking the wrath of a jealous God.

The Sunday newspaper is also a great sinner. It is at this moment the head and front of our offending with respect to the holy day. Observe some of the points in the indictment.

(1.) It is the worst paper of the week. No pretence is made that its columns are adjusted to the needs of the holy day. On the other hand, all items peculiarly abominable or salacious are tossed upon the desk of the Sunday editor. If this issue were made up of material proper to be read on the Sabbath not a hundred copies could be disposed of.

(2.) Its preparation involves a vast amount of Sabbath work. To throw this blame upon the Monday issue is to resort to a very diaphanous subterfuge, for if there were no Sunday newspaper the Monday's issue could and would be prepared as formerly, without the necessity of working on the Lord's day.

(3.) It is training up an army of lads for Sunday work. To buy a paper of a newsboy seems a small matter to you. The average business man—not to say Christian—would hesitate to sell a corner lot on the Sabbath; but he forgets that to a newsboy the selling of his paper is a matter of as much importance as the larger transaction would be to him. And this boy, remember, is being encouraged to believe that business may be properly transacted on the Sabbath. There are thousands of these boys in New York who are certain to carry that impression through life. And the people who patronize them are responsible for it.

(4.) It drags the world into our Sabbath life. You say you must have the news. Yet the news is the very thing that we should most desire to escape from on the Lord's day. " The world is too much with us." We are like the starling in the " Sentimental Journey," that, beating against its cage, cried, " I can't get out! I can't get out!" God's purpose in instituting the Sabbath was to give our souls an opportunity of quitting the world for a season and resting from the worry of it.

(5.) It keeps up traffic on the sacred day. The Sunday newspaper is sustained most largely by the income from its advertising columns. The merchant who patronizes them may delude himself with the idea that he has arrested his business for the Sabbath; but he has done nothing of the sort. He may have turned the key in the lock on Saturday night, but he has taken effective means of continuing his traffic another way. If he were to send a bell-man up and down Broadway to cry, " Hear ye! hear ye! my place of business is closed for the Sabbath as becomes a Christian man, but it will be open to-morrow morning with such bargains as never were heard of!" it would be obvious that he was making a pretty fair thing of his Sabbath rest in a financial way. But this is the very thing you are doing through your advertisements in the Sunday press. The fact is that so far from resting, you are doing a very vigorous and profitable business on the Lord's day.

II. To return now to Christ's manner of keeping the Sabbath, observe that he desisted from secular amusements. If proof be called for, we reply that it goes without proving. To suggest that he might, possibly, have gone to an amphitheatre to witness a gladiatorial show on the Sabbath would be in the nature of gross impiety. We know him too well to entertain the thought.

The drift in our time is towards the opening of places of Sabbath amusement. The French people tried that experiment under the most favorable circumstances and are to-day groaning under it. The German people have also tried this experiment; and their Sunday beer-gardens are a weariness and an abomination. It is a poor time for Americans to institute the custom. The proposition is made as if in behalf of the workingmen, but this is mere pretence. In 1883 when a vigorous and persistent effort was made in England to open the museums and other places of amusement on the Sabbath, a canvass was made of the various labor guilds and associations with the following result: For Sunday opening, sixty-two organizations with a membership of 45,482. Against Sunday opening, two thousand four hundred and twelve organizations with a membership of 501,705.   This ought to be conclusive as to one point, namely, that if we are to open our places of secular amusement on the Sabbath it is not for the benefit of the workingmen.   Our wage-earners are well aware that Sunday amusements are the entering wedge for Sunday work, and that Sunday work means six days' wages for seven days' toil.   Every place of amusement thrown open to the public means a relay of workmen to carry it on.   The encroachment is gradual but the result is sure.   Our wage-earners are familiar with the logic of the situation; if the holy day is to be made a holiday it is not because they desire it.

III. Our Lord attended church on the Sabbath.   It was his custom to worship in the synagogue.   The Sabbath is preëminently a time for the cultivation of the spiritual graces.   Six days in the week we are in the midst of the world's work and worry.   Brain and sinew are under the utmost tension.   Matters of eternal moment go largely by default.   This is preëminently true of the American people.   Our ordinary business man is moderately sure of breaking down under the continuous strain.   Our most common ailment is nervous debility.   Possibly our disregard of Sabbath rest has something to do with it.   God means that we shall quit the world one day in seven, lay off its cares and burdens and come up out of its mists and miasms to breathe the mountain air with him.   Why is it that a sea voyage is so frequently prescribed for worn-out business men?   The moment the ship hoists anchor the world recedes.   Then follows a week of substantial exile. No more news now.   Stocks may go up or go down, kingdoms may rise and fall, but the voyager knows it not.   Oh blessed rest!   The horizons of our life are pushed back.   Our hearts are enlarged.   There are depths above and deeps beneath.   We are out of the world! Every Sabbath ought to be like a sea voyage. It should carry us away from the hum and roar of traffic, from the distracting pursuits of the madding crowd, away from the world into the spiritual .ealms. This is the day of devotion, the day for spiritual growth and enjoyment in communion with God.

IV. Our Lord devoted himself on the Sabbath to charitable work. Many of his most helpful miracles were wrought upon that day. And why not? This is the day of days for mercy—to lift up the fallen, comfort the bereaved, feed the hungry, visit the sick, and impart instruction to such as are ignorant of spiritual things. If it cannot be said that philanthropy is worship it is certainly true that our Lord is pleased with kindness rendered to the least of his little ones. The Legend Beautiful has a lesson for us. To the monk kneeling in his chamber alone came

> the Blessed Vision
> Of our Lord, with light Elysian
> Like a vesture wrapped about him.

Never had the monk known such transport. He knelt in rapt adoration. Then, on a sudden, the convent bell tolled the hour of charity. The poor were waiting at the monastery door for their accustomed dole; and to-day this monk was almoner.

> Deep distress and hesitation
> Mingled with his adoration;
> Should he go or should he stay?
> Should he leave the poor to wait
> Hungry at the convent gate
> Till the Vision passed away?
> Should he slight his radiant guest,
> Slight this visitant celestial,
> For a crowd of ragged, bestial
> Beggars at the convent gate?

But a voice within reminded him that God required mercy and not sacrifice.   Reluctantly he arose from his knees and with a last look at the Vision went forth to duty. He dispensed the daily alms, received the thanks of the poor and suffering, and then in haste returned.   On entering his cell he paused with unspeakable delight,

> For the Vision still was standing
> As he left it there before,
> When the convent bell appalling,
> From its belfry calling, calling,
> Summoned him to feed the poor.
> Through the long hour intervening
> It had waited his return,
> And he felt his bosom burn,
> Comprehending all the meaning,
> When the Blessed Vision said,
> " Hadst thou stayed, I must have fled !"

Two words, in closing. *First*, " The Sabbath was made for man ;" not, surely, that he might abuse it, but that he might apply it to his spiritual and eternal good. The day is a holy trust and we shall be held responsible for the right use of it.

Second, " The Son of Man is Lord also of the Sabbath." He has a property right in it. Time is his, for he made it. By a special and explicit designation the Sabbath is set apart as " the Lord's Day." The man who appropriates it to his own selfish uses is guilty of grand larceny indeed ; for he is guilty of robbing God. Let us therefore use the day as not abusing it.

— ◆ —

THE

CENTURION'S STORY.

PREACHED BY DR. BURRELL, APRIL 3, 1892.

I AM an old man now; the burden of fourscore years is resting upon me. But the things which happened one April day in the year 783 A. U. C., full half a century ago, are still fresh in my memory.

At that time I was stationed in the Castle of Antonia. On the morning of the day I mention, I was summoned to take charge of the execution of a culprit who had just been sentenced to death. Of the men in the garrison I selected twelve of such as were hardened to the sight of blood and with them I proceeded to the Prætorium. All was hurry and excitement there. It being the time of the Jewish Passover, the city was crowded with strangers. A multitude of people was gathered and clamoring for the death of this malefactor. On our arrival he was brought forth. He proved to be that Prophet of Nazareth whose oracular wisdom and wonder-working power had been noised everywhere. He was a man of middle stature, with a face of striking beauty and benignity, eyes of mingled light and warmth, auburn hair falling over his shoulders. He was now pale and haggard, having passed through three judicial ordeals since the last sunset, besides being scourged with the *flagellum horribile* and exposed to the rude sport of the midnight guard. He wore the cast-off purple of the Roman procurator and a crown of thorns. But, as he issued from the Hall of Judgment, such was his commanding presence that the multitude was hushed and separated to make way. The cross, constructed of transverse beams of sycamore, was brought and laid upon his shoulders. About his neck was suspended a *titulum* on which were written in three languages his name and the indictment against him. My quaternions fell into line, and at the signal the procession moved. I rode before, clearing the way. The people thronged the narrow streets, crying more and more loudly as we proceeded, "*Stauroson !* Crucify him !"

The Nazarene, weak from long vigils and suffering, bowed low under his burden. A woman in the company, by name Veronica, it is said, pressed near and wiped the dust and blood from his haggard face, and the napkin when withdrawn bore the impress of his face, marred but divinely beautiful.

It is reported also that as the multitude surged on towards the Jaffa gate, a certain cobbler, named Ahasue-rus, moved by a malignant spirit, thrust his foot before the prisoner, who stumbled thereat and fell. In punish-ment for that cruel deed he is said to be a wanderer upon the earth even to this day with no rest for his weary feet. This too is a mere legend ; but within it dwells the truth that retribution ever like a Fury pursues the pitiless.

We passed through the Jaffa gate and entered upon the steep road leading to the place of execution. The sun flamed down upon us ; we were enveloped in a cloud of dust. The prisoner at length, overborne by his cross, fell under it. We seized upon an Ethiopian in the com-pany and placed the burden upon him. Strange to tell, he assumed it without a murmur, insomuch that he was suspected of being a follower of the Nazarene. As we moved on with din and uproar, a group of women, standing by the wayside, rent the air with shrill lamentations, on hearing which Jesus said, "Daughters of Jerusalem, weep not for me, but for yourselves and your children, for behold the days come when they shall say to the mountains, Fall on us! and to the hills, Cover us!" It was a weird prophecy, and ere a generation passed it was to the letter fulfilled. There were those in that company who lived to see the Holy City compassed about by a forest of hostile spears. Its inhabitants were brought low by famine and pestilence; mothers cast envious eyes on the white flesh of their children. On the surrounding heights crosses were reared whereon a multitude of Jewish captives died the death. Despair fell upon all. And in those days there were not a few who called to mind the ominous words of the Nazarene, "Weep not for me, but for yourselves and for your children after you."

The way we journeyed has since been called *Via Dolorosa*. It led to the round knoll called Golgotha—from its resemblance to a skull. As we drew nigh we perceived two crosses already reared, on which two thieves of Barabbas' band had been suspended for some hours. Our prisoner, as a token of obloquy, was to be crucified between them. Our spears and standards were now lowered, and Jesus being stripped of his outer garments was laid prostrate upon his cross. A soldier approached with hammer and spikes, at sight of whom the frenzied multitude ceased for a moment their revilings and pressed near. The prisoner preserved his calm demeanor. A stupefying draught was offered him, but he refused it, preferring to look death calmly in the face. He stretched out his hands; the hammer fell. At sight of the blood the mob broke forth again, crying, "Stauroson!" but not a word escaped the sufferer. As the nails tore through the quivering flesh his eyes closed and his lips moved as if he were holding communion with some invisible One.   Then with a wrench the cross was lifted into the socket prepared for it.

At this moment the first word escaped him.   With a look of reproach and an appealing glance to heaven, he cried, " Father, forgive them ; they know not what they do !"   It was as if he were covering our heads with a shield of prayer.   In this he practised his own rule of charity and doctrine of forgiveness, " Love your enemies, bless them that curse you, do good to them that hate you, and pray for them that despitefully use you."

His prayer, however, seemed but to rouse the fury of his Jewish enemies.   They broke forth in mockery, " Come down ! come down from thy cross !   Thou that destroyest the temple and buildest it in three days, save thyself !"   The priests and rabbis, standing by, joined in the mockery, saying, " He saved others, himself he cannot save.   Let him come down if he be the Messiah, the chosen of God !"   My soldiers, meanwhile, were disputing as to the apportionment of his garments ; I noted the rattling of their dice in a brazen helmet wherein they cast lots for his seamless robe.

The thieves upon either hand joined for a time in the mockery ; but presently a change came over the one upon the right, named Dysmas.   The demeanor of Jesus had touched his heart ; and after long silence he entreated, " Lord, remember me when thou comest in thy kingdom !"   The Nazarene turned upon him a look of compassionate love, saying, " To-day thou shalt be with me in Paradise."   It was not long after when this robber's head sank upon his breast, but in death his face wore a look of indescribable peace.   The time came when Jesus' word of pardon to him was full of comfort to great sinners.

He who saved Dysmas in the article of death, plucking him from the edge of the abyss, was thenceforth known to be able to save even unto the uttermost all who would believe in him.

Not far from the cross stood a company of women wringing their hands in helpless pain. Among them was the mother of the Nazarene. When her son as a child had been brought to the Jewish temple, an old priest took him from his mother's arms and prophesied, "This child is set for the fall and rise of many in Israel," then looking upon the mother said, "A sword shall pierce through thine own soul also." At this moment his word was fulfilled; the iron entered her soul. Her dying son beheld her, and, with his eyes directing her to one who was known as his favorite disciple, said, "Woman, behold thy son," who thereupon bore her fainting away.

It was now noon, a clear, scorching Syrian noon. But a veil seemed gathering before the sun. Shadows fell from the heights of Moab. Night rose from the ravines, surging upward in dark billows, overwhelming all. A strange pallor was upon all faces. The gleam on shield and helmet faded out. It was night, Egyptian night at high noon! What meant it? Manifestly this was no eclipse, for the paschal moon was at its full. The Jews had ofttimes clamored for a sign, a sign whereby they might test this sufferer's Messianic claim. Had the sign come? Was nature sympathizing with her Lord? Were these shadows the trappings of a universal woe? Was God thus manifesting his wrath against sin? Or was this a stupendous figure of the position in which this dying Nazarene stood with respect to the deliverance of the race from sin? Once in a Jewish synagogue I heard a rabbi read from the scroll of Isaiah a prophecy concerning the Messiah; He was to be wounded for our transgressions and bruised for our iniquities; and by his stripes we should be healed. It was predicted that when Messiah came he should, bearing the world's burden of sin, go into the outer darkness in expiatory pain. Was it at this awful moment that he carried that burden into the region of the lost? Did he just then descend into hell for us? Hark! a cry from his fever-parched lips, piercing the silence and the darkness, "*Eloi, Eloi, lama sabachthani?* My God, my God, why hast thou forsaken me?" But for that terrific cry of anguish the silence was unbroken for three mortal hours. I have known other victims of the cross to vent their rage in impotent wrath, to spit their hate like asps, to harangue the crowd with helpless protestations, or to beg for the death-stroke; but this Jesus preserved a majestic silence. The people also seemed wrapped in a weird terror. Naught was heard but the rattling of armor as some soldier jostled his comrade, a sob escaping from some woman's heart, the dropping of the blood.

Thus until the ninth hour of the day. It was the hour of the evening sacrifice, and the darkness began slowly to lift. It was then that the Nazarene uttered his only word of complaint. " I thirst," he said. Whereupon a strange thing happened. One of my soldiers, trained in the arena and in gladiatorial contests—one who had never been known to spare a foe, delighting in the sack of cities, looking on unmoved when children were dashed against the stones—this man dipped a sponge in the sour wine which was provided for the guard, and would have raised it to the sufferer's lips. The Jews cried out, " Let be, let be, and let us see if Elias will come to his relief!" For a moment the soldier hesitated, even joined in the cry, then giving way to the better promptings of his heart, lifted the sponge and assuaged the thirst of the dying man. It was the only deed of kindness I noted on Golgotha that day.

In return for it the Nazarene cast upon his benefactor such a look of gratitude that his nature seemed ever afterwards to have been transformed by it.

Then Jesus cried with a loud voice, "*Tetelestai!* It is finished!" Did it signify that his pain was over? Well might he after such anguish utter a sigh of relief. Or was it that his work was accomplished? So have I seen a laborer turn homeward from his day's work with pleasant anticipation of rest. So have I seen a wayfarer quicken his footsteps as at eventide he came in sight of the village lights. So have I seen a soldier, weary with the stress of conflict and wounded unto death, bear the standard aloft as he climbed the parapet and with his last voice shout for victory!

And then the last word. It was spoken softly, as if coming from the threshold of the other world, " Father, into thy hands I commend my spirit!" Then, as he yielded up the ghost, a look of surpassing peace fell upon his upturned face which lingered there when death had put its rigid seal upon it. Thus he fell on sleep. I have ofttimes since been reminded of that look when I have seen an infant lulled in its mother's arms, or when, walking through a Christian cemetery, I have noted upon the tombstones of martyrs the word "*Dormit.* He sleeps."

The supernatural darkness had now given way to the calm twilight. The sky was covered far towards the zenith with a golden splendor crossed with bars of crimson light. It looked as if heaven's gates were opened, and one gazing through could almost seem to see the flitting of superhuman shapes and hear far-away voices calling, " Lift up your heads, O ye gates; even lift them up, ye everlasting doors; and the King of glory shall come in!"

At that moment the earth rumbled under my feet; a shudder seemed to pass through nature. It was said that as the high priest was kindling the lamps in the Holy Place of the Temple, this being the hour of the evening sacrifice, the great veil hanging before the Holy of Holies was rent from the top to the bottom as if by an unseen hand. This happened at the instant when the Nazarene' yielded up his spirit; and his followers are wont to say that when he passed from earth to resume his heavenly glory a new and living way was opened up for penitent sinners into the Holiest of All.

The execution being over, the people slowly dispersed to their homes. The twilight settled down on Golgotha. A group of wailing women lingered for a while, then went their way. Against the sky stood forth the outlines of the three crosses. On the face of Dysmas the moonlight showed the look of peace that had settled upon it at Jesus' word of pardon. The robber on the left had dropped his face in anguish upon his breast. In the midst Jesus looked upwards, dead but triumphant! Long and steadfastly I gazed upon him. The events of the day crowding upon my mind, my conviction deepened that this was no common man. My conscience was sorely smitten; my heart was inexpressibly touched by the memory of the things which had happened. A tide of grief overwhelmed me. I dismounted from my horse, my soldiers looking on in wonder. I knelt before the middle cross; I prostrated myself upon the earth. The truth went surging irresistibly through my soul, until at length, able to restrain myself no longer, I confessed, "*Verily, verily, thou art the Son of God!*"

I am old now. The end draws near. For half a century have I loved and served him. In my body are the marks of the Lord Jesus. Fears have sometimes compassed me about. But never have I known the moment when I would recall my vow of devotion to him. Trials

and sorrows have but deepened my conviction; for he
has given me songs in the night. I have seen men and
women for his name's sake die without a murmur, heroic
amid the flames, triumphant when cast to lions. I have
heard them with their last breath protest with joy, "*Chris-
tianus sum !*" The Master himself seemed to be holding
them up with his everlasting arms—a living Christ, an
omnipotent Christ, an ever-present Christ, even as he
promised, "Lo, I am with you alway, even unto the end
of the world."

The cross in my time has been transformed from an
emblem of shame into a symbol of victory. And the
Christ who suffered upon it has been made unto me wisdom and righteousness and sanctification and redemption.
I have learned somewhat of the meaning of his life and of
his death and of his glorious resurrection. Many glorious
hopes have I, but the most earnest is that I who crucified
him may yet behold his face in peace—that I, who bowed
that night with broken heart beneath his cross, may some
day see the King in his beauty and fall before his throne,
crying, "My Lord and my God!"

PAUL'S

EASTER SERMON AT ANTIOCH.

PREACHED BY DR. BURRELL ON EASTER SUNDAY, 1892.

" Then Paul stood up, and beckoning with his hand, said —" Acts 13:16.

THIS was in the synagogue at Antioch of Pisidia.   At the further end stood a desk for the reader.   Above that was the women's gallery ; their faces could be seen behind the partition of lattice-work.   On the side of the room nearest Jerusalem was the ark or chest for the sacred scrolls.   Seats for the worshippers were arranged according to station, those for the rabbis being nearest the reader's desk.   As each attendant entered he cast a scarf over his shoulder, the sacred tallith with its four tassels.   Among the worshippers on this particular day were two strangers. One was a man of imposing presence and benignant countenance, with clear, kindly eyes,—a gracious man whom we know as "the Son of Consolation."   His companion was of smaller stature, described as a man " of mean presence," with stooping shoulders and defective sight.   These two found their way to the rabbinical seats.

The service commenced with a prayer recited by the reader or "Angel of the Assembly."   Then the Chazan brought from the ark the sacred scroll, from which was read the Scripture for the day.   Then singing from the Psalter, which was the Hebrew hymn-book.   After that the service was thrown open, according to custom, to such as occupied rabbinical seats. A special invitation was extended to the two strangers. "Men and brethren," said the leader, "if ye have any word of exhortation for the people, say on."

Then Paul arose and beckoned with his hand. He was a master of dialectics. In this very beckoning with his hand we note an evidence of his rhetorical skill. It was his first sermon. He had been familiar with forensic disputation in the Sanhedrin in former years. But to-day he was to make his maiden effort as a minister of the gospel.

If you have ever spent a week in London it is safe to say that on Sunday morning you betook yourself, possibly by an omnibus marked "To the Elephant and Castle," across London Bridge to the Metropolitan Tabernacle. From all directions the crowds were going that way to hear the greatest of modern preachers whose voice has recently been hushed in death. In him there was little of the pomp and circumstance of the homiletic art. It was a delight to hear him in the midst of the vast assemblage—his hands grasping the rail before him in the attitude of a jury pleader—simple, earnest, grandly eloquent, setting forth the glorious gospel of the blessed God. It minded one of the wish of quaint Nicholas Breton:

> "I would I were an excellent divine
>   That had the Bible at my fingers' ends,
> That men might hear out of this mouth of mine
>   How God doth make his enemies his friends."

But this greatest of our modern preachers is scarcely to be compared with the apostle who arose in the Pisidian synagogue and beckoned with his hand that day. His sermon was a masterpiece; it will bear analysis.

I. *His text.* He found his text in the sixteenth Psalm,

which was probably the Scriptural lesson of the day: "I have set the Lord always before me: because he is at my right hand, I shall not be moved.   Therefore my heart is glad, and my glory rejoiceth: my flesh also shall rest in hope.   For thou wilt not leave my soul in hell; neither wilt thou suffer thy Holy One to see corruption."   The title of this Psalm is *Michtam*, or hiding.   Christ hides behind the lattice of this prophecy uttered a thousand years before the world saw him.

II. *His exordium*.   He began with an historical resumé, tracing the footsteps of Messiah from the Exodus to the Cross.   The striking feature of this introduction is its resemblance to a speech which Paul had heard twelve years before in the Hall Gazith.   He was at that time a member of the Sanhedrin.   The deacon Stephen was brought before that tribunal for trial.   In making his defence he began with the call of Abraham, and followed the golden thread of Messianic prediction through the history of Israel until, overcome with indignation at the people's hardness of heart and casting prudence to the winds, he cried out: "Ye stiff-necked and uncircumcised in heart and ears, ye do always resist the Holy Ghost!   As your fathers did, so do ye.   Which of the prophets have not your fathers persecuted?   They have slain them which showed before of the coming of the Just One; of whom ye have been now the betrayers and murderers!" At this point the audience, cut to the heart, gnashed on him with their teeth and ran upon him with one accord. They cast him out beyond the city walls and stoned him. As he bowed his bruised and bleeding face before the storm of missiles, he cried, "Lord Jesus, receive my spirit!" and again, "Lord, lay not this sin to their charge!" While this was transpiring the clothes of the ringleaders were held by young Saul of Tarsus, who to-day in the synagogue at Antioch preaches the gospel of Christ. His words are an echo of Stephen's, as if his voice had fallen upon the sensitive plate of a phonograph to be kept and reproduced in due time. So true is it that, though the saints rest from their labors, their words as well as their works do follow them.

The historical resumé of St. Paul, which brought him to the death and burial of Jesus, was concluded with the abrupt words, "But God raised him from the dead!" And he continued, "We thus declare unto you glad tidings, how that the promise which was made unto the fathers, God hath fulfilled the same unto us their children in that he hath raised up Jesus again, as it is written, 'Thou art my Son; this day have I begotten thee.'"

III. *The argument.* In stating this proposition of the Resurrection, observe how Paul begins with God. It is impossible to proceed with the argument otherwise. For only upon the assumption of Omnipotence can we frame an antecedent probability or even possibility of a resurrection from the dead. But Paul's brain and conscience and heart were filled with the consciousness of God. His life was overarched by the truth of the divine presence. In his philosophy all things are of God and through God and for God.

Then, having shown the resurrection possible by the affirmation of almighty power, he reviews the Messianic prophecies. Three in particular are referred to: "Thou art my Son; this day have I begotten thee" (Psa. 2:7); "I will make an everlasting covenant with you, even the sure mercies of David" (Isa. 55:3); and, "Thou wilt not suffer thy Holy One to see corruption" (Psa. 16:10).

This anticipation of Messiah's triumph over death was known as *the hope of Israel.* It lay in Scripture like Aaron's rod in the Ark of the Covenant: cut off from mother earth and from the parent stem, shut out from air and sunlight, yet in fulness of time putting forth tokens of newness of life.

Men have always feared Death. They have called him the King of Terrors. They have seen him stalking through palace gates and bowing low to enter the cottage door. They have known that the time was coming when they—every one—must bow before him. This fear was relieved by the hope of the coming of One who would conquer Sin and bind at his girdle the keys of Death and of Hell. He was to be the "death of Death and Hell's destruction." All human-kind were in bondage under sin and in subjection unto death, like the garrison of a beleaguered city, gaunt and desperate, gazing wistfully afar off with one forlorn hope. The story of the bursting of the sepulchre in Joseph's garden was like a bugle-blast on the distant hills, the footfall of an army come for deliverance, the waving of banners to tell that One mightier than Death drew nigh to save his people. "We declare unto you glad tidings," said Paul, "how that the promise made unto the fathers is fulfilled unto us!"

Observe, he does not undertake to prove the resurrection of Christ. The reason is obvious. It was beyond the necessity of proof. Had one risen in the assembly and cried, "I doubt it!" scores of witnesses could have been summoned to certify that they had seen Jesus alive after his crucifixion, had seen his scarred face and wounded hands, had talked with him, bowed under his benediction, and seen him vanish in the opening clouds of heaven. Scores? Ay, hundreds upon hundreds, for this thing was not done in a corner. He was seen "by above five hundred at once." We are now eighteen hundred years beyond the event; and yet the proofs of the resurrection of Jesus are so striking that no fair-minded man

will resist them.   Dr. Arnold of Rugby, one of the profoundest students of history, said truly, "I do not know
of any historical fact more substantially proven by cumulative evidence than the resurrection of Jesus Christ."

IV. *The application.* The practical importance of this
doctrine is set forth by St. Paul, here and more elaborately
elsewhere, as a sign and a seal.

(1.) *It is a sign of the divinity of Jesus.* His enemies
were continually clamoring for a sign.   He professed to
be their Messiah.   "Show us a sign," they cried, "and
we will believe thee."   He answered, "There shall no
sign be given but the sign of the prophet Jonas, for as
Jonas was three days and three nights in the whale's
belly, so shall the Son of man be three days and three
nights in the heart of the earth."

On this grand miracle the Lord adventures the truth
of his Messianic claims and the integrity of his redemptive
work.   He showed himself to be the Son of God with
power by his resurrection from the dead.   Rom. 1 : 4.

It is related that Charlemagne was buried by his own
desire in a sitting posture, clothed in purple and ermine,
his crown upon his head and his sceptre in his hand.   Long
afterwards his tomb was opened by the Emperor Otho,
but alas! little was left of the imperial glory!   The crown
had fallen from Charlemagne's bleached brow, his sceptre
lay in the dust, his royal robes had rotted and fallen about
him.   *Sic transit gloria mundi.*   But not so with Jesus.
It was prophesied that God would not leave him in the
grave nor suffer his Holy One to see corruption.   By this
was he proven to be far above all principalities and powers.   Being superior to the King of Terrors, he hath upon
his vesture and upon his thigh written a name, *King of
kings and Lord of lords.*   In this he presents his credentials ; by this he corroborates his teaching ; and hereby

he for ever certifies the effectiveness of his redemptive work.

(2.) *This miracle is also a seal of the covenant of life.* Because he lives, we shall live also. We stand gazing out towards an unknown world, bewildered and questioning, " If a man die, will he live again ?" Our fathers dreamed of life and immortality—dreamed and hoped and wondered; but now since Christ has risen the shadows are gone; we dream no more; in him life and immortality are brought to light! When Madame de Gasparin went through the burial crypts under Palermo, her faith for the moment forsook her. Walking amid the heaped up bones of centuries, treading upon the dust of the multitudinous and forgotten dead, oppressed by the mould and the chill, she was moved to ask like the prophet in the Valley of Vision, " Can these slain live ?" But as she came from the crypt into the sunshine, turning backwards she saw above the archway, *Jesu Nazaret, Rex Judæorum*—the very words that were written upon the cross. Jesus of Nazareth is King of the whole Israel of God. And beholding that, her faith came back as in a sun-burst, flooding her heart with indescribable joy. Ah, beloved, with him all things are possible. He was dead, but liveth and is alive for evermore, and hath the keys of Death and Hell! And because he lives we shall live also.

Paul elsewhere (1 Cor. 15) elaborates the argument on this wise, " Now if Christ be preached that he rose from the dead, how say some among you that there is no resurrection of the dead ? For if there be no resurrection of the dead, then is Christ not risen : and if Christ be not risen, our preaching is vain, and your faith is also vain. Yea, and we are found false witnesses of God ; because we have testified of God that he raised up Christ ; whom he raised not up if so be that the dead rise not. For if the dead rise not, then is not Christ raised; and if Christ be not raised, your faith is vain; ye are yet in your sins. Then they also which are fallen asleep in Christ are perished.   If in this life only we have hope in Christ, we are of all men most miserable.   But now is Christ risen from the dead, and become the firstfruits of them that slept. Behold I show you a mystery: we shall not all sleep but we shall all be changed, in a moment, in the twinkling of an eye, at the last trump.   For the trumpet shall sound and the dead shall be raised incorruptible, and we shall be changed.   For this corruptible must put on incorruption, and this mortal must put on immortality.   Then shall be brought to pass the saying that is written, Death is swallowed up in victory.   O death, where is thy sting?   O grave, where is thy victory?   The sting of death is sin; and the strength of sin is the law.   But thanks be to God which giveth us the victory through our Lord Jesus Christ. Wherefore, my beloved brethren, be ye steadfast, immovable, always abounding in the work of the Lord, forasmuch as ye know that your labor is not in vain in the Lord."

V. *The peroration.*   This Easter sermon concludes with an impressive offer of salvation in the name of the risen Christ: "Be it known unto you, therefore, men and brethren, that through this man is preached unto you the forgiveness of sins."   He who conquered death is able to save unto the uttermost all who by faith will come unto him.

I greet you this morning, beloved, in the name of the living Christ.   The Lord is risen!   The Lord is risen indeed!   It makes a great difference to those who love him.   After his death and burial the disciples were overcome with grief.   They had hoped that it had been he who should deliver Israel.   But they had suffered a sad disillusioning. He was dead; and with him hope had died. They went about with slow steps and downcast faces. Then on a sudden came a change. There was running to and fro. John ran; Peter ran; the women came running down the slopes of Olivet. One to another they cried, " The Lord is risen! The Lord is risen indeed!" It transformed their lives. They went everywhere preaching it. Oh let us make more and more of the doctrine of the risen Christ. He is not dead! He is alive and liveth for evermore! He hath the keys of Death and Hell! Peace be with you in his name. Into the upper chamber he came in the calmness of his great triumph, and lifting his pierced hands in benediction, said, " Peace be unto you." It is the greeting of the Easter morning. The peace of God which passeth all understanding keep your minds and hearts through Christ Jesus. Amen.

"THE GREAT REFUSAL."

PREACHED BY DR. BURRELL APRIL 24, 1892.

" And when he was gone forth into the way, there came one running
and kneeled to him, and asked him, Good Master, what shall
I do that I may inherit eternal life? And Jesus said unto him,
Why callest thou me good? there is none good but one, that
is God. Thou knowest the commandments, Do not commit
adultery, Do not kill, Do not steal, Do not bear false witness,
Defraud not, Honor thy father and mother. And he answered
and said unto him, Master, all these have I observed from my
youth. Then Jesus, beholding him, loved him, and said unto
him, One thing thou lackest: go thy way, sell whatsoever thou
hast, and give to the poor, and thou shalt have treasure in
heaven: and come, take up the cross, and follow me." Mark
10:17–21.

THE key-note of our Lord's preaching was life. " I
am come," said he, " that ye might have life and that ye
might have it more abundantly."   He was speaking of a
life above and beyond that of mere breathing and eating
and toiling and sleeping and rising again to mingle in
the affairs of the workshop and the market-place.

" We live in deeds, not years ; in thoughts, not breaths ;
　In feelings, not in figures on a dial.
We should count time by heart-throbs."

And again he said, " Except ye eat the flesh and drink
the blood of the Son of Man, ye have no life in you."
That is, in order to attain and enjoy the higher life, we
must enter into participation with the best and noblest.
To our Lord food and raiment were minor considerations;
he was ever seeking the kingdom of God and righteousness. His meat and drink were to do the will of the Fa-

ther and to serve the welfare of his fellow-men. And again he said, "What shall it profit a man if he gain the whole world and lose his life (New Version), or what shall a man give in exchange for his life?"   It is possible, then, to continue an animal existence for ever and still be utterly and for ever devoid of life.   To fall short of glory is, in a dreadful sense, to enter into the regions of death, which is but another way of saying to be exiled from God.   It is the divine will that all who have fallen from their original estate of God-likeness should return and be again with and like God.   To this end Christ came into the world, as it is written, " For God so loved the world that he gave his only-begotten Son, that whosoever believeth in him should not perish, but have everlasting *life.*"

The young man in this narrative was worth looking at. To begin with, he was young, and youth is always interesting.   Then he was rich, "very rich," and "a ruler" besides.   Better still, he was of upright character, claiming a due respect for the divine law.   He was amiable also, for when the Lord looked ·upon him he loved him. But the best of all was his earnestness.   A young man in earnest, and in earnest with respect to spiritual things! The sight is not so common but that we may profitably pause to admire and ponder it.

This youth had doubtless heard the preaching of Jesus with respect to the kingdom ; had heard him set forth the excellency of the spiritual life—that higher life which we share with the Infinite: and his heart went out after it so fervently that, as Jesus was passing, he ran and prostrated himself before him, crying, " Good Master, what shall I do that I may inherit eternal life?"

Fasten your eyes here, O frivolous youth—you that chase thistledown and butterflies while the world rolls on to judgment. Do you remember Froude's description of the young men whom Catiline gathered about him? "Smooth-faced, with curled hair and redolent with perfumes, as yet beardless or with the first down upon their chins, wearing scarves and veils and sleeved tunics reaching to their ankles, industrious but only with the dice-box, night-watchers but in the supper-rooms, in the small hours before dawn, immodest, dissolute boys, whose education had been in learning to love and to be loved, to sing and to dance at the midnight orgies." Was it a wonder that Catiline failed in his great conspiracy when his comrades and counsellors were of such a character? It was to be seen from the beginning that his effort would be a fiasco; for earnestness is ever the earnest of success; frivolity, of failure. When Cæsar saw Brutus for the first time and heard him pleading in the Forum, he said, "Yon youth is destined to make his mark, because he intends strongly." The youth who here prostrated himself before Jesus intended strongly. But, alas, there were grave difficulties in the way. The heavenward path is ever steep and rugged. Three serious mistakes he made, any one of which would have nullified his pursuit of spiritual things. It is much to be feared that together they cost him his life.

I. With respect to Christ. At this point he was an Arian. He addressed Jesus as "good Rabbi," and would probably have been willing to pronounce him the most excellent of men. But Jesus would have none of it. "Why callest thou me good?" said he; "there is none good but one, that is, God." The alternative, put in syllogistic form, was like this:

God alone is good:

Thou dost not believe me to be God;

Ergo, Call me not good.

Or,

> God alone is good :
> Thou callest me good ;
> *Ergo*, Go further and pronounce me God.

In any case, as merely a "good Rabbi," He could not receive it. The compliments of those who esteem him anything else or lower than he claimed to be are, in the nature of the case, an affront to him.

All through these eighteen hundred years there has been no lack of such vain adulation. Pilate in the act of sentencing Jesus to death pronounced him "a faultless man." Porphyry the Neo-Platonist, who rejected all his divine claims, was fond of calling him "a pious man." Spinoza, who flouted his divineness, was still willing to call him "the temple of God." The infidel Rousseau referred to him as "a man of colossal dimensions, of wonderful sweetness and purity of life." Goethe, who was possibly the most unchristian of poets, went so far as to say that Jesus "was as divine as ever the divine appeared on earth." Channing the Unitarian said, "His was a character wholly removed from human comprehension ; I know not what can be added to heighten the reverence and love due to him." Theodore Parker said, "His was the mightiest heart that ever beat in a human breast." John Stuart Mill, who can scarcely be said to have had any consistent religious belief, spoke of Jesus as "a unique figure, a man charged to lead mankind to truth and virtue." The freethinker Richter said, "Jesus was purest among the mighty and mightiest among the pure ; who with his pierced hand has raised empires from their foundations, turned the stream of history from its old channel, and still continues to rule and guide the ages." David Strauss said "he was the highest model of religion within the reach of human thought." And Ernest Renan, "We believe him to be in the front rank of the great family of the sons of God. He was an incomparable man, greater than any in the past and probably than any to come. Whatever the surprises of the future may be, Jesus of Nazareth will never be surpassed. All ages will proclaim that none greater than he has been born among the children of men." All this is adulation rendered by such as utterly rejected the divine claims of Jesus. It is robing him in mocking purple, placing in his hand an impotent reed, and crying, "Hail, O King!"

If any of you have been disposed to think of him in this manner it will be profitable to recall the amazing pretensions which were made by him as the claimant of Messianic honors. All through his ministry he insisted that he was the long-looked-for Christ, and as such the very Son of God. He arrogated to himself all the divine attributes and distinctly made himself equal with God. For this he suffered death. On the last fatal morning when he was brought into the presence of the Sanhedrin the high priest Caiaphas said to him, "I adjure you by the living God, tell us plainly whether thou art the Christ, the Son of the living God!" And Jesus answered, "I am; and ye shall, I say unto you, hereafter see the Son of man sitting on the right hand of power and coming in the clouds of heaven." (Mark 14:62.) The impression made by this avowal at the time is manifest from the fact that the high priest rent his garments, crying, "Blasphemy! blasphemy!" while the other members of the court joined in the ominous response, *Ish Maveth!* "He is worthy to die!" A little later he was brought before Pilate, that the sanction of the Roman Government might be put upon the finding of the Jewish court. Pilate in turn took him aside and asked, "Art thou the King of the Jews?" that is, Art thou Messiah, the long-promised Prince of the House of

David? And Jesus answered (using the strongest form of affirmation which was possible in those days), " Thou sayest it. But now is my kingdom not from hence. To this end was I born and for this cause came I into the world, that I might bear witness of the truth." He thus distinctly claimed to be Messiah. At mention of that claim the Jews in sudden fury cried, " Crucify him! crucify him!" Calmly Pilate answered, " Will ye crucify your Messiah?" He sent him to Golgotha apparelled like a king, and over his cross was the *titulum*, " This is Jesus, the King of the Jews." In view of these things, I say that to ascribe mere human virtues to Jesus is to fall infinitely short of the truth. Arianism is anti-Christ. He was either what he claimed to be or he was an impostor. " Good Rabbi" he certainly was not. There is no middle ground. Was Voltaire right when he cried, "*Ecrasez l'infame!*" or Peter when he said, " Thou art the Christ, the Son of the living God"?

II. The second mistake made by the young ruler was with reference to himself. At this point he was a Pelagian. He had no comprehension of his own moral character. When reminded of the commandments he said, "All these have I kept from my youth up." He had in fact kept none of them. Nor have you. Nor have I. The first of them is, *Thou shalt have no other gods before me*—no love nor passion nor ambition coming between us and the Infinite One. Let each for himself answer, Guilty or not guilty? *Thou shalt not take the name of the Lord thy God in vain*—a precept covering all forms of impiety in thought, word, or deed. Guilty or not guilty? *Remember the Sabbath day to keep it holy*. To-day is the Sabbath: have you kept it thus far? *Thou shalt not kill:* to hate one's brother without a cause is murder. *Thou shalt not commit adultery:* an unclean glance is adultery.

Thou shalt not steal. Thou shalt not lie. Thou shalt not covet. Guilty or not guilty? Ah we all alike hide our faces with shame. No one of us has kept one of the commandments!

This youth was under a sad delusion. In one of Hogarth's cartoons a demented prisoner sits in the straw, chained like a beast to his dungeon wall; but he smiles and sings as if he were the happiest of mortals. The straw is his throne, his jailers are his courtiers; he deems himself the envy of crowned kings. Not greater is his self-deception than that of the self-righteous man who deems himself worthy to appear in judgment before God. For all such the message addressed to the Laodiceans has a peculiar interest: "Because thou sayest, I am rich and increased with goods and have need of nothing, and knowest not that thou art wretched and miserable and poor and blind and naked; I counsel thee to buy of me gold tried in the fire that thou mayest be rich, and white raiment that thou mayest be clothed and that the shame of thy nakedness do not appear, and anoint thine eyes with eye-salve that thou mayest see."

III. The third mistake made by this young man was with respect to salvation. At this point he was a Legalist. "What shall I do," said he, "that I may inherit eternal life?" There was indeed nothing for him to do. Had he but known it, life is a gracious gift. If we are ever saved it will not be on account of our doing, but by God's giving. He is not a merchant that he should sell his precious wares; he is a king and gives right royally. He does indeed bow the heavens and come down; he stands at the corners of the streets, like a vendor of wares, crying, "Ho, every one that thirsteth, come ye to the waters; and he that hath no money; come ye, buy and eat; yea, come, buy wine and milk without money and without price!"

But while salvation is free it is conditioned. God who gives it has been pleased—as was his obvious right—to affix a condition upon its bestowal, to wit, *He that believeth shall live.* To believe is to accept. Faith is the hand stretched out to grasp God's grace. Salvation is free—free as air, as water, as the manna which lay like hoar-frost on the ground. But if the Israelites had not gathered up the manna they would have died of hunger. And though a man stood on the bank of the Amazon, were he to refuse to drink he would perish of thirst. There is an atmosphere fifty miles deep around this earth of ours, but a man who will not breathe must strangle. So I say salvation is free; but it saves only the man who reaches forth and takes it.

This story is called "The Great Refusal." Yonder goes the young man, turning his back on life—"very sad, for he was very rich." He loved something better than life. Whether he ever changed his mind we know not. The curtain falls; we may not lift it. The important consideration is that life is just now offered to every one of us. It is to be had for the taking. But unless we take it we shall not have it. The word of the Master comes to you as to this young man, "Go sell all that thou hast—put away everything, gold, pleasure, unholy ambition, everything that separates between thee and holiness—and come and follow Me."

OUR PASSOVER.

"Then Moses called for all the elders of Israel and said unto them,
Draw out and take you a lamb according to your families and
kill the Passover. And ye shall take a bunch of hyssop and
dip it in the blood that is in the basin and strike the lintel and
the two side posts with the blood that is in the basin; and
none of you shall go out at the door of his house until the
morning. For the Lord will pass through to smite the Egyptians; and when he seeth the blood upon the lintel and on the
two side posts, the Lord will pass over the door and will not
suffer the destroyer to come in unto your houses to smite you.
And ye shall observe this thing for an ordinance to thee and
to thy sons for ever." Exod. 12:21-24.

"For even Christ, our Passover, is sacrificed for us; therefore let us
keep the feast, not with old leaven, neither with the leaven of
malice and wickedness, but with the unleavened bread of sincerity and truth." 1 Cor. 5:7, 8.

IT is a noteworthy fact that of the sacred times and
seasons of the Old Economy we have nothing left but the
feast of the Passover. The perpetuation of that feast was
provided for and announced in its original institution; as
the Lord said, " Ye shall observe this thing for an ordinance to thee and to thy children for ever."

It is recorded that on that memorable night when Jesus
was betrayed he ate the Passover with his disciples, and
at the same time established the Holy Communion as its
successor, the broken bread representing the flesh, and
the wine the blood of the Paschal lamb. "Do this," he
said, "in remembrance of me." He thus rescued the
Passover feast from among the vanishing shadows of
the ceremonial economy, and gave it in simpler form but
with unbroken continuity a perpetual place among the

ordinances of the new dispensation. So Paul writes to the Corinthians, "Christ, our Passover, is sacrificed for us; therefore let us keep the feast with the unleavened bread of sincerity and truth."

It will be interesting to note some of the points of resemblance which seal the identity of this feast with the Eucharist of the Christian Church.

I. The original Passover feast was observed at night. It was the night of the fourteenth of Nisan. A serene calm followed the boisterous day. The land was lighted by the benignant rays of a full moon. King and people were asleep, unmindful of approaching danger. But the Hebrews were awake; lights glimmered in their homes. They had been forewarned that in their behalf the Lord was about to make bare his arm. The four hundred and thirty years of their oppression were at an end. They had passed their last day in the brick-kilns. As the night wore on a sudden light gleamed in the window of the king's chamber, and the cry of the queen-mother rang out. Death had smitten the heir-apparent to the throne! Then another cry in the beggar's hut where a wretched mother pressed her hand upon the-cold and pulseless breast of her firstborn. Presently lights were kindled in all the Egyptian homes, for the avenging Angel had breathed upon them all. A wail of mingled sorrow and anguish from ten thousand breaking hearts gave the signal to the waiting bondmen. Staff in hand they crossed the threshold, passed along the streets and out through the gates into the wilderness, then on through toil and danger and weariness to the land that flowed with milk and honey, of which the Lord had said, "Behold, I will give it you."

It was a darker night than that when our Lord hung dying on his cross. At high noon the shadows closed around him. Earth never saw so deep a darkness, nor was night ever pierced with a cry so dismal, *Eloi, Eloi, lama sabachthani!* At that moment he, bearing our sins, like the scape-goat on its way to the desert, went into the outer darkness for us. At that moment "he descended into hell" for us. His cry of abandonment was the signal of our deliverance. When his anguish had reached its utmost we, healed by his stripes, passed forth into the glorious liberty of the children of God.

II. The Passover feast was kept within doors. This was true of no other of the great festivals. At Pentecost the husbandmen with their sheaves and baskets of olives came from all directions to wave them, as their offering of first-fruits, before the altar. At the feast of Tabernacles the people, who dwelt in temporary booths upon the mountain slopes, passed along the roads and through the streets of Jerusalem waving lulab branches and shouting hosannas. But at the Passover each family was assembled within its own doors. This was preëminently the home festival; it was the Jewish Thanksgiving day, the time for the "hame-bringing," when absent sons and daughters came back and when the beloved dead were remembered. On other days the ties of kinship might be ignored, but on that day blood was always thicker than water. It was a time for praising the Lord because he hath set the solitary in families. The father presided, the children hearkened to his counsels and joined him in gratitude for the blessings of the roof-tree.

The Lord's Supper is our family feast. Here the Elder Brother takes our hands and places them in the strong grasp of the Infinite One, bidding us say after him, "Abba, Father." We here commune with one another in the household of faith and with him who is the God and Father of us all.

> "Blest be the tie that binds
> Our hearts in Christian love ;
> The fellowship of kindred minds
> Is like to that above."

III. The Lamb was at the centre of the Paschal feast. It must be a lamb of the first year and without blemish. The four days previous to the Passover were set apart for careful inspection. The lamb was placed in the hands of judicious persons, who were instructed to see that there should be no spot nor blemish in it.

By a curious coincidence the four days previous to our Lord's crucifixion were days of peculiar trial. They are known as "the days of temptation." On Monday of Passion Week the Lord made his triumphal entry into Jerusalem, was rebuked by his enemies for permitting the hosannas of the people, healed the sick, taught in the temple-porch, and was approached by certain Greeks who "desired to see him." On Tuesday he purged the temple, thereby provoking the Jewish leaders to more vigorous measures against him. On Wednesday the rabbis called his divine authority in question, and sought to entrap him by a query respecting the baptism of John. The Herodians tried him with a difficult and dangerous question as to the payment of tribute; the Sadducees sought to ensnare him in the problem of the "sevenfold widow;" and a certain lawyer tested him with reference to "the first and greatest commandment." The day closed in with a council of conspirators, among whom Judas appeared and covenanted to betray him. On Thursday he remained at Bethany beyond the immediate reach of his enemies, but came in the evening into Jerusalem to keep the Passover with his disciples. All day his enemies had been awaiting him, and when he left the upper chamber they followed him to the Garden of the Wine-press.

Thus the days of preparation, known as *the Paraskeue*, were strictly kept with respect to this Lamb slain from the foundation of the world. The eyes of many were upon him to discover any possible spot or blemish. And when the preparation was over he was led as a lamb to the slaughter, and as a sheep before her shearers is dumb, so he opened not his mouth.

IV. The blood of the Paschal sacrifice was sprinkled on the door-posts and the lintel. It was not enough that the lamb should have been slain. The head of the household must arrange for the sprinkling of the blood where the destroying Angel might see it. For so it had been promised, " When I see the blood I will pass over you." The rabbis tell, in one of their sacred books, of a sick girl who on that memorable night was troubled with apprehension lest due precautions had not been taken. She called her father to her couch, saying, " Father, I greatly fear lest the blood hath not been sprinkled on the lintels of the door. I pray thee, see to it." He laughed at her fears, but at her persistent entreaty he went and looked, and lo, his servant had neglected his task. The basin and the branch of hyssop were speedily brought, the blood was sprinkled, and the household saved.

In like manner the merits of the Saviour's blood are effective only for such as appropriate it. The lamb slain has power to save only as his blood is sprinkled on the sinful heart. He that believeth shall be saved; he that believeth not shall be damned. Faith is the condition of life. Faith is the hand that appropriates. Faith is the hyssop branch that sprinkles the lintels of the door. O beloved, I pray you see to it that the sprinkling has not been overlooked. The night is dark, the black-winged angel is above us; but we are quite secure if we have entrusted our welfare to the only-begotten Son of God.

The promise is sure: "When I see the blood, I will pass over you."

V. The lamb was eaten with bitter herbs and unleavened bread. The bitter herbs were a reminder of the toil and weariness of Egypt. The unleavened bread was a symbol of the sinless life. The two together set forth the nature and necessity of repentance. For repentance is, on the one side, sorrow for sin, and on the other, an abandonment of it. On the night of the ancient Passover it was the custom, and is still in many Jewish homes, for the head of the household to go with lighted candle searching for leaven in every nook and cranny. Leaven is the type of sin. The Egyptians used it. The Israelites were to be for ever separated from Egypt by abjuring it.

At the Lord's Supper we remember with sorrow our Lord's passion for us and with joy his breaking of our bonds. In memory of his sacrifice we renew in this *sacramentum* our vows of devotion and signify our abhorrence of and departure from sin. Wherefore Paul enjoins upon us to purge out the old leaven. "Let us keep the feast, not with old leaven, neither with the leaven of malice and wickedness, but with the unleavened bread of sincerity and truth."

I beseech you, brethren, to put aside this day every weight and the sin which doth so easily beset you. As we in repeated Eucharists cast off more and more our Egyptian bondage, let us leave farther and farther behind us the leaven with the leeks and flesh-pots. For we are called to be a separate and peculiar people. "Be not conformed to this world, but be ye transformed by the renewing of your minds, that ye may prove what is that good and acceptable and perfect will of God."

VI. The children of Israel ate their Passover with sandals on and staff in hand. They were ready for the signal of departure. It is much to be doubted whether they would have gone so cheerfully had they known what was before them—the forty years of wandering, the blazing suns, the scorching sands, the thirst and hunger, flying serpents and flaming arrows, weakness and weariness, and multitudes of graves along the way. Had they known of these, they would have thought twice ere they exchanged the brick-kilns for the wilderness. But blessed be God, the future is not revealed to us. The divine guidance is like a lantern which throws a dim light only a single step ahead. At this distance it is plain to see that the long journey of the Israelites was needful to the making of the nation. So, we may rest assured, all things are working together for our good. We are asked to bind on our sandals, uplift our banners, and march out of Egypt in the name of the living God. The life to which we are called is no sinecure, but its tasks and crosses will be adjusted to our ability. "As thy days so shall thy strength be."

> "Oh blissful lack of wisdom;
>   'T is blessed not to know;
> God holds me with his own right hand,
>   And will not let me go;
> My troubled soul is lulled to rest
>   In him who loves me so.
>
> "So on I go not knowing;
>   I would not if I might;
> I 'd rather walk in the dark with God
>   Than go alone in the light;
> I 'd rather walk by faith with him
>   Than go alone by sight."

That night when the children of Israel went out of Egypt was momentous in many ways. It meant not only the deliverance of six hundred thousand men with their women and children from a bondage that was like a living death; it meant also the building of a nation which was to uplift the torch of progress and civilization through all the future ages.   As they passed out of the Egyptian cities they threw off, avowedly, the worship of the Egyptian deities and put on loyalty to Jehovah who was thenceforth to be their only God.   The Passover marked their utter surrender of life and possessions to him.

The Eucharist is a feast of glad consecration.   Here we renounce the idols of the world and put on more and more devotion to our God.   Not long ago a foreign potentate was received with much pomp and circumstance by the Lord Mayor of London.   He came along the Strand with courtiers and attendants to Temple Bar, at the borders of the old city, where the Lord Mayor met him and delivered to him the keys of London, so signifying that he was welcome not merely to the freedom of the city but also to the custody of it.   As we at this sacramental gateway of promise pass out into the larger and better life, let us turn over the keys to our Prince.   Come in, thou Blessed One!   Come in and possess thine own.

> "Take my life and let it be
> Consecrated, Lord, to thee;
> Take my hands and let them move
> At the impulse of thy love.
>
> "Take my feet and let them be
> Swift and beautiful for thee;
> Take my voice and let me sing
> Always, only, for my King.
>
> "Take my moments and my days,
> Let them flow in endless praise;
> Take my intellect and use
> Every power as thou shalt choose.
>
> "Take my love; my God, I pour
> At thy feet its treasure store;
> Take myself, and I will be
> Ever, only, all for thee."

CHARITY THINKETH NO EVIL.

PREACHED BY DR. BURRELL MAY 8, 1892.

"Love thinketh no evil."   1 Cor. 13:5.

THIS chapter has been called "the Psalm of Love." It occurs in the midst of a spirited argument respecting the fundamental doctrines of our religion. It is like the song that was sometimes introduced in the course of a gladiatorial struggle. For a time the athletes rested while a singer in tinsel robes charmed the multitudes with flowing melody. Here however it is the athlete himself who, resting upon his blade, sings the praises of Love. For the writer it was an unusual theme. Had he pronounced a panegyric on logic or eloquence, on rhetoric or dogmatics, it would have been a matter of course; but behold, Paul the dialectician lifts his voice in eulogy of Love.

He has just been discoursing on *charismata*, or spiritual gifts. They were necessary to the church in the early, formative days. Tongues and interpretation, healing and prophecy, these were special endowments vouchsafed to the church while she was struggling for a foothold on earth. It was a blessed thing to be possessed of any of these. One of the current questions in the apostolic church was, "Which is the greatest of the *charismata?*" Paul says, "Covet earnestly the best of them, *and yet I show unto you a better way.*" The better way is Love. All other gifts are incomparable with this: for Love is the fulfilling of the law. It o'ertops all the *cha-*

rismata, outshining and surviving them all. "Now abide Faith, Hope, and Charity, but the greatest of these is Charity."

"The night has a thousand eyes, and the day but one,
  But the light of the whole world dies with the setting sun :
The mind has a thousand eyes and the heart but one,
  But the light of the whole life dies when love is done."

In this disquisition on Love the apostle names fifteen distinctive features of it. For our present purpose we select but one of these: "Love thinketh no evil." We are here advised as to the duty of looking on the bright side of character. It is an old proverb, "Faults are thick where love is thin." If we walk in the "better way" we shall not hastily impute evil, or put a wrong construction on well-meant words, or misunderstand motive or suspect the sincerity of those around us. If we walk in the "better way" we shall not gossip or backbite or give place to a censorious spirit. As far as possible we shall speak favorably of our neighbors; and as to their errors, unless a definite purpose is to be answered by an exposure, we shall prefer not to mention them.

This is not to say that love is blind to iniquity or slow, on occasion, to reprove it. The most scathing denunciation that ever was heard, "Woe unto you, scribes and Pharisees, hypocrites, how shall ye escape the damnation of hell!" fell from the lips of Incarnate Love. You remember how Hannah Dustin, held as a prisoner by the Indians in a little island of the Merrimac, rose in the middle of the night while her savage guards were sleeping, gazed on the faces of her children bound and reserved to death, then drew a tomahawk from the girdle of a sleeping brave as gently as if she were plucking a feather from the wing of a sleeping dove, and passing around the circle fiercely brained one after another until ten lay dead. It was love that nerved her arm, it was love that kindled the fire in her eyes. In like manner he who walks in the "better way" will be aggressive for the public good, will not hesitate to denounce evil in high places and low places, will "cry aloud and spare not." He who loves the youth of this city will, by the token of that love, make war unceasing on the dives and dramshops and all strongholds of iniquity. Love is the most fierce and fearless of the graces. It hates evil, and, for love of souls, it leaves nothing undone to destroy it. Because it loves the sinner it hates the sin and can make no allowance for or compromise with it.

But love has nothing in common with a censorious spirit. An habitual fault-finder is disqualified for the *role* of a reformer. Love and fault-finding are at constant variance. Love puts the best construction on everything it sees. It thinketh no evil. Let us note some of the reasons why we should as far as possible speak well of our fellow-men.

I. It is Christlike. How sympathetic and gracious and helpful he ever was! He had a kind word for the magdalen, a pitying glance for the dying thief. In one of the apocryphal Gospels it is related that a mad dog having been slain in one of the streets of Jerusalem, while the bystanders were thrusting it with their feet and finding themselves at a loss for epithets, they saw Jesus coming. His habit of kind speaking was proverbial. "Now," said they, "let us hearken what he will say of this despicable thing." He stood looking on in silence for a moment, then said, "His teeth are like pearls." Was anything lost in speaking thus graciously? Would anything have been gained by another foot-thrust? And why, beloved in Christ, should we not follow in his steps, passing kindly judgment as far as possible upon all?

II. Consider our ignorance.   Who are we that we should assume to know what passes in a human breast? How little we understand the conditions, the environment, the sore temptations, of those who fall into sin.

> "O ye wha are sae guid yoursel',
>   Sae pious and sae holy,
> Ye 've nought to do but mark and tell
>   Your neebor's fauts and folly;
> Whase life is like a weel-gaun mill,
>   Supplied wi' store o' water,
> The heapèd happer 's ebbing still,
>   And still the clap plays clatter.
>
> "Then gently scan your brother man,
>   Still gentler sister woman;
> Though each may gang a kennin' wrang,
>   To step aside is human.
> One point must still be greatly dark,
>   The moving why they do it;
> And just as lamely can ye mark
>   How far perhaps they rue it.
>
> "Who made the heart, 't is He alone
>   Decidedly can try us;
> He knows each chord—its various tone,
>   Each spring—its various bias:
> Then at the balance let 's be mute;
>   We never can adjust it;
> What 's done we partly may compute,
>   But know not what 's resisted."

We speak of justice, but what do we know of it? "Vengeance is mine, saith the Lord; I will repay." How many and lamentable are our mistakes whenever we undertake to administer justice.   We sometimes try offenders by lynch law and hang them up at eventide only to discover before break-of-day that we have hung the wrong man.   And, alas, it is too late to cut him down.

The ruin is done. Of justice we know little or nothing. Let us leave that to an omniscient God. Our function is with mercy. That falls measurably within our sphere of knowledge, and we are safe to administer it. But to speak as if we were sitting on the wool-sack is to be vastly presumptuous. It is falling into the error of Phaeton who sought, unskilled, to drive the chariot of the sun.

III. We work incalculable injury by our uncharitable treatment of others. There are people who would not prick their neighbors with a bodkin, yet do not hesitate, as Swift says, to

> "Convey a libel with a frown,
> And wink a reputation down."

They would not steal a farthing, but rob their neighbors without scruple of that which is better than life.

> "Good name in man or woman, dear my lord,
> Is the immediate jewel of their souls.
> Who steals my purse steals trash ; 't is something, nothing ;
> 'T was mine, 't is his, and has been slave to thousands ;
> But he that filches from me my good name
> Robs me of that which not enriches him
> And makes me poor indeed."

It is related that when the martyr Taylor was dying at the stake one of the bystanders cast a flaming torch which struck his eyes and blinded them "and brake his face that the blood ran down his visage." This was base, cowardly, brutal beyond words. But it was not more base, more brutal, or more cowardly than to injure a man in his reputation, to put him to an open shame by blackening his honor. This is the very climax of inhumanity; baseness can no further go.

IV. We live in glass houses. The old proverb, " People who live in glass houses should not throw stones," had its origin in our Master's words respecting the woman taken in adultery.   The Rabbis had dragged her up the temple steps and cast her upon the pavement, saying, "Moses in the law commandeth that such shall be stoned, but what sayest thou?"   He stooped for a moment in silence and seemed to be writing on the marble floor, then quietly said, "Let him that is without blame among you cast the first stone."   Why do n't they throw?   O master of Israel with the broad phylacteries, so circumspectly pious, cast thou a stone at her!   O venerable Sanhedrist, having the law written upon thy frontlets, against whom no breath of calumny has ever come, why dost thou falter?   Cast thou a stone at her!   O illustrious priest, minister at God's altar lo, these many years, famed for thy immaculateness, why is thy face flushed with sudden crimson, and wherefore dost thou not cast a stone?   It is written that they which heard the Master's word, being convicted by their own conscience, went out one by one, beginning at the eldest even unto the last.

We are none of us any better than the law requires, none of us any better than we ought to be.   We have all sinned and come short of the divine glory ; and, strange to tell, the faults which we are most prone to criticise in others are those which are most deeply seated in ourselves. Tell me the general drift of a man's aspersions and I will show you his darling sin.   It would be prudent in us all to take advantage of that provision which in courts of justice excuses a witness from testifying against a culprit when to do so would incriminate himself.   It takes a rogue to catch a rogue.   All captious criticism is in the nature of State's evidence.   "Why beholdest thou the mote that is in thy brother's eye, but considerest not the beam that is in thine own eye?   Or how wilt thou say to thy brother, Let me pull out the mote out of thine eye, and behold a beam is in thine own eye?   Thou hypocrite, first cast out the beam out of thine own eye, and then shalt thou see clearly to cast out the mote out of thy brother's eye."

V. We are on our way to Judgment. And here we are making the rule which will apply to ourselves at that great day. "Judge not," said the Master, "that ye be not judged. For with what judgment ye judge ye shall be judged, and with what measure ye mete it shall be measured to you again." We may have what we will at the Great Assize, mercy or justice. If we here minister justice it will there be ministered unto us. But, blessed be God, heaven is full of mercy, if we will have it. The Moslems say that two spirits are set to guard the actions of every man. At night they fly up to heaven and report to the recording angel. The one says, "He hath wrought this good, O angel! Write it ten times!" The other says, "He hath wrought this evil; but forbear, O angel, yet seven hours, in order that he may repent!" It is true that God delighteth in mercy. But if we want it we must here accord it.

How otherwise may we offer the prayer, "Forgive us our trespasses as we forgive those who trespass against us"? How otherwise can we with heart and understanding sing,

> " Teach me to feel another's woe,
> To hide the fault I see;
> The mercy I to others show,
> That mercy show to me."

VI. In dealing ungraciously with others we lose the blessed opportunity of kindness. There is no telling what good may be done by a word of sympathy and helpfulness, one of those "words in due season" which are like apples of gold in pictures of silver.

In the prison at New Bedford there is a man serving out a life sentence who some years ago had a strange experience. He had previously been regarded as one of the most desperate and dangerous inmates. He had planned outbreaks and mutinies and been repeatedly punished in vain. His heart was full of bitterness. But one day in June a party of strangers came to visit the institution, an old man with several ladies and one little girl. It happened that this prisoner had just been assigned for some misdemeanor to the menial task of scrubbing the corridor. The warden, leading the visitors about, saw him, sulky and morose, at the top of the stairway. "Jim," he called, "come and carry this little girl up." The convict scowled and hesitated. The little girl at the foot of the stairway held out her arms and said, "If you will, I 'll kiss you." He looked at her seriously a moment, then slowly came down, and lifting her upon his shoulders as tenderly as any father could have done, carried her to the upper corridor. She raised her face. He gravely stooped and kissed it, then returned to his task. And they say at the New Bedford jail that he has never been the same man since that day. The kindness of that child in some way transformed his life.

The meanest of proverbs is, *De mortuis nil nisi bonum.* It were even better to say, "Speak only good of the living." A word of encouragement to a living man is worth the best Latin epitaph that ever was carved on a granite shaft. A blossom put into a living hand is better than the treasures of all the conservatories laid on a mound in Greenwood. This was the substance of our Lord's teaching when he said of the woman who broke the alabaster-box of ointment, "Let her alone. She hath anointed me aforetime for my burial." Oh for more of the aforetime anointing! Oh for more of kindness towards those who are bearing the heat and burden of life's busy day!

There are some of you who remember Blondin. In making his dangerous journey along the wire stretched below the Falls of Niagara he sometimes carried a man upon his back. The shores were lined with spectators. Did they shout and applaud when they saw him poised above the abyss? Did they loudly reprove his folly? Did they obtrude unnecessary counsel upon him? If he stumbled and seemed to lose his balance, wavering for an instant, what then? Ah, they held their breath! Their very hearts stood still! Every one of us on life's journey bears his burden, oftentimes so heavy as to tax his utmost strength, along a path as narrow and dangerous as the sword-blade in the dream of Mirza. Every one of us needs the kindly word, the helping hand. Oh for the spirit of charity! All the graces have done virtuously, but thou, O Charity, excellest them all!

ON THE STORMY SEA.

PREACHED BY DR. BURRELL MAY 15, 1892.

"They that go down to the sea in ships, that do business in great
waters, these see the works of the Lord and his wonders in
the deep. For he commandeth and raiseth the stormy wind,
which lifteth up the waves thereof. They mount up to the
heaven, they go down again to the depths: their soul is melted because of trouble. They reel to and fro and stagger like
a drunken man, and are at their wits' end. Then they cry
unto the Lord in their trouble, and he bringeth them out of
their distresses. He maketh the storm a calm, so that the waves
thereof are still. Then are they glad because they be quiet;
so he bringeth them unto their desired haven. Oh that men
would praise the Lord for his goodness and for his wonderful
works to the children of men!" Psa. 107:23-31.

In 1830 the ship " Lady Holland " on her way to India
struck on a bar stretching out from the Cape of Good
Hope, and after making a brave struggle went to pieces.
All the passengers were saved. Among them was Alexander Duff, on his way to missionary work among the
Hindoos. Everything that he possessed in the world had
gone down with the ship, including a library of eight hundred volumes. As he walked along the shore drenched
and discouraged he caught sight of a book which had
been washed in by the waves. It was a Bible, the sole
remnant of his precious library. He opened it at this
" Traveller's Psalm " and read, " Oh that men would praise
the Lord for his goodness and for his wonderful works to
the children of men!" The words made a profound impression upon him and were an inspiration to all his sub-

sequent life. He knew thereafter many periods of trial and difficulty, but never one of despondency. When the winds were fierce his heart recurred to the Traveller's Psalm. It may be that there are some here whose hearts are sore and weary. If so, God give them comfort out of his blessed Word and help them to join us in singing, " Oh that men would praise the Lord for his goodness and for his wonderful works to the children of men !"

Life is here portrayed in six picturesque panels.

First: The ship sails forth. As it is written, " They that go down to the sea in ships, that do business in great waters, these see the works of the Lord and his wonders in the deep."

Our life is a voyage. We all go down to the sea in ships, to a life of mystery and danger, of glorious privilege and responsibility. We set out with high hopes and splendid aspirations. The skies are fair, the winds favorable, the waters smooth. We look down into the clear depths and dream dreams; we gaze up into the overarching blue and see visions. Our hearts are full of happiness as of new wine. Ah it is a glorious thing to live ! Praise God for the exuberance of youth, for bright days, for life's commencement under the rainbow arch of promise ! Far be it from us to reprove the young for their merry-making. Rejoice, O young man, but *remember !* Be mindful of the sublime things. Be mindful of immortality and of the Judgment ! Let your gladness be as sweet and harmless as the laughter of a child. Rejoice ! but *remember* that when life's pleasures are over there are sweeter pleasures at God's right hand for evermore.

Far yonder is a fleck on the horizon—a mere bit of floating fleece, a puff of rising mist. Does it portend trouble ? What matter ? What matter if the heart be right and the conscience clean ? Yet look to the sheets, the cordage, the anchors! It is well to be ready for whatever may chance upon the open sea.

Second: The wind rises. As it is written, "He commandeth and raiseth the stormy wind, which lifteth up the waves thereof."

Has it come to you already? Has there been a turn in your prosperity? Are things going wrong? Is it sickness, bereavement, financial stringency? Are the winds whistling through the cordage? Fear not! God holds the trident; the winds are in his fist. Trouble springeth not up out of the ground. God reigns. God rules and overrules. There are some anchors that will hold in the fiercest stress of Euroclydon. One is the Wisdom of God. There is nothing that happens without his cognizance. No storm comes haphazard. God understands the end from the beginning; and *he makes no mistakes.* Another is God's Goodness. He doth not afflict willingly. Whom the Lord loveth he chasteneth, and scourgeth every son whom he receiveth. But never too much. "He sitteth as a refiner of silver." The fire shall never burn too fiercely. Let him but see his image on the molten metal and it sufficeth. Pain and trouble must work together for our good. And another is God's Omnipotence. He is able in our behalf to do whatsoever he will; the opposing spirits of earth and hell cannot thwart him.

> "The Lord our God is clothed with might,
>   The winds obey his will;
> He speaks, and in his heavenly height
>   The rolling sun stands still.
>
> "His voice sublime is heard afar,
>   In distant peals it dies;
> He yokes the whirlwind to his car
>   And sweeps the troubled skies.

> "Howl, winds of night, your force combine;
>   Without his high behest
> Ye shall not in the mountain pine
>   Disturb the sparrow's nest."

Third: The sailors are at their wits' end. "Their soul is melted because of trouble. They reel to and fro and stagger like a drunken man, and are at their wits' end."

In the margin it is, "All their wisdom is swallowed up." Then there is hope! For when I am weak, then am I strong. My strength is made perfect in weakness. Most gladly let me glory in my infirmities, that the power of Christ may rest upon me. No man is ever ready to be saved until his own wisdom is all swallowed up. The prodigal was content to abide in the far country until his last farthing was spent, his last garment pawned, and he a menial in a swine-field, coveting the husks which the swine did eat. Then visions of home came before him— the riches of his father's house, the loaded table, the laughter, the merry-making. "Why should I perish of hunger?" he cried. "I will arise and go to my father!" Jacob was never submissive to the divine purposes concerning him until one night, alone, he wrestled with a supernatural Athlete, and fell down crippled, worsted, but victorious. He triumphed through his weakness, and was blessed in his humility as he never could have been in self-conscious power. The dying thief was not salvable until he found himself at his wits' end; his feet nailed, so that they could run no more into evil; his hands nailed, so that they could no more be stretched forth in his own behalf. Then, dying and desperate, he prayed, "Lord, remember me!"

It is related of William Brown, who died at Smithfield, that at the last moment, while the flames were consuming him, he, looking for a friendly face and finding none, asked one of his priestly executioners to pray for him. "I will no more pray for thee," was the answer, "than for a mangy dog." Then the martyr, being at his wit's end, cried, "Son of God, I have none beside thee; shine thou upon me!" And at that moment, tradition says, the sun shone full upon his face, and so remained until he yielded up the ghost. Oh blessed are they whose wisdom is all swallowed up, and who as to self-righteousness and self-confidence are utterly at their wits' end. For man's extremity is God's opportunity.

Fourth: They are on their knees. "Then they cry unto the Lord in their trouble, and he bringeth them out of their distresses."

Our Lord said that men ought always to pray and not to faint. But alas, men do not always pray. They will not. But they pray when the storm breaks. There are men in this company, doubtless, who have not prayed to-day, who have not offered a prayer perhaps for years. But if the death-angel were to walk through this aisle and lay his hand upon them, saying, "The hour is come!" every one would fall upon his knees in an instant, crying, "God, have mercy!"

And, strange to tell, God is willing to hear even the cry of desperation. He is of great loving-kindness and forbearance. For some men prayer is their vital breath, their native air. To others it is like the bell in the coal-mine, used only in time of danger. If the cord be pulled it says to the watcher at the shaft's mouth, "Fire-damp! Come!" So is the prayer that ascends to God in sudden exigencies. How many there are who, having forgotten God in their prosperity, remember him when driven in flight like a partridge upon the mountains. Then they pray and God hears. "This poor man cried, and the Lord heard and saved him out of all his trouble."

"There is an eye that never sleeps
    Beneath the wing of night;
There is an ear that never shuts
    When sink the beams of light.

"There is an arm that never tires
    When human strength gives way;
There is a love that never fails
    When earthly loves decay.

"That eye is fixed on seraph throngs;
    That arm upholds the sky;
That ear is filled with angel songs;
    That love is throned on high.

"But there's a power which man can wield
    When mortal aid is vain,
That eye, that arm, that love to reach,
    That listening ear to gain.

"That power is prayer, which soars on high,
    Through Jesus, to the throne,
And moves the hand which moves the world,
    To bring salvation down."

Fifth: The storm is assuaged. " He maketh the storm a calm, so that the waves thereof are still. Then are they glad because they be quiet."

How calm it is whenever Christ lifts his hands over the raging sea. How pains and sorrows flee at his word, Peace, be still!

The rule, after all, is fair weather. The storm, rage it never so fiercely, will soon be spent. Our "light afflictions" are "but for a moment." Weeping may endure for a night, but joy cometh in the morning. How many will lie down on sleepless beds to-night. Their nerves will be tingling, their hearts will be aching. Oh the pain of insomnia! Their griefs and troubles come like ghosts, gigantic in the night-time, shaking their gaunt fingers at them. They cannot sleep. They toss from side to side and moan, "Would God it were morning!" They rise and sit by the window, their hot eyes cooled by the grateful night air. Yonder the last star is fading. The first beams of the sun appear. A golden glory is shining through the gray. Arrows of crimson light shoot up into the heavens. The mists are flying. The birds begin to sing. The flush of the morning now suffuses all. The dew is glistening on the grass and "jocund Day stands tiptoe on the mountain-tops." It always comes. There is no night without a dawn. This is the gracious ordinance of both nature and grace. Weeping may endure for a night, but joy cometh in the morning.

Sixth and finally: The ship sails in. "So he bringeth them unto their desired haven. Oh that men would praise him for his goodness and for his wonderful works to the children of men!"

On April 2, 1513, Ponce de Leon, cruising in the Gulf of Mexico in search of an imaginary island which he was to christen *Bimini* when he should discover it, came in sight of the mainland. Never had a vision of such glorious beauty greeted his eyes. The land was in its vernal splendor. The melody of birds filled the air. The perfume of gardens floated far out to sea. The palm-trees were waving their fronds as if in welcome. Eight days he cruised along these shores, and then landing, planted the Red Cross banner. And he christened the land not Bimini but Florida—the Land of Flowers. But what, think you, will the shores of Canaan be like when, after a stormy voyage, we by God's grace come sailing in? Oh sweet music of angels and archangels, greeting us from afar! Oh rare odors of the King's gardens! Oh light of the great throne flooding and suffusing all! Oh welcome voices of saints triumphant whom here we loved and lost a while! In that day the sorest troubles of the earthly life will seem insignificant as we look back upon them. We shall understand then what the apostle meant when he called our afflictions "light" and spoke of them as "enduring but for a moment." It will be in our hearts to bless God for all the storms and the trials. Our song will be, "Oh that men would praise the Lord for his goodness and for his wonderful works to the children of men!"

> "Safe home, safe home in port!
> Rent cordage, shattered deck,
> Torn sails, provisions short,
> And only not a wreck;
> But oh the joy upon the shore
> To tell our voyage perils o'er!"

Not long ago, on entering my study I found a man awaiting me with his face buried in his hands. He looked up and said, "I am in desperate trouble; I must have help or die." A letter has recently come to me, undated and unsigned, beginning with these words, "My heart is breaking; pray for me." It may be that there is some one in this company in desperate trouble—some one whose heart is breaking. It may be that there is a wanderer here who from a pleasant home, a mother's love, a family circle of prayer, has gone away into the far country and wasted his substance. Perhaps there is one whose soul is troubled with "a certain fearful looking for of judgment." The heart knoweth its own bitterness. Each of us bears his own burden. But, friend, whatever yours may be, God is here and ready to help. Earth has no sorrow that heaven cannot heal. The light from the Cross, where the kind Father has manifested his love towards all the sorrowing and the lost, falls helpfully and graciously over us. Let us believe in Him. Let us believe that He is and that he is the rewarder of all that diligently seek him. Let us believe that having spared not his only-begotten and well-beloved Son, he will with him freely give us all things. Is thy heart sore, my brother? Has the storm burst upon thee? Look to the heavens! ˙ God is our refuge and strength, a very present help in trouble. Therefore will not we fear, though the earth be removed, and though the mountains be carried into the midst of the sea; though the waters thereof roar and be troubled, though the mountains shake with the swellings thereof. There is a river, the streams whereof shall make glad the city of God, the Holy Place of the tabernacles of the Most High. God is in the midst of her; she shall not be moved : God shall help her and that right early. The Lord of Hosts is with us; the God of Jacob is our refuge.

THE
SILENT ARCHITECT.

PREACHED BY DR. BURRELL MAY 22, 1892.

"And the house was built of stone made ready before it was brought thither: so that there was neither hammer nor axe nor any tool of iron heard in the house while it was in building."

1 Kings 6:7.

WHEN the children of Israel had ended their wanderings and were settled in the land of promise it would naturally occur to them at once to build a temple in honor of the God who had guided them for forty years by his pillar of cloud. But for many reasons this was not to be. The times were inauspicious and the people were unprepared for it. At first they were employed in driving out the aboriginal tribes, and it was not in the nature of things that temple walls should rise amid the turmoil of strife. Then came the period of the judges. But who among them was fitted for the task? Gideon, marshalling the clans of Abi-ezra with his trumpet blast? Jephthah dragging the vanquished princes of the children of Ammon at his chariot wheels? Samson shouting out his fierce battle song? Shamgar with his ox-goad? Nay, all these were bloody men. Then came the period of the kings. But where among them was the architect? Saul reading battle omens in the witch's cave? David girding on his armor for Baal-perazim? During these reigns the air was laden with the stench of carcasses and the roads were red with bloody footprints. It did indeed occur to David that he ought not to dwell in a house of cedar while the Ark of the Lord was within curtains. But when he purposed to build a house for God that should be exceedingly magnifical, his plan was interrupted by the divine voice saying, " Thou shalt not build me an house to dwell in, because thou hast been a man of war." The holy fabric must be raised by bloodless hands in quiet days. At length, five hundred years after the exodus, in the reign of Solomon, there came a season of absolute rest. " In the fourth year of his reign were the foundations of the house laid and in the eleventh year was the house finished throughout in all parts thereof. So he was seven years in building it." Never were grander preparations, never a more magnificent temple—simple, beautiful, from massive foundation stones to fine-twined curtains. And all was divinely planned. The basilica of St. Peter's bears the impress of the mind of Michael Angelo; St. Paul's at London of the mind of Sir Christopher Wren; but the temple on Zion was projected and reared by the Architect of the universe; and in wondrous beauty it was not unworthy of him. During the period of its erection there was peace throughout the land. Silently, majestically, its walls rose towards heaven "without the sound of hammer or of axe," for its stones had been chiselled at the quarry and its beams had been fitted to their places amid the forests of Lebanon. There was no busy hum or clamor, no echo of implements among the rising timbers, no voice of the mason calling to the carpenter, no running to and fro. It was like a grand Sabbath service.

> "No workman's steel, no ponderous axes swung;
> Like some tall pine the noiseless fabric sprung."

And this is God's method everywhere—in nature, in history, and in grace. He walks with stately steppings.

He performs his tasks in quiet patience as if ever mindful that the eternal years are his.

I. *In nature.* When he created the heavens and the earth there was heard no sound of hammer or axe. The slow revolving ages, the six grand epochs with their alternate lights and shadows, graduated one into the other, marking off his successive creative acts.

We speak of the creative *fiat* as if God did, with an audible voice, call out of nothing the things which are.

> " He said, Let there be light !
> Grim Darkness felt His might
> And fled away.
> Then startled seas and mountains cold
> Shone forth all clad in blue and gold
> And cried, 'T is day ! 't is day !"

Not so : there was no audible voice. The *fiat* is but a figure of speech. In fact the beginning of Light may have been in the trembling of a dim electric force occasioned by atomic friction. Long æons may have passed before the first beams of the heavenly luminaries shone through the lifting clouds of vapor. Slowly the darkness faded into twilight, the twilight into dawn, until at length the earth was flooded with the splendor of day.

And God said, " Let the dry land appear." He might indeed have wrought it with a word. He might indeed have summoned the continents and islands as a captain calls the muster-roll of his army ; and they would have come crowding to meet him, shouldering each other aside like the lost titans in Dante's Sea of Ice. In fact, however, the beginning of the dry land was in the slow upheavals and crumblings and noiseless convulsions of primitive chaos. What if a million years were needed for the laying of a single stratum ? The splintered obelisks and pinnacles of the Alps have been wrought by th . imperceptible might of the atmosphere, by the slow action of frost and sun. God might have tossed them up with his right arm. But to him a thousand years are as a single day. Not the avalanche, but the glacier that moves so slowly as to seem immovable, is the apt figure of his stupendous power. "Hast thou not known, hast thou not heard, that the everlasting God, the Creator of the ends of the earth, fainteth not neither is weary?" He is never restless, never in haste. In the depths of the ocean there are numberless infinitesimal creatures at work, each living but a day and when it dies leaving a tiny shell as its monument. Generations come and go, accomplishing their tasks with only the patient eyes of God and the sleepless stars to watch them. Centuries pass by, incalculable æons; and then from the bottom of the sea there emerges the outline of a coral reef. Thus God makes the dry land appear. There is no sound of hammer or axe. But what a temple to the glory of the Ancient of Days!

In the processes of nature there are three factors: *First:* Force, an infinitely impressive something which defies definition. Force is "whatever sets matter in motion." But the word "whatever" suggests the problem. An apple falls from the bough. We say it falls by the force of gravitation. But what is that? A tree is shattered by a bolt of lightning; we call it electrical force; but what is that? A mushroom grows up in the night; the power within is vital force; but what is that? The fact is obvious; but who shall explain it?

Second: Law. Force works through law. We are compassed about by law. With a silent presence it envelopes us. We call for a miracle, a sign with a sound. But a miracle is not above law or beyond it. A miracle is simply force working through law without the intervention of second causes. The miracle of Cana is as silent as the distillations of the vineyard. When Joseph feeds the multitude from the storehouses of Egypt, the outrunners announce him and the people hail him " Zaphenath-Paneah! O Saviour of the world." But when God goes forth to feed the nations of the earth there are no acclamations. Not a seed germinates except as he guards and fosters it. The fields grow yellow under his care. He sends the loaded wains to the waiting granaries. He spreads our tables everywhere. But not a voice declares his goodness until the grace is said, " For what we now receive the Lord make us truly thankful."

Third: Mind. Here we touch the argument from design. That the forces which operate through law are superintended by an infinite Intellect is attested by the adjustment of all things to their uses: the eye to seeing, the eagle's wing to mounting aloft, the nightingale's throat to melody. If I place an æolian harp in my window I can tell from the result whether or no an intellect controls it. If it produces only a mingling of sweet sounds without a theme, I say, The wind blows through it; but if there be a theme in the melody, I say, A human hand has touched it. In like manner as I look abroad in nature I behold everywhere the convincing proofs of a superintending intellect—*Anima Mundi*, the Soul of the World. This God does not cry aloud nor lift up his voice, but in impressive silence he manifests himself. How noiselessly the world passes over from summer to winter, from seedtime to harvest. Who ever heard the opening of a rose-bud or the falling of snowflake? In the phenomena of nature the rule is quiet. If we travel on the railway at the rate of sixty miles an hour, our ears are filled with the noise of hissing steam and rumbling wheels, and we are in momentary dread of burning axles, derailment, or collision : we cling to the seats in terror of life. But we are living on a world that rolls through space at the rate of sixty thousand miles an hour; yet in the midst of this tremendous whirl we can hear an infant's wail, the singing of a bird, the beating of our hearts !

II. *In history.* We speak of Providence. By this, again, we understand a force working through law under the supervision of an infinite Mind. All the world's a stage indeed. Tragedies are being enacted everywhere; but no crier reads the prologue, no chorus explains between the acts, no bell rings down the curtain. The profoundest episodes in the life of men and nations are without scenic effect.

We are accustomed to speak of the epochs of history. There are none; or, in any case, the real epochs are not those which are marked by uproar and confusion and garments rolled in blood. The landing of Cæsar with his hosts in Britain was not so significant an event as the landing of St. Augustine bearing a white Christ on a silver cross. The marching forth to the Crusades of Richard Cœur de Lion was not so important in its ultimate issues as the quiet demand of Stephen Langton in the meadow at Runnymede. The victories of Drake upon the high seas were of less real moment than the embarking of a few pilgrims from Delft Haven in search of religious freedom. The charge of the Light Brigade at Balaklava was not so worthy of immortality in song as the play of a bare-legged lad in an English village, who at about that time was making clay engines furnished with hemlock sticks for pipes. The best history of Anglo-Saxon civilization is Green's " History of the English People," which is constructed on the assumption that the victories of peace are more renowned than those of war.

The most memorable event that ever occurred on earth,

out of which flowed the issues of universal life and immortality, was celebrated only by a mother's cradle-song and the angels' anthem, " Glory to God in the highest !" The earthly life and ministry of Jesus were characterized by the same absence of display. Their theatre was a carpenter's shop, an upper chamber, an accursed tree. No hosts were marshalled around him, no banners waved above him. It had been prophesied, " He shall not cry nor lift up his voice in the streets." In his death he was led as a lamb to the slaughter, and as a sheep before her shearers is dumb, so he opened not his mouth. Living and dying he was true to his name, Shiloh, Prince of Peace. His church in like manner—fair as the moon, clear as the sun, and terrible as an army with banners—has conquered thus far by a silent force as irresistible as her Lord's right arm. She wields no sword but the sword of the Spirit, sheds no blood but her own, rears no standard but the Red Cross; yet with these she has triumphed over thrones and dominions, banns and interdicts, the violence of flame, the Prince of Darkness, the gates of hell. All along the pages of history is written this parable, " The Kingdom of Heaven is like to a grain of mustard-seed, which a man took and sowed in his field; which indeed is the least of all seeds; but when it is grown it is the greatest among herbs, and becometh a tree, so that the birds of the air come and lodge in the branches thereof." As the seed germinates in silence, and as all the benignant influences of air and earth and water are made to minister unto it, so the Church, which is God's Kingdom among men, is fostered by his care, and will of a certainty in due time fill the earth with his glory as the waters cover the deep. But this kingdom cometh not with observation. No man can say, Lo here! or, Lo there! The victories of truth and righteousness are celebrated with less of pomp and pageantry than was a triumph of a petty centurion in the ancient times.

III. *In the soul of man.* Here we are in the province of grace. By grace we understand, again, a force inscrutable, working through law mysterious, under the superintendence of a Mind Infinite. The beginning of the Christian life is commonly without observation. It is true that Saul of Tarsus was felled to the earth, blinded by a sunburst, and addressed by a voice from heaven. But even of this case it is written, " Those that were with him saw the light but heard not the voice." The operation of the Spirit in the human heart is not with violence. He cometh down as rain upon the mown grass. To the majority of believers their passing out of darkness into the light is as when a traveller crosses the tropics; he cannot mark the instant. We are not scourged but wooed into the divine arms. "I have drawn thee," he says, "with the cords of a man;" that is, with leading-strings.

> "I heard the voice of Jesus say,
>   'Come unto me and rest;
> Lay down, thou weary one, lay down
>   Thy head upon my breast.'
>
> "I came to Jesus as I was—
>   Weary and worn and sad;
> I found in him a resting-place,
>   And he has made me glad."

And all the subsequent life of the Christian is passed under the same gentle influence. Our sanctification is like the shining light that shineth more and more unto the perfect day. As of old, the Lord is not in the wind that rends in pieces the rocks, nor in the earthquake, nor in the fire, but in the still small voice. To the beasts of the field and cattle and creeping things, to the rolling worlds, the lightning, the tempest, he says, Go! and they obey him. But to his children he says, "Come now, let us reason together." Thus he stoops to conquer. The symbol of his Spirit is a brooding dove. Our gracious God would build up our souls into temples fit for his indwelling; but he would build without the sound of hammer or of axe.

He comes to us this day, not blowing a trumpet at our gates, but waiting upon our scant courtesy. I pray you, grieve him not. The fears and relentings, the hopes that are stirring within you, are kindled by his Spirit. At this moment a slender thread is let down from heaven along which runs the electric current of everlasting life. You may put it aside if you will—alas, how easily! Or you may take hold of it and be thrilled and quickened as by a breath from the flaming lips of God. O Thou that standest waiting, thy locks wet with the morning dew, waiting in silence patiently at our closed doors, enter this day and spread thy table of wine and manna—the wine of consolation, the hidden manna of thy peace—and sup thou with us!

THE TRUE KNIGHT.

PREACHED BY DR. BURRELL MAY 29, 1892.

" Thou therefore endure hardness as a good soldier of Jesus Christ."
2 Tim. 2:3.

IN the year 1094 A. D. a man of dwarfish stature, robed and tonsured, might have been seen riding upon an ass through the thoroughfares north of the Alps. He had been at one time a soldier in the army of Boulogne, but, moved with penitence for deeds of blood, had retired to a cloister. As time passed rumors came to him of infamous deeds wrought by Moslems at the holy sepulchre, and at his devotions he fumbled at his rosary as if it were a sword-hilt. The passing herald told at the monastery gate how Christian pilgrims had been seized and immured in dungeons or sold into a bondage worse than death—whereat the old martial passion shot from under his cavernous brows. He could endure this life of dreamy devotion no longer. Voices came to him from over the sea calling for help. He mounted and rode forth. His head and feet were bare; in his hand he carried a white Christ on a cross. Passing through the hamlets and villages he told the story of the Christian captives and of the Lord's sepulchre. His auditors responded with sobs and groans and vehement protestations. " To the rescue!" he cried. " *Deus vult!* It is God's will!" He tore his red scarf into cross-shaped fragments, which his followers affixed to their breasts. They grew in numbers as he passed from town to town until sixty thousand were riding after him.

Thus under Peter the Hermit began the Crusades, that strange movement in which were enlisted some of the noblest spirits that ever unsheathed a sword. There was Robert of Flanders; there was Tancred the Good; there were St. Louis and Cœur de Lion and Godfrey of Bouillon and St. Bernard and Blondel the minstrel—the time would fail me to tell of the mighty ones who won immortal fame in the marches and conflicts of those days.

> "Their bones are dust,
>   Their good swords rust;
>   Their souls are with the saints, we trust."

A vindication of the Crusades at every point is not to our present purpose; we have to do with the permanent heritage they have left us in the name and character of the True Knight. His ambition was to be "without fear and without reproach"—a good soldier of Jesus Christ.

For this knight of the olden time was distinctly and preëminently a Christian. The initiatory rites of his order were celebrated within the sacred confines of the church. All night he prayed, and received the sacrament at break of day. With the cross upon his bosom and the oriflamme waving above him he went forth singing—

> "Fairest Lord Jesus,
>   Ruler of all nature,
> O Thou of God and man the Son,
>   Thee will I cherish,
>   Thee will I honor,
> Thou my soul's glory, joy, and crown!

> "Fair are the meadows,
>   Fairer still the woodlands,
> Robed in the blooming garb of spring;
>   Jesus is fairer,
>   Jesus is purer,
> Who makes the woful heart to sing.

> "Fair is the sunshine,
>   Fairer still the moonlight
> And the twinkling starry host;
>   Jesus shines brighter,
>   Jesus shines purer,
> Than all the angels heaven can boast."*

The character of the true knight is set forth in the chivalric star, a star of five points, each representing a chivalric grace. To these let us address our thought.

I. *First of knightly qualities is Truth*—truth that expresses itself not merely in ingenuous words but in a character of transparent honesty. Its word is *esse, non videri;* to be, not seem to be. For a falsehood may be told with a nod or wink, the lifting of the brows or beckoning of the hand, as well as in articulate speech. It is much to be feared that one of our besetting sins is disingenuousness. "'T is as easy as lying," quoth Hamlet. But a true man shrinks from every shape and form of it. His character is truthfulness itself. When the Commons demanded of Charles I. that to a certain promise he should give them his royal word, he answered, "Nay, but I will give you somewhat stronger and surer, the word of a Christian Knight."

II. *The second of the chivalric graces is Purity.* An old writer in setting forth the knightly character says among other things, "Nothing he cometh upon is to him common or unclean, because there is no mordant in his nature for an evil thing." This "mordant" was the chemical factor used in a dye-vat to make the colors fast. It is derived from a Latin word signifying to eat or bite. A true man has nothing in him to grasp, to apprehend, to appropriate a low or common thing. This is the prime

---

* This hymn from the German, "Schönster Herr Jesu," sung by the Crusaders of the twelfth century, has come into new popularity in recent years.

quality of a gentleman. He not merely avoids the grosser contacts of impurity; he shrinks from it with an instinctive disrelish and repugnance, as the sensitive plant trembles and withdraws itself from an unfriendly touch.

III. *The third of the manly graces is Courtesy.* This is something above fine breeding. It is something more than common culture. You cannot get it from a " Handbook of Etiquette." Sir Philip Sydney defines it as "high thoughts seated in a soul of honor." It is a large and manly grace. Its other name is magnanimity. It is the going out of soul in a large sympathy towards all. It is the finest expression of the Golden Rule. I know not where to find a better illustration of it than in the case of two rough sailors who were once walking in a seaside town. No one would have taken them for gentlemen by any test of outward garb or graceful carriage. As they rolled along on their sea legs, gazing and wondering, a thing happened which suddenly fastened their attention. A funeral came down the street—four bearers carrying the dead upon a bier. There were no mourners, no friends or kindred. The sailors looked into each other's faces, silently read each other's thoughts, then stepped into the street, fell into line, and went following after the friendless dead. That was the prompting of true courtesy; and rude and homely as those sailors seemed, they were possessed of the truest instincts of gentlemen.

IV. *A fourth of these manly graces is Patience.* It is indeed the drudge of the graces, the Cinderella of them all. And yet there is something strong and admirable in it. We think of it as a grace for womankind, for sick people and prisoners. It is, however, no less becoming in a true and stalwart man. To "endure hardness" is the part of a good soldier. The field of battle never knew a braver man than General Grant; in the field of politics he showed himself a wise counsellor and statesmanlike ruler; but his character shines brightest of all, it seems to me, in the story of those dreadful days when he sat waiting for the King of Terrors. He wrote his "Memoirs" while the anguish of an incurable disease was tearing at every nerve and sinew; but no murmur escaped him. Ah, that was patience! And at last, having completed his work, he relinquished his pen as he had laid down his sword in calm and gracious submission to the higher Will.

V. *The fifth knightly grace is Valor*. In Peter's catalogue of the marks of Christian character he begins in this wise, "Add to your faith virtue." The virtue here referred to is the Latin *virtus*, which meant the courage of a Roman soldier. It is cognate with *vir*, which was the title of a nobleman of those early times. "Add, therefore," said Peter, "to your faith the courage of a soldier." And Paul, in his order of equipment, urges the importance of the same unflinching spirit: "Finally, my brethren, be strong in the Lord and in the power of his might. Put on the whole armor of God, that ye may be able to stand against the wiles of the devil. For we wrestle not against flesh and blood, but against principalities, against powers, against the rulers of the darkness of this world, against spiritual wickedness in high places. Wherefore take unto you the whole armor of God, that ye may be able to withstand in the evil day, and having done all, to stand."

Let us be grateful that the days of war are drawing to a close. It is much to be doubted if the great nations will ever again be brought into serious collision. The means which are being used to make war effective to the utmost are reasonably certain to make it impossible. When explosives are brought to such a degree of perfection that with a few score of dynamite bombs a whole army may be annihilated or the mightiest of fortresses lifted into the air, it is incredible that the nations should much longer use such methods for settling their disputes. And why, indeed, at this stage of civilization, should it be deemed more proper for nations to resort to the barbarous arbitrament of battle than for men to settle their differences by fisticuffs? But God is working out the problem in his own way. We think it important to be making great guns, while he, smiling at our narrow plans and purposes, goes on with the beating of swords into ploughshares and of spears into pruning-hooks. We bend our energies to preparation for war; he makes all things work together for peace. The doors of the Temple of Janus are closing fast; the coming of Shiloh is near.

Are we therefore to imagine that chivalry is obsolete or that knightly courage is of no further use? Nay. Manliness of the best sort is needed for the trials and temptations of our daily life. Oftentimes it takes more courage to speak the truth than it does to lead battalions into battle. It takes more courage oftentimes to stand before a pointed finger than it does to face a loaded cannon. To say "No!" on occasion tests our manhood more effectively than to ride down "into the valley of death, into the jaws of hell." He who would keep his knees unbent before the great image in the vale of Dura when sackbut and psaltery are ringing, needs to make a more vigorous call upon his manhood than were he answering the beat of drum. The three Babylonish youths who refused the meat and wine of the king's table, preferring pulse and water, had in them the stuff that heroes are made of. The same sort of bravery is shown by the young man of these times who turns down his glass at the banquet or refuses to cross the threshold with boon companions when they enter an iniquitous place.

We need courage now-a-days for the defence of truth. The "infidel" whom the crusader went forth to meet was armed and harnessed for conflict on the open field; but the infidel in these days wears a scholar's gown. No battle axe can cleave his crown. His pen is more keen and more disastrously cruel than the Moslem's sword. And those who stand up against him defend not a Holy Sepulchre but that body of living truth which is dearer to Christ's disciple than the blood throbbing in his veins. Our natural disposition is to take the peaceful course, to avoid trouble at all hazards. But this is not the part of a true soldier of Jesus Christ. He cannot nor will he seek to excuse himself from a manful defence of the principles of the gospel of Christ.

It is written of Sir Hugh Talbot that, being sentenced to death by his Moslem captors, life and liberty were offered if he would signify an abandonment of his faith. He was at length brought out for execution: and again he was offered release if he would bow under the Crescent and say, "God is God, Mahomet is his prophet." It was a sore temptation, for life was very dear to him. He bowed his head, and saw in the far-away castle his wife gazing wistfully towards the east and murmuring a prayer for his return; he saw his children playing about the home and prattling of him. Then lifting his heart in prayer he shook off weakness. He arose and bared his breast, saying, "I am ready. *Deus vult!*" Oh blessed is the man, here and hereafter, who counts life of less value than rectitude, and freedom of less worth than a clear conscience!

We need courage also for a manly assault upon all entrenched forms of evil. There are so many wrongs to be righted; there are so many castles to be levelled with the earth. These are times for vertebrate Christians. The dram-shop, the gambling-hell, and infamous resorts

of every name and nature are fortresses that must be re-
duced in the name of the Most High God. Never was
valor more needed than in our onslaughts upon these
frowning strongholds of the enemy. It is so easy to abide
in our comfortable places and let the few faithful—who are
not afraid to be called fanatics—march out in more or less
effectual attempts to reduce these haughty forms of sin.
The good Lord give us the courage of the right! The
good Lord make us willing to be, if necessary, in the right
with two or three! The good Lord help us to make our
influence felt to the very uttermost of its measure against
all forms of sin!

We need courage for the defence of the weak. The
spirit of knighthood is the spirit of humanity. There is no
chivalry which does not recognize the Golden Rule. There
is no true man, no gentleman, whose heart does not thrill
at the faintest cry for help. We smile at the devotion of
the true knight of the olden time to his ladye fayre; but
the glove which fluttered from his spear-point spoke of a
nobler sentiment than gallantry; it was the symbol of a
glorious espousal, the espousal by the strong of the defence of the weak. The same spirit finds expression now-
a-days in our great enterprises for the evangelization of the
world and in every lesser endeavor for the uplifting of the
fallen, the deliverance of the helpless, the feeding of the
hungry, the wiping away of tears. There is no higher expression of puissant courage than this. And its noblest
exemplification was in our own Lord Jesus, who came
from heaven as the Knight-Errant of a ruined race. He
crossed the drawbridge into human life and conflict at Beth-
lehem. He mingled in the fray while a lad in the carpenter-shop. He was storming castles and delivering captives when he seemed to be preaching and healing a few
blind and withered folk. He knew the hardships of the

campaign, forced marches, fierce engagements in the high places of the field. There was no vulnerable point in his character, no joint in his harness, no blot on his escutcheon. He bared his breast at the trumpet call, saying, in the front of the enemy, "Whom seek ye? Jesus? I am he!" He set his face steadfastly towards Golgotha. Yonder on the heights he died. Six mortal hours he hung there in anguish, bearing a solitary pain which found its best similitude in the treading of the wine-press. Nothing could appall him. Straight on he went for truth and for humanity. Never for an instant did his courage forsake him—never until the word of death and victory escaped him, "It is finished!" Never was such knighthood as that. Behold the man!

All other heroes of the olden time are dead. The Crusader's tombstone bears the transverse cross and sword, and "Dormit," he sleeps. But the great Knight-Errant lives—lives more gloriously than ever, and leads on through trial to victory an innumerable company of knightly men. "Lo, I am with you always," is his word, "always—even unto the end of the world." Let us follow him. "In His name," was the countersign of the knights of St. John. At that word the blade flashed from its scabbard in a comrade's defence. At that word the drawbridge was lowered to the hard-pressed fugitive. Our watchword is the same. With that upon our lips and in our hearts let us go about doing good, defending the weak, opposing the wrong, and standing for the right until our Lord shall open the gates of the kingdom unto us. Let us quit ourselves as men, as gentlemen, as knights without fear and without reproach, as good soldiers of Jesus Christ.

THE

RESPECTABLE SALOON.

PREACHED BY DR. BURRELL JUNE 5, 1892.

"Woe unto him that giveth his neighbor drink, that puttest thy bottle to him, and makest him drunken also, that thou mayest look on their nakedness!" Hab. 2:15.

IT is not my purpose to call in question the right of any man to use intoxicating drink. No doubt there are many excellent people who reserve to themselves the right of taking a social or convivial glass. I suggest to them that the noblest of all rights is that which our Lord exercised when he counted not even his Godhood as a thing to be cherished, but putting aside all divine rights and prerogatives, made himself of no reputation and became obedient unto death for us. The highest form of human freedom is the liberty to deny ourselves for the good of others. But whether or no any of you insist upon your personal privilege in this matter, we shall all agree that the dram-shop is an evil thing and we can make common cause in assaulting it. The dram-shop has done evil and only evil all the days of its life. We are at no loss to define it: A place where intoxicating drink is sold over the counter, by the glass. The presiding genius of the institution is a man in his shirt sleeves with an unctuous face, an inviting smile, a solitaire in his bosom front—the bar-keeper—he is the presiding genius of the place and he is the malefactor of all malefactors. There are culprits and wrong-doers and reprobates, but this man who presides over the dram-shop is the worst of criminals, for he makes ninety per cent. of them all.

It is my purpose to make a reasonable presentment of the influence of the saloon, and so doing I shall ask you to consider how it affects man in all the various relations of his life.

I. As an individual. Note its baneful touch upon his flesh. Man's body is God's masterpiece, erect and sovereign. But drink is its ruin. Drink blears its eyes, reddens and be-pimples its face; unstrings its nerves and sinews, weakens its limbs, and sends it reeling, staggering, muttering, hiccoughing, drivelling, by way of the gutter, to the grave.

And how does it affect his brain? Men say, "When the wine is in the wit is out." Drink would make a fool of an angel. Not long ago one of our leading legislators arose in Congress to speak upon a matter of the greatest importance. He steadied himself by his chair and for a while his lips poured forth a stream of maudlin foolishness, profanity, and uncleanness like the exudations of a festering sore. "Oh that men should put into their mouths an enemy to steal away their brains!"

But most of all does the blight of the dram-shop fall upon his spiritual nature. It robs him of self-respect, dulls the sense of duty, and makes wreck of character. There is a multitude of drunkards at this moment, larger than the standing army of the most formidable nation of the earth, reeling down to death. If we could but stand on the edge of the abyss as they vanish into the night of endless despair we should hear the voice of retributive justice, " No drunkard shall inherit the kingdom of God."

II. Observe the evil influence of drink upon a man in his domestic relations.

He is the house-band, vowed to love, honor, and protect the wife and care for his little ones. But the dram-shop is the great home-breaker. The sweetest song that ever was sung touching the joys of domestic life was written by a man whose hand shook while he penned it and whose home was ruined by drink.

> " His wee bit ingle, blinkin' bonnily,
> His clean hearth-stane, his thriftie wifie's smile,
> The lisping infant prattling on his knee,
> Does a' his weary carking care beguile,
> An' makes him quite forget his labor and his toil."

Two miles away from Alloway cottage was Tam O'Shanter's Inn. It was this inn that broke the heart of the poet's wife and robbed his weans of their bread. As time passed Burns, wrecked ánd impoverished by drink, betook himself to Dumfries, where, as exciseman, he fell lower and lower until, in the very prime of his life, gazing out of his windows at the Nithsdale hills and moaning that he was friendless and penniless, he breathed his great soul out, leaving his dear ones to the mercy of a cold world. John Barleycorn did it, and John Barleycorn is breaking up ten thousand happy homes. It is the same story always and everywhere. In an article on the " Tenement Houses of New York," in one of our recent periodicals, are the pictures of two neighboring apartments. The one is the home of a widow. The room is clean and comely. Her face is sad but lighted by a sweet hopefulness. The children are playing merrily beside her. The other apartment is next door and, alas, the man of the house is living—a drunken brute. His wife is there, bowed down and shame-faced, cheeks sunken and pinched, a poor despairing thing. The children are ragged and unkempt, shrinking from him with tears. The brute scowls upon them all. The picture is sad enough, but sadder still the thought that any Christian should seriously propose to adorn the dram-shop for the comfort of this drunken brute. If the church has aught of time or treasure to expend, let it go towards the comfort of that sorrowful wife and those worse than orphaned children. Let us make the tenement houses more comfortable and allow the brute to shift for himself.

III. How it affects him as a neighbor. For we all owe something to the vicinage. Did you ever have the habitué of a saloon for your next-door neighbor? If so, how did you like it?

Why is it that the people of the West End of New York city are so persistent in excluding all dram-shops? Why is it that respectable business men leave their shops and offices and spend days together to prevent the dram-shop from coming near? Why? Because, to begin with, a saloon is an injury to real estate. Every square foot of ground in the vicinity loses value by reason of it. Not only so, but the dram-shop, when it enters a neighborhood, does not come alone; it brings on either arm its two boon companions, the gambling-hell and the den of nameless infamy—three furies with serpentine locks. And with the saloon comes danger unmeasurable. You are not willing that your wife or daughter should pass the door of the saloon at night. Why? Because it is the dram-seller's business to brutalize his patrons. Nor are you willing that your boy should come within the influence of the place.

Here is a brief calculation that is likely to be of interest to parents. There are more than nine thousand saloons in New York city, i. e., one for every one hundred and twenty-five people, or one for every twenty-five families. It is not to be supposed that less than twenty-five habitual topers are needed for the support of each saloon. So then the dram-shop expects and receives on an average a patron from every household. The twenty-five topers are rapidly dropping into their graves and their places must be filled from the ranks of the rising generation. The saloon cannot live unless the people furnish the boys to support it. One from every household! If yours does not furnish one, some other must cover the deficit. One boy from every household. Are you ready to furnish a boy? You take your chances.

IV. With respect to man in the still larger circle of industrial life. There is not one leader among the guilds of the working-men to-day who does not utterly and uncompromisingly denounce the dram-shop. Powderly is one of its worst enemies. But alas, a tremendous part of our working-men are enrolled as its best patrons. The American working-man is the best and most prosperous laborer on earth. The yeoman of England with his five acres of ground is not to be compared with him. The French peasant dressed in wooden sabots and smock frock and owning a little vineyard on the sunny hillside is not to be compared with him. The German farmer content to live from hand to mouth is not for a moment to be compared with him. Our American is a self-respecting man, ambitious, energetic, hopeful. He expects to make his way and is resolved that his children shall be happier and more prosperous than he. All this is true of the sober American workman. There is no doubt, however, that the vast majority of the laboring class in our country are habitual patrons of the saloon. The average outlay for drink is said to be $120 per annum. Tell me, how could a working-man expect to prosper when laying out so large a percentage of his earnings for drink? It is our tippling laborers who complain that the rich are growing richer and the poor are growing poorer. It is these who are responsible for strikes and lock-outs and who give countenance to

wild dreams of socialism. It is true that the rich are growing richer, and the Lord be praised for it! It is true also,
however, that the sober working-men of our country are
growing richer every hour and every day, and the Lord
be greatly praised for that! And, alas, it is true that multitudes of our working-people are growing poorer and
poorer. How could it be otherwise when they squander
in drink so large a proportion of their wages, their sa-
vings, their houses, and their lots, yea, their food and
their clothes and their necessary comforts? It is now proposed in some quarters that these toilers shall have the
saloon made more inviting and comfortable for their ac-
commodation. I do believe that for the working-man who
has no home it would be wise to provide reading-rooms,
restaurants, and other places of wholesome resort ; but for
a man, whether married or single, who has a home, his
place is there at eventide and he has no business to have
any other resort. The thing we need to do is to encourage thrift through temperance and economy on the part
of our working-men, to erect savings-banks and provide
building associations and the like. It is an easy thing in
this country for a sober man to get on. He cannot do
otherwise if he will avoid the dram-shop and put away
his surplus in a safe place.

> "Not for to hide it in a hedge,
> Nor for a train attendant,
> But for the glorious privilege
> Of being independent."

The outlay in our country for drink and liquors, every
way, is estimated at one billion two hundred million of
dollars, and the largest part of this comes from the pock-
ets of the working-men. Allow yourself to think for a
moment what a tremendous increase there would be in
the health and comfort and happiness of our entire coun-

try if only our working-men could be persuaded to let the drink alone for a single year.

V. As to the influence upon man as a citizen.   In our own city of New York it is a proverb that every department of politics is corrupted by the rum power.   At every point the rum power antagonizes law and order.   Our police superintendent, in his recent report, states that the larger number of the nine thousand saloons in this city are run by habitual and flagrant violators of the excise laws.   The logical consequent of such an announcement would seem to be the resolution to mete out retributive justice to these malignant law-breakers.   But, strange to tell, the superintendent proceeds to say that the excise laws are very difficult of enforcement because of their unpopularity among those who believe it to be an infringement of personal freedom.   Unpopular indeed!   A law is always unpopular with a law-breaker.   Our magistrates are not chosen to commend themselves to those who defy the law. Let the superintendent poll the churches and the institutions of learning and the respectable business houses and the homes of this city, and he will discover that the unpopularity of the excise law is confined to those who are carrying on the rum-traffic and their patrons.   The wholesome portion of our population are all in favor of the enforcement of the excise law.

Let us go a little further in determining the influence of the dram-shop on our political life.   Here is a startling computation.   Of the nine thousand saloons in New York city more than five thousand are under chattel mortgage. The saloons boast that they control forty thousand votes. This fact, if indeed a fact, gives them without doubt the balance of power.   These chattel mortgages are said to be held in the hands of about twenty men.   These twenty men dominating the saloon-traffic control the balance of power. The vote of New York city determines the political complexion of the commonwealth, and "as New York State goes, so goes the country." This means that twenty men, who are brewers, distillers, and wholesale liquor-dealers, have at this moment within their hands the control of the Republic. A most portentous fact of which it behooves all good citizens to take note.

VI. With respect to man as a cosmopolitan or citizen of the world. For every man is debtor to all, and it devolves upon every man, according to his influence, to make the world a better place to live in. The missionary, Dr. Livingstone, characterized slavery as the open sore of the world. But slavery is dead, and the open sore of the world to-day is the traffic in drink. No nation has escaped it. Poor Ireland has been shamed and embarrassed and robbed of her political rights by reason of it. Scotland, land of stalwart and brainy men, is groaning under it. And England—shame on an Englishman conscious of the fact that London air is dense with stale odors of "'alf and 'alf" and London fog is tinged with the florid reflection of the bar-maids' faces, conscious that the English physique is proverbially heavy with drink, and yet presuming to suggest the Americanization of the spirit-house! It is English, thoroughly English, and we Americans can get on without it. In Germany the complaint is made in official circles that, owing to the effect of beer through progressive decades, it is scarcely possible to replenish the army with sound men. In France the national legislature is at this moment wrestling with the question, " What shall be done to arrest the progress of the evils of intemperance?" It is indeed a poor time for Americans to think of adopting the saloon as a respectable institution when all the nations of the earth are wearied to death with it.

VII. We now come to man in his widest relation, as a

son of God. He is an immortal being, put here to prepare for a higher and better life, and to that end needs the clearest brain and the cleanest conscience. The church is a divine institution organized to help man on in the world towards a higher and a better life. The great enemy of the church to-day is the dram-shop. In New York city there is one church to five thousand people and one saloon to one hundred and twenty-five people. Note the disparity and reflect how the church is handicapped in her beneficent purposes by this horrid enemy of the souls of men.

It is obvious that the church has nothing to gain and everything to lose by striking hands with this arch-enemy. Compromise? Nay! not till Christ compromises and forms a coalition with the "prince cf this world." "For what fellowship has light with darkness or righteousness with unrighteousness?" Wherefore come out from among them and be ye separate, saith the Lord. Touch not the unclean thing. The church is fair as the moon, clear as the sun, and terrible as an army with banners. The rum demon is foul as filth, black as night, and the eternal foe of God and goodness. A church in Bristol, England, rented a building which it owned for a wine and spirit store. The church stands on a hill and is approached by a flight of stone steps, which connect the street and the wine-shop with the temple of God. But some godless fellow passing by and noting the incongruity which had escaped the sight of the preacher and his people, wrote upon those steps:

> "There is a spirit above and a spirit below,
> A spirit of love and a spirit of woe;
> The spirit above is the spirit divine,
> And the spirit below is the spirit of wine. .,

It is manifest that the attitude of the church must be one of unflinching hostility to the dram-shop. There are some things, as Sir Walter Scott says, "O'er good for banning and o'er bad for blessing, like Rob Roy;" but the saloon is not one of them. It is bad, always and altogether bad, and irretrievably bad. There is no white-washing it. There is nothing left for us but to join with God in laying a curse upon it.

As to a respectable saloon, if that were possible, we should not want it. That way lies danger. If the choice must be between the gilded barroom, in which ninety per cent. of our inebriety begins, and the low dives, with their sawdust, their reeking fumes of stale drink and exudation from perspiring inebriety, let us by all means encourage the dives. Boys do not commence their downward course in the dives, but in the gilded saloons. There they serve their apprenticeship, not with whiskey, but with beer. The low dive gets them only after the respectable saloon has used them up and thrown them out. There is no such thing as a respectable saloon. As soon speak of a pure devil or a comfortable hell or clean offal or wholesome fire-damp. It is bad, always and everywhere, and there is only one thing to do with it—exterminate it.

We are told that the saloon has come to stay and that philosophy suggests that we make the best of it. What if it has come to stay? So have snakes and tigers. So have small-pox and yellow-fever. So have infidelity and uncleanness and every evil thing. They have come to stay until God, working through us, through his wise and zealous people, shall in the fulness of time take this earth into his own hands, and to use the figure of the Psalmist, as a woman shakes the crumbs out of the tablecloth, shall so shake all evil out of our world. In the meantime let us fall into line with God and refuse to serve as coparceners with any evil thing. Let us set our faces as a flint against this mighty and iniquitous thing and do our utmost to destroy it. Let us have faith to believe that, thus withstanding its bold front, it will yet be expelled from the earth.

> "For right is right as God is God,
>   And right the day must win;
> To doubt would be disloyalty,
>   To falter would be sin."

A DAY OF WONDERS.

PREACHED BY DR. BURRELL JUNE 12, 1892.

"And he said unto the woman, Thy faith hath saved thee; go in peace." Luke 7:50.

It had been a day of wonders. In the early morning a company of wayfaring men came up through the rocky defile leading to the village of Nain. By the way they talked of the Hope of Israel, of their Leader's succession to the throne. Their hearts were full of holy joy and purpose. At the gate of the village they came upon a funeral procession. A widow was following to the tomb the body of her only son. The heart of Jesus was touched with compassion as he beheld her. "Weep not," said he. Ah, lonely, breaking heart! Who is this that, with a pitying word, would assuage the flood of nature's grief! She looked into his face and beheld somewhat there that set her heart throbbing with a speechless hope. He approached the bier, touched the dead body, and said, "Arise!" The word echoed through the dominions of death. The lad arose, rubbed his eyes, smiled in a bewildered way, saw his mother, stretched out his arms; and while these two were foretasting a little of the joy of the great reunion "there came a fear upon all." Thus began this day of wonders; but stranger things were to follow.

The Lord passed into the village and began to preach in the market-place. It is probable that at this time he uttered those gracious words, "Come unto me, all ye that labor and are heavy laden, and I will give you rest." The sick were brought on couches and he healed them. At this juncture a company of the disciples of John the Baptist desired a hearing. John was a prisoner at the Castle of Machærus. Alone and desolate, gazing through his barred windows on the desolation of the land beyond Jordan, it was little wonder if "the eye of the caged eagle had begun to film." It may have been to seek confirmation of his wavering faith that he had despatched these friends to inquire of Jesus, "Art thou he that should come, or look we for another?" The answer of Jesus was characteristic. He did not enter on a rhetorical demonstration of his credentials, but went on preaching and healing the sick. Then presently he said to the delegation, "Go your way and tell John what things ye have seen and heard: how that the blind see, the lame walk, the lepers are cleansed, the deaf hear, the dead are raised, to the poor the gospel is preached." Here was a display worthy indeed of this day of wonders; but greater things were coming.

As the day wore on an invitation was received by the Master to dine at the house of a certain Pharisee. As yet there was no open rupture between him and that most respectable class of pietists. He accepted the invitation, for he was ready ·to go anywhere in pursuance of his work. He was like a physician in a city of the plague. The houses of the lofty and the lowly were alike to him if only duty called. The house of the Pharisee was open to the street; on three sides were tables and couches. On occasions like this it was customary to keep open house. Nor was it unusual for strangers to stand on the piazza or in the doorway hearkening to the conversation of the guests. On this day no doubt many came to hear the table talk of Jesus. At length one entered on whom all eyes were turned. She was an unwelcome guest, a well-known woman of the town. She made her way noise-lessly to the couch where Jesus was reclining, and after a moment's pause—her face marked with mingled emotions of grief, penitence, and gratitude—she drew from beneath her cloak an alabaster vase of spikenard—how often she had perfumed her locks with it!—and bending over his feet she anointed them, while wiping away with her di-shevelled hair the tears falling upon them. Meanwhile the Pharisee looked on with cold disapproval. Had the woman approached him on this wise he would have known how to repel her: "Stand aside, for I am holier than thou." He said within himself, "This Jesus cannot be a prophet, or else he would have known this woman, and knowing must have spurned her." Ah how little he knew of the heart of Jesus!

"Simon," said the Master, perceiving his thought, "I have somewhat to say unto thee."

His host replied, "Say on."

"There was a certain creditor which had two debtors: the one owed five hundred pence and the other fifty. And when they had nothing to pay he frankly forgave them both. Tell me, therefore, which of them will love most?"

"I suppose," said Simon, "he to whom most was for-given."

And He said unto him, "Thou hast rightly judged. Simon, seest thou this woman? I entered into thy house; thou gavest me no water for my feet; but she hath washed my feet with tears and wiped them with the hairs of her head. Thou gavest me no kiss; but this woman, since the time I entered, hath not ceased to kiss my feet. My head with oil thou didst not anoint; but she hath anoint-ed my feet with ointment. Wherefore I say unto thee, her sins, which are many, are forgiven; for she loved much."

Then turning to the woman, he said, "Thy faith hath saved thee: go in peace." And this was the most wonderful of all that happened on this day of wonders. Healings are wonderful; the raising of the dead is more wonderful still. But there is nothing so divine as the deliverance of a soul from sin.

Thus the record ends. The woman goes her way forgiven. What a day this has been for her! In the morning she was burdened with shame and hopelessness. Now the music of heaven is ringing in her soul. She has come out of darkness into light, out of the shadow of death into newness of life. God hath put a new song into her lips, even the song of salvation.

We note in this incident a procession of three graces—the three redemptive graces following ᐧeach other in the logical order of the spiritual life.

I. *Faith.* This is the saving grace. "Thy faith," said the Master, "hath saved thee."

This woman had stood in the company that listened to his discourse on truth and goodness, had felt within her the stirring of better hopes and aspirations, had seen the ghosts of the past go trooping before her, had longed and despaired and hoped against hope—until that blessed word was uttered, "Come unto me, all ye that labor and are heavy laden, and I will give you rest." Thereat her soul started up and took hold on the promise. She believed. And her faith that instant saved her.

What is faith? It is taking God at his word. It is the assent of brain, conscience, heart, and will to the divine overtures. It is the reaching out of the soul, without question or murmuring, to accept the unspeakable gift.

One day as Napoleon was reviewing his troops the

reins fell from his grasp and his charger galloped away. A private sprang from the ranks, caught the frightened horse, and placed the bridle again in the Emperor's hand. "I thank you, Captain," said Napoleon. "Of what regiment, Sire?" was the quick reply. Pleased with his ready wit, Napoleon answered, "Of the Imperial Guard," and rode away. The soldier thereupon laid down his musket and walking over to a group of staff officers, assumed his promotion. "He said it," was enough. The Emperor's word was final. So is our great Leader honored by an instant assent and obedience. There is not a person in this company who cannot be saved in sixty seconds. "Only believe." He that believeth in the Son hath life.

But how does faith save? ʻBy bringing the soul into vital union with God. A train of cars is standing on the track. The engine has full pressure of steam. The bell rings. The locomotive moves, but the cars stand still. What is the trouble? It backs up and tries again, but with the same result. What is the trouble? The coupling has not been made. A link makes all the difference. There are foolish people who are acting thus all the while, trying to reach heaven without the coupling of faith. It is impossible. Faith is the *sine quâ non* because it brings us into oneness with God through our Mediator Christ Jesus, so that our destiny is bound up with his for ever and ever. When once we believe, our life is for evermore hid with Christ in God.

II. *Then follows Love.* Love is the complement of faith. The expression, "For she hath loved much," would seem to favor the view that love rather than faith is the saving grace. But the word "for" in this connection is not causative but illative. Moreover Christ himself says presently, "Thy faith hath saved thee." Faith and love—this is the logical and chronological order. For, as Tyndale said, "Faith is the mother of love."

We love Him because he first loved us. It is his loving-kindness in delivering us out of the horrible pit and the miry clay that attunes our heart to the song of salvation.

> "Love I much? I've much forgiven;
> I'm a miracle of grace."

Behold how this woman loved him! Her emotion was beyond words. She kissed his feet. The word is intensive; she kissed them again and again. And her gratitude was grateful to him. God's heart hungers for our love. Love is the fulfilling of the law. Let us make much of it. Behold what the Lord hath done for us. We are great sinners; he is the great Saviour. "Bless the Lord, O my soul, and all that is within me, bless his holy name. Bless the Lord, O my soul, and forget not all his benefits!" The box of spikenard is not too precious to be lavished upon him. Nothing is too good for him. Our gratitude, however, finds its best expression not in thanksgiving, but in thanksliving. "Beloved, if he hath so loved us we ought also to love one another." Lip-service is good as far as it goes, but life-service is better. We cannot minister to Jesus in the flesh, but we can minister to his little ones. Tradition says that this woman of Nain spent all her after life in self-forgetful service. She accompanied Christ, assisting in his labor of love; and after his death she devoted herself to the reclaiming of her fallen sisters. This is the sort of gratitude that commends itself to the Master. His word is, "Inasmuch as ye have done it unto one of the least of these my brethren ye have done it unto me."

III. *Then Peace.* Faith is the root, love the tree, and peace the sweet consummate fruit. "Go in peace," said Jesus to this woman. Rather, "Go *into* peace." Luther thanked God for the pronouns; let us thank him for this preposition. It suggests that she was entering upon a new manner of life. Old things were passed away; all things—joys, tasks, hopes, and purposes—now became new. God's peace thenceforth was hers. What a change! She had been at war with herself, with her fellow-men, and with God. Her conscience had been up in arms. Her life had been filled with a weary, desperate strife. Now the dove of peace brooded over her and the bells of heaven made music for her. The smile of the Lord was like sunshine upon her. "Go into peace!" Oh blessed be God for that legacy! "Peace I leave with you, my peace I give unto you."

There is no peace in sin. "It is a merry world, my masters!" But wait a moment. Stop and think. You dare not? Have you lulled your fears to sleep and must you keep them slumbering? Are you a sinner unforgiven? If your knell rang to-night would your soul stand un-shriven before God? Do you try to persuade yourself that all is well when in your inmost soul you know that all is ill? When God speaks to you, as he did to Adam in the garden, do you run and hide from him? When you awake in the watches of the night do your fears like spectres shake their gaunt fingers at you? "There is no peace, saith my God, to the wicked." Your soul is full of war and war's alarums. You cannot be at rest while you abide in sin.

And sedatives are all in vain. He is a foolish man who expects to cure a deep-seated malady with morphine. There was a time when God was angry with his people Israel. He afflicted them until the whole head was sick and the whole heart faint. "From the sole of the foot unto the crown of the head there was naught but wounds and bruises and putrefying sores." Then came the false prophets saying, "This is but a temporary matter. Do not fret, do not worry; the trouble will pass." So the altars burned for Baal and the people suffered on until Jeremiah came; and he cried, "Woe unto you, false prophets, who have healed the hurt of the daughter of my people slightly, saying, Peace, peace, when there is no peace!" They had put a plaster on a wound that needed cauterizing. The Lord deliver us from such "slight healing." And alas for the prophet who lulls to sleep the well-grounded fears of the awakened sinner, who teaches a philosophy shallower than repentance or narrower than the gospel of the cross !

There is no peace except in Christ. He that believeth on the Son hath life; but he that believeth not is condemned already. Acquaint thyself, therefore, O sinner, with this salvation and be at peace. This is "the truce of God." The woman of the city, on this occasion, received a definite assurance of pardon. The work had really been wrought when, standing among the auditors of Jesus, she heard him say, "Come unto me," and accepted the proffer. At that instant her sins which had been many were forgiven her. But now she receives assurance in the Master's word. It is blessed to be forgiven, but oh how joyous to know it! Let us pray that the Master will bend over us and say, "Son, daughter, thy sins are forgiven thee."

A bird in mid-ocean all day long went circling around the ship on weary wing—nearer and nearer as if it would alight and then away again in sudden alarm, rising and circling afar—until at last, in utter weariness, it settled down to rest. We stood upon the deck and watched it as, flying to and fro, it spent its strength in needless conflict with its fears. So do we resist our hopes and longings and hold out against the overtures of heavenly

love. Why not suffer the dear Lord to have his way
with us ?

> " Oh cease, my wandering soul,
> On restless wing to roam ;
> All this wide world, from pole to pole,
> Hath not for thee a home.

> " Behold the ark of God,
> Behold the open door ;
> Hasten to gain that blest abode
> And roam, my soul, no more."

The Master speaks, " Come unto me and rest." Return unto thy rest, O my soul, for thy Lord hath loved thee ! Acquaint thyself with him and be at rest.

www.ingramcontent.com/pod-product-compliance
Lightning Source LLC
Chambersburg PA
CBHW031020120726
47905CB00007B/1980